Ethnic Conflict and Political Development

ETHNIC CONFLICT AND POLITICAL DEVELOPMENT

Cynthia H. Enloe

Clark University

UNIVERSITY
PRESS OF
AMERICA

LANHAM • NEW YORK • LONDON

Copyright © 1986 by

University Press of America,® Inc.

4720 Boston Way
Lanham, MD 20706

3 Henrietta Street
London WC2E 8LU England

Copyright © 1973 by Little, Brown and Company, Inc.

Library of Congress Cataloging in Publication Data

Enloe, Cynthia H., 1938-
Ethnic conflict and political development.

Reprint. Originally published : Boston : Little
Brown, 1972, c1973.
Originally published in series: The Little, Brown
series in comparative politics.   An analytic study.
Includes bibliographical references and index.
1. Minorities.   2. Pluralism (Social sciences)
3. Ethnic groups.   4. Federal government.   I. Title.
[JF1061.E54   1986]   305.8   86-7801
ISBN 0-8191-5359-1 (pbk. : alk. paper)

All University Press of America books are produced on acid-free
paper which exceeds the minimum standards set by the National
Historical Publications and Records Commission.

To my mother and father

Foreword

The Little, Brown Series in Comparative Politics has three main objectives. First, it will meet the need of teachers to deal with both Western and non-Western countries in their introductory course offerings. Second, by following a common approach in analyzing individual political systems, it will make it possible for teachers to compare these countries systematically and cumulatively. And third, it will contribute toward re-establishing the classic relationship between comparative politics and political theory, a relationship which has been neglected in recent decades. In brief, the series seeks to be global in scope, genuinely introductory and comparative in character, and to broaden and deepen our understanding of the nature and variety of political systems.

The series has two parts: the Country Studies and the Analytic Studies. The Country Studies deal with problems and processes deriving from a functional, as compared with a purely structural, approach to the study of political systems. We are gratified that the participants, all mature scholars with original insights, were willing to organize their discussions around a common set of functional topics in the interest of furthering comparisons. At the same time, each author has been urged to adapt the common framework to the special problems of the country he is discussing and to express his own theoretical point of view.

An introductory book, *Comparative Politics: A Developmental Approach,* by Gabriel A. Almond and G. Bingham

Powell, provides an analytic supplement to the Country Studies. It also opens our set of Analytic Studies, which offers basic discussions of such topics as political change in the emerging nations, comparative analyses of interest groups, political socialization, political communication, political culture, and the like. These books are useful and stimulating supplements to the Country Studies as well as points of departure in more advanced courses.

Development and modernization have recently become the subjects of sharp polemic. Industrialization and urbanization, once thought to be proper measures of their growth, have been charged with leading to ecological disaster. In the political science literature, the identification of development with the centralization of power and authority in the nation-state, the expansion of bureaucracy, and pluralistic, democratic politics, has been attacked as an extrapolation of Anglo-American and European experience, and as favoring existing distributions of power and privilege. Finally, sociologists' identification of modernization with secularization and rationality, and with the attenuation, or even disappearance of primordial and traditional institutions and attachments, has been criticized on the grounds that the vitality of traditional institutions, as well as human needs for primary group and communitarian attachments, substantially limit these trends.

Cynthia Enloe's *Ethnic Conflict and Political Development* bears on several of these important themes. She challenges development theory's exclusive focus on the nation-state, arguing that even in many of the established states ethnicity defines one of the most significant planes of political cleavage. She shows the fallacy of assuming that as the nation-state develops, ethnicity attenuates. Ethnic identity responds to some of the influences affecting national identity. In the new nations as well as the old, ethnicity typically affects political organization and the territorial distribution of power. One explanation for the survival of ethnic identity is that it meets primary and communitarian needs in a world increasingly dominated by large-scale organization.

In developing her arguments Cynthia Enloe draws on an extraordinary range of examples, including ethnic phenomena from North and South America, Europe, Asia, and Africa; and manifestations from tribalism to linguistic-cultural forms. Her book is an important contribution to development theory, as well as to our understanding of ethnic politics.

Gabriel A. Almond
James S. Coleman
Lucian W. Pye

Preface

When picking up a book purporting to analyze development and ethnicity — not to mention the relationship between them — a reader must be on his guard. No two social science concepts are more slippery or more subject to parochial definition. This is such a book. I myself am skeptical of what I have set down here, and I trust that students and colleagues will go over the following chapters in a similar spirit.

At two points in the investigatory process intellectual caution can be exercised. Until recently most caution had been concentrated at the writing end of scholarly enterprise, often to such a degree that social scientists have been charged with rehashing the commonplace and avoiding significant human concerns because of professional timidity. Now readers — students as well as their teachers — are beginning to exercise caution or, better, aggressive skepticism. Perhaps this portends a healthier academic situation, in which writers leave safe harbors, raise fundamental questions, and take more risks with their data, and readers read more energetically, not simply "digesting" a book but tracking down its unstated assumptions and long-range implications.

Nowhere are contemporary readers becoming more "participant" than in political development and ethnic group affairs. Thanks to the disillusionments born of the Vietnam War and to the new self-consciousness stemming from the international black power movement, even the driest, most theoretical social science studies are being picked over carefully by

readers no longer willing to permit authors to take cover
behind shields of professionalism and scholasticism. Critics
of America's (and other great powers') policies in Asia as well
as black militants in the United States knew well before the
rest of us that the abstractions of social science were shaping
governmental perceptions of problems and alternative solutions. In an era when political scientists wield influence once
confined to precinct captains, criticism of social science cannot be left to academics alone, particularly when the study
claims to dissect human goals — development — or to analyze
human identity — ethnicity.

My first debt is to social critics in and out of academia, but
especially to members of caucuses within professional social
science associations. They have revealed the extent to which
Anglo-Saxon ethnic values pervade an allegedly objective discipline and to which American national interests have warped
our notions of legitimacy and efficiency in development. One
does not have to be in perfect agreement with the accusation
of every caucus to realize that sociology, political science,
anthropology, and history all are more vital and exciting
enterprises today thanks to their stimulation.[1]

My second debt is to three sets of students. My first investigation of a multi-ethnic society focused on the Federation of Malaysia. When I was doing research in Kuala
Lumpur, I would sit in the University of Malaya's library
watching Malay, Indian, and Chinese undergraduates read-
ing assigned books, so many of them authored by Englishmen
or Americans, and I would become quite nervous at the prospect of their one day taking my own study of Malaysia off the
shelf. Would it ring true to them, or would it sound as
though I had conducted research in some country quite un-
related to their own?

1 Four volumes that bring together many of the professional dissidents'
charges and recommendations are Philip Green and Sanford Levinson,
eds., *Power and Community: Dissenting Essays in Political Science* (New
York: Vintage Books, 1970); Irving Louis Horowitz, ed., *The Use and
Abuse of Social Science* (New Brunswick, N.J.: Transaction Books, 1971);
Norman K. Denzin, ed., *The Values of Social Science* (Chicago: Aldine,
1970); Marvin Surkin and Alan Wolfe, eds., *An End to Political Science*
(New York: Basic Books, 1970).

Imagining an audience can paralyze a writer, but it can also keep him on the straight and narrow. This has been the service performed by students at Berkeley, Northeastern, and Miami who have taken my courses in American, Asian, and, most recently, American black politics. Finally, there are students at the University of Guyana whom I taught during a one-year lectureship. They too live in a society coming to grips with the problems of ethnic communalism and the pressures of economic and political development. Their ears are at least as sensitive to American and Anglo-Saxon misperceptions as are those of professional critics.

Research for this book began with the study of Malaysia, funded by the Fulbright Commission and later by the National Endowment for the Humanities. In addition I am grateful to Miami University for its Faculty Research Grant.

Among those colleagues who have read the manuscript I am particularly grateful to David Abernathy for his suggestions on the African sections, Mustapha Rejai and Warren Mason for their advice on style and organization, and Douglas Frisbie, an astute officemate who has given up hours to listen to half-formulated ideas.

Gretchen Meyers, Cynthia Rejai, and Peter Downs have come to my aid with typing and have done extra duty clearing up my worst editorial atrocities. Bob Schuette graciously let me use his Oxford restaurant as a study when my own office became intolerably cluttered.

Gene Farmer has made valuable editorial suggestions, and Basil G. Dandison and David W. Lynch have guided me and this manuscript through the intricacies of publication. It goes without saying that, despite all these direct and indirect debts, any errors and misinterpretations marring the following chapters are my own.

C.H.E.

Contents

Ethnic Conflict and
Political Development

CHAPTER I

Introduction

EVERY HISTORICAL ERA has its peculiar preferences and phobias. Taken together, they define the period. The two hundred years since the American Revolution have worn many labels, each meant to pinpoint a distinctive quality: the age of revolution, the age of progress, the age of the machine, the age of nationalism. Which label is most nearly accurate provokes endless debates at scholarly conventions. With the year 2000 now in sight, observers already are referring to this era in the past tense, looking back on it as a cluster of trends that have run their course. These two centuries have shaped not only societies but the social sciences that purport to analyze them. Social scientists who forecast conditions in the next era still wear mental spectacles fashioned by the current era, whatever it is labeled. The "end of an era" attitude prevails especially among observers preoccupied with the advanced nations of the world. When they speak about the latest phase of development, they usually avoid historically biased labels and refer to the twilight of modernization.[1] "Modern" seems more neutral than other terms, and it embraces them all. Industrialization, faith in progress, belief in man's power of reason, the sanctity of the nation-state, and the exhilarating though traumatic

[1] Cynthia H. Enloe, "Beyond Modernization: The Implications for Underdeveloped Nations," *Journal of Developing Areas* 3, no. 3 (April 1969): 313–18.

penchant toward revolution — all are hallmarks of modern life.[2]

Peoples of the world can be divided roughly between those currently entering modernity and those about to leave it behind. This notion abstracts modernity from a strictly chronological context, and we find ourselves describing not so much a particular period of time as a phase of social development that some countries experience early, others late. Nevertheless, the historical implications persist, even in the writings of the least historically conscious social scientists. What we call "modernity" crystallized as a mode of life at a peculiar point in time and bears the markings of that time — from the eighteenth into the twentieth century. Furthermore, "modernity" refers to those centuries as experienced by only one part of the world, Europe and North America. Thus "modernity" may be abstracted from time and place, but never completely. For this reason social science — itself a Western artifact of the nineteenth and twentieth centuries — constantly struggles under the burden of cultural parochialism while it preaches universal values.

If periods of development were labeled according to their *disinclinations,* the modern era might be called the age of the craftsman's decline, the age of disappearing countryside, or the age of demythology. These are awkward (positive attributes are always more pleasing to the phrase-maker), but they help to clarify the biases — not just the facts — of modern men. Indeed, cities and suburban tracts are invading the countryside. Yet rural ways of life and rural inhabitants are still facts of life, frequently carrying formidable political influence. But the values prized by modernizers are fundamentally contrary to ruralism and impose pressures on it even where it does manage to survive. The same two-pronged attack confronts craft shops and religious myths: whether they persist, they are

2 Among descriptions of modernity are C. E. Black, *The Dynamics of Modernization* (New York: Harper Torchbooks, 1967); Kenneth S. Sherrill, "The Attitudes of Modernity," *Comparative Politics* 1, no. 2 (January 1969): 184–210; David E. Apter, *The Politics of Modernization* (Chicago: University of Chicago Press, 1965).

considered by the majority to be out of joint with prevailing social needs.

The relationship between modernization and ethnic groups has been somewhat more ambiguous. Ethnic identity can be a building block, but also a potential stumbling block, on the road to modernity. On the one hand, the sentiments of ethnic groups are considered drags on modernization. They are said to divert energies, fragment the nation-state, and conserve irrational patterns of behavior. On the other hand, where one community is dominant, ethnicity has been the cornerstone of nationalism. Where an ethnic group is only one among several, modernity's promotion of equality has given ethnicity protection under minority rights. All too often ethnic groups are analyzed only in the context of minority rights, but they have been standard-bearers of the nation-state as well. A pertinent American illustration of this point involves the Eskimos, Aleuts, and Indians who call themselves Alaskan natives. Ramsay Clark, former attorney general, has said:

> The intrusion of our [American] society on theirs [Alaskan natives'] is inescapable, regardless of who owns title to the land. . . . It is impossible in this world today to maintain an isolated culture. We must seek mutual enrichment. They have qualities that we need. And they need meaningful opportunities for self-determination. If Alaska develops now, they will develop. If not, it passes them by.[3]

Clark was defending claims pressed by Alaskan natives on the United States federal government. But as their chief counsel he cited what he and most pragmatic politicians see as the irrefutable fact of modernization: no ethnic group can remain isolated. This is deemed good. Modern development, such as the discovery of oil, opens opportunities for all men, in this instance Alaskans of all ethnic groups. Modernization is not only inescapable, it has its rewards.

Nevertheless, Emil Notti, president of the Alaskan Federation of Natives and on Clark's side in the congressional lobbying effort, took exception to the Anglo-Saxon lawyer's analysis.

[3] *Washington Post,* August 9, 1970.

Notti argued that the alternatives presented by development are broader than supposed: they do permit a choice between ethnic differentiation and absorption into the mainstream:

> Our goal is not merely dollars and cents, but to give each native the opportunity to join the mainstream of American life on equal terms if that is his wish, or the opportunity to continue the traditional way of life while enjoying the full benefits of modern science, if that is his wish.[4]

As the Clark and Notti statements suggest, most debates about the relative merits of ethnic identity and modern development are complicated. It is more than simply a stand-off, pitting isolationism against assimilation or tradition against modernity. The conflict between the claims of Alaskan natives, on the one hand, and the ambitions of state legislators and petroleum companies, on the other, provoked still a third perspective. William Van Ness, special counsel for the United States Senate Interior Committee, was more pessimistic than either Notti or Clark about the chances for ethnic survival in the midst of the intensive development of Alaska:

> Their culture has been disintegrating for one hundred years. . . . [The young native Alaskans] are not going to go back to igloos and trap lines. . . . The white guys are going in there [to native villages] with liquor stores and grocery stores and becoming dominant with these placid, unaggressive people. . . . The old culture is already gone.[5]

Each of these projections of Alaskan natives' future assumes something about development, modernity, and ethnicity. At one extreme is the presumption that development is synonymous with modernization, which in turn so pervades men's lives that peculiarities defining ethnic groups necessarily vanish. At the other extreme is the conviction that development can be encouraged in such a way that modernity does not infringe on cherished ethnic distinctiveness. The latter belief also assumes that expanded opportunities and ethnic survival are not directly opposed to one another and that ethnicity is

4 Ibid.
5 Ibid.

hardy enough to adapt. When development is so deeply affected by public policy, the truth of either position depends on the relationship of political power and ethnic mobilization. For this reason oil surveyors, native spokesmen, and state and federal officials engaged in discussion fit for a social science symposium before lights and cameras in a Senate hearing room. How development, modernization, and ethnic loyalties affected one another would depend in large part on the workings of the political process. Conversely, American politics would be shaped by the ability of ethnic leaders to mobilize their communities to exert pressure on the system.[6] At the very time Americans were beginning to refer to "ethnic politics" in the past tense, the most contemporary crises — energy needs and the threat of environmental pollution — were being discussed in terms of Alaskan ethnic demands.

Movements toward convergence or separateness have been going on among peoples for centuries. The world's population has always included a myriad of distinct cultures, each vulnerable to absorption and fragmentation. Every instance of intercultural contact, whether in northern China or on the British Isles, raised the possibility of the creation of new human capacities for satisfying needs and aspirations — that is, development. There is an unfortunate tendency, however, to discuss development in the context of the transition from "tradition" to "modernity" as if no major changes occurred during previous generations. Transformations of ethnic groups alert us to the wealth of change contained within the "traditional" period of any area: migrations from southern China continually altered the cultural and political frameworks of

---

[6] In early 1971, the Nixon administration acceded in part to native demands. In a bill sent to Congress the administration proposed that Eskimos, Indians, and Aleuts received a grant of 40 million acres of land, with all mineral rights in the state reserved to the natives. In addition, $500 million would be paid into a native corporation over a nine-year period, instead of a twenty-year span as originally suggested. Finally, the Nixon bill proposed a 2 per cent royalty on all gross revenues from oil and mineral resources developed on all land in the state. The Alaskan Federation of Natives responded by saying that although the plan fell short of the autonomy and financial control natives desired, it was a step forward. The federation would seek amendments in Congress. *New York Times*, March 28, 1971.

Southeast Asia before Portuguese and Dutch ships ever passed through the Straits of Malacca; Jews migrated from the Mediterranean northward to become critical factors in many European polities; the slave trade brought thousands of Negroes to North America as early as the seventeenth century; Arab traders carried Islam below the Sahara and helped create distinctive communities among black Africans.

Four aspects of the transition to modernity intensify the political implications of interethnic contact. Modern change is characterized by rational deliberateness founded on a belief that men can engineer societies just as in the past they engineered irrigation systems. Moreover, modern change is noted for its rapidity, due to faster communication and tighter functional interdependence. Modern change is international, hard to confine within geographical limits. These qualities make it difficult to deal with an issue or group in a vacuum or for its own sake. Political calculation is raised to a higher level of abstraction. Gradualism and piecemeal solutions are harder to justify. As the California naturalist John Muir remarked, you try to pick out anything by itself and find it hitched to everything else in the universe. As we have become increasingly conscious of this interrelatedness in modern change, we have looked for a theoretical construct that would take it into account. The result is systems analysis, for a system is a stable pattern of interdependencies. In a system everything is "hitched" to everything else, and thus each change has some impact on every subunit in the system. Armed with this sensitivity to the peculiar nature of modern change and with the notion of systems, observers see ethnic groups to be significant mainly as they relate to the larger community. The claims of Alaskan natives must be weighed because they organized themselves well enough to exert pressure on politicians, but the analytical significance of the claims is determined within a frame of reference larger than the native community or even the Alaskan community. The nation-state becomes the point of reference. Likewise, regardless of the validity of demands and what they reflect about the ethnic group's own condition, the significance of, for instance, the Basques must be analyzed in the context of Spain's development, Quebeckers in the context of Canadian development, Meos in the context of Laotian development. Before long, the scientific observer joins the central policy-maker in perceiving ethnic phenomena as problems — that is, as challenges to the integration of some larger system.

System and development by themselves are neutral concepts and have served political investigators well. However, because of the historical and cultural biases of political science, "system" has often become synonymous with nation-state and "development" has been defined as nation-building. The nation is considered the chief vehicle for modernization. Development and modernization have merged so that political development depends finally on effective national mobilization. This confusion has led to a peculiar perception of ethnic politics. The political scientist begins to worry chiefly about "system maintenance," by which is meant national political durability.[7] He unconsciously adopts the point of view of the political elite — the people directly responsible for national stability. His vantage point gives him a "king's-eye view" of ethnic politics. Most political scientists are sensitive to the pitfalls of American and democratic assumptions and try to guard against them in comparative studies. However, a basic nation-state bias persists. It relegates ethnic groups to the status of dependent variables or policy problems. The danger is that, in assuming the nation-state to be natural and the national elite's problems to be the primary challenges for development, the outside observer implies that integration and assimilation are by definition good. In one of the few efforts at comparative theorizing about ethnic relations, R. A. Schermerhorn criticizes system analysts for their nation-state orientation. He holds that

> applying system analysis to comparative ethnic relations actually centers attention on the functions the ethnic group performs for the entire system, viewing the ethnic group itself

[7] For example, see the imaginative use of comparative data to determine political performance in Ted Robert Gurr and Muriel McClelland, "The Performance of Political Systems: A Twelve-Nation Study" (Paper prepared for the annual meeting of the International Studies Association, San Juan, Puerto Rico, March 17–20, 1971, forthcoming in the Sage Professional Papers in Comparative Politics.) One of the best discussions of the problems posed by ethnic loyalties for nation-builders is Clifford Geertz, "Primordial Sentiments and Civil Polities in New States," in Geertz, ed., *Old Societies and New States* (New York: Free Press, 1963), pp. 105–57.

as a subsystem gradually fitted into the entire society by a
series of adaptive adjustments regulated by the norms and
values of its institutions that eventually become internalized
by members of the ethnic group involved.[8]

The notions of system and development, then, at least in the
hands of many modern observers, generate not only national
but assimilationist biases.[9]

The concept of development is fraught with intellectual
dangers because an analyst can so easily use it to impose his
own personal or cultural values. Samuel Huntington, among
the foremost students of political development, recently mused
that the concept might be more appropriate for a missionary
than for a disinterested scholar. Huntington writes:

> The principal function that political development has in fact
> performed for political scientists is neither to aggregate nor
> to distinguish, but rather to legitimate. It has served as a way
> for political scientists to say, in effect: "Hey, here are some
> things I consider valuable and desirable goals and important
> subjects to study.". . . The concept of political development
> thus serves in effect as a signal of scholarly preferences rather
> than as a tool for analytical purposes.[10]

Taking a close look at ethnic groups as they struggle to use
politics to articulate and advance their communal interests
may alert us to the pitfalls of development theory and enable
us to neutralize it. One way to immunize development against
our own subtle biases is to see it as one kind of change among
several. Not all change represents development; development

8 R. A. Schermerhorn, *Comparative Ethnic Relations* (New York: Random House, 1970), p. 51.

9 Blacks and Chicanos have been among those American social scientists exposing their discipline's tacit commitment to assimilation. See, for instance, Raymond A. Rocco, "The Chicano in the Social Sciences: Traditional Concepts, Myths, and Images" (Paper prepared for the sixty-sixth annual meeting of the American Political Science Association, Los Angeles, Calif., September 8–12, 1970).

10 Samuel P. Huntington, "The Change to Change: Modernization, Development and Politics," *Comparative Politics* 3, no. 3 (April 1971): 304. Huntington's own application and interpretation of development theory are spelled out in his *Political Order in Changing Societies* (New Haven: Yale University Press, 1968).

is a very particular sort of change. On a spectrum of social change having generality at one end and particularity at the other, development would fall toward the latter. The spectrum might look something like this:

Most
general
concept

Social change · Growth · Development · Modernization

Most
particular
concept

Although development is a rather special kind of social change, modernization — another kind of change — is even more special. In other words, modernization is a peculiar kind of change or syndrome of changes. *There can be development without modernization.* Much of the unacknowledged bias that infiltrates the analysis of development is the consequence of confusing development with modernization and measuring a group's or nation's development by the special criteria of modernity — for example, secularization, mobilization, mass participation, functional bureaucratization. If development is unleashed from modernity's requisites its utility to the social observer can be increased; it is applicable to more periods of history and to a greater variety of cultures.

Development refers to change that takes place in stages. Furthermore, it refers to successive transformations that enable the unit — an individual, an organism, a nation, a subnational group — to cope with new demands upon it. The key words in this definition are "to cope with." Can we measure a unit's ability to cope by its stability, its happiness, its physical well-being? Or, perhaps, merely by its survival as a distinct entity? So long as we were blurring modernity with development these questions were not so bothersome. After all, the outside observer had an objective set of measurements to employ in his evaluation, and these were supposedly relevant to individuals and communities everywhere. But once we define development as a more general phenomenon, these neat criteria become less useful. We must look more closely at the subject's response to its current status. Thus the study of development becomes intimately related to the study of desires, goals, aspirations, and perceptions of the national or communal polity. The political scientist interested in *political* development must therefore concentrate on the interaction of public power and public policy as they stimulate and react to local desires and needs.

Life would be easier if we could ignore the conceptual gap between modernization and development. It would be easier for national and ethnic group leaders. While known — though, admittedly, still debated — criteria for modernity posed cruel dilemmas and often impossible standards, at least the prescribed ends were relatively clear: we knew where we were heading and could measure our progress along the way. This kind of political development was filled with frustrations and often alienation, but a leader could calculate and plan. However, when development is freed from the narrow confines of modernity, the road signs fade, and a great deal of time and energy must be spent just in getting the polity to agree on goals and priorities. Nevertheless, the generalized notion of development as the creation of capacities relevant to group needs is liberating: it frees polities and their leaders from standards and goals imposed from outside. Religion, for example, may be severed from politics, or it may not have to be, depending on what the developing community wants in the long run. Of course, the ultimate goals of some political groups will sound like an academic's model of modernity. Naturally, no group hammers out its ends in a vacuum. Development criteria still have to take account of external pressures, and since World War II those pressures certainly have been in the direction of modernity.

Detaching political development from political modernization makes the former a much more uncertain tool for analysis, perhaps even impractical. The general development concept adds not only to the political leader's problems but to those of the social scientist as well. The universe in which the latter operates — commonly referred to as "the field" — becomes a strange, less predictable place. So long as he had a shopping list of modern criteria in his pocket, he could go into a black ghetto, an Indian reservation, or a foreign capital still feeling somewhat at home. Without that list — or at least not being sure how applicable it is in a given place — the social scientist immediately is more reliant on local data to serve as guideposts and bases of judgment.

This could be very good for social scientists and their disciplines. They necessarily will keep their ears closer to the ground as they study development because development now is defined largely in terms of a group's perceptions of demands to be satisfied. Detaching the development concept from modernization could help restore the credibility and reliability of both concepts by reducing their ideological content and re-emphasizing empirical observation.

The cases discussed in the following chapters suggest that understanding political development requires at least double vision: the political system of the United States as viewed from Washington and from Harlem, the political system of Bolivia as viewed from La Paz and from an Indian village in the Andes. On the one hand, the nation-state is indeed a potent political reality; any hypotheses about political behavior that pretended it was merely a chimera would be shallow. On the other hand, nation-states are not the sole realities. Other political entities are capable of choice and innovation. As ethnic groups are politicized — though politicization is not inevitable — they, like nation-states, can pursue political development. It is one thing to acknowledge the existence of national polities; it is quite another to assume that they are the logical goal of all political development. Actually, nation-states have shown themselves to be fragile, and there is no guarantee that their preeminence is any more than a passing phase. Investigation of the politics of ethnic groups underscores the delicacy and possible transitoriness of the nation-state and compels us to reexamine the origins of now apparently established nations. Perhaps we have fallen into the belief that nations are logical modes of political community because we have neglected their histories. For example, if we devoted more attention to pre-eighteenth-century Britain would we conclude that its present makeup is quite remarkable and thus use it as a measuring rod for newer nations with far more caution? The historical point at which we start our political analysis largely determines the factors and relationships we consider important. There has been a tendency to start political analyses of most Western countries with the beginning of the Industrial Revolution, but by that time most of these countries had subdued ethnic communalism and had consolidated political power at the national level. Thus we miss the English colonization of Ireland, the Great Russian conquest of Muslim peoples to the east, American displacement of Indians and enslavement of blacks. Ethnic factors do show up in our studies of non-Western and Latin American countries because there nationalism came later. Political scientists had their analytical tools sharpened and ready for use when Burma and Kenya started to nationalize, whereas those tools were just being fashioned when Britain, Russia, and the United States were formed. As a result, ethnic variables seem much more critical in non-Western than in Western political development. This may be due merely to our own historical shortsightedness.

Today events are sharply reminding us of the tenuousness of the nation-state. Basque separatists are challenging the authority of the Spanish national regime; Flemish and Walloon militants are questioning the practicality of Belgian unity; foreign workers from Italy and Yugoslavia are straining the ties that bind Switzerland together; Scottish and Welsh nationalists are forcing Westminster to consider a radical decentralization of British political authority. All of a sudden, the allegedly established and advanced nation-states appear as fragile as those in Asia and Africa, and we find ourselves wondering whether the nation-state is logical or natural after all. Ethnic activists have moved political scientists to confront two factors in political life that we have either forgotten or have preferred to ignore. First is the element of oppression present in most political systems: integration is not by socialization alone. When an ethnic group rises up to challenge national legitimacy, the coercive dimension of national politics is blatantly revealed. Second, ethnic mobilization alerts an observer to the adaptive and innovative qualities inherent in all sorts of human groups. Just when an ethnic group appears to have outlived its utility, it finds new issues to rally around or new institutions to give it cohesion. Of course, the same thing is true of national groupings; on the brink of disintegration, many nations discover new modes of resolution. The emergence of ethnic separatism, in fact, often reinforces a sense that nationhood is the natural form of political community. Militant ethnic spokesmen frequently are ardent advocates of nationalism; they just want the boundaries redrawn. Today it is common for blacks in Newark, New Jersey, to greet each other with this question and answer: "What time is it?" "It's Nation Time!" [11]

One savant has said that the only problems are those caused by solutions. What we may be witnessing today in places as dissimilar as Pakistan and Canada is the surfacing of ethnic problems caused by the "national" way to modernity. The ethnic conflicts threatening the stability not only of Pakistan and Canada but of numerous other countries are not just a reflection of traditional sentiments that stubbornly refuse to die. They stem in part from the successes of modernization. Modern developments have equipped ethnic communities, as well as national elites, with new political resources and aspirations. When an Alaskan Eskimo presses for a larger share of oil royalties, we are witnessing not the vestiges of traditionalism but rather the emergence of a new kind of ethnic politics.

Political science grew out of the European Enlightenment. So did the nation-state and the values of modernity. Perhaps only now are we becoming conscious of the extent to which our cultural background and historical environment determine the direction of our inquiry. Reassessing approaches and interests means looking anew at the kinds of questions we ask — and do not ask. Gabriel Almond warned:

> what the enlightenment did was to reject systematically a whole set of answers to enduring human questions which the ancient regime and traditional religion had provided. The enlightenment rejected these answers, because they could not stand up to the light of reason, and because they constrained man's potentiality for understanding and control. But the enlightenment

---

[11] Discussions of the artificiality of the nation-state are in Mostafa Rejai and Cynthia H. Enloe, "Nation-States and State-Nations," *International Studies Quarterly* 13, no. 2 (June 1969): 140–58; Walker Connor, "Self-Determination: The New Phase," *World Politics* 20 no. 1 (October 1967): 30–54; E. K. Francis, "The Ethnic Factor in Nation-Building," *Social Forces* 46, no. 1 (September 1967): 338–46.

went further than this. It tended to reject the legitimacy of these questions themselves. And now, when the clerical-traditional answers have lost their vitality, the questions are coming back to plague us.[12]

Almond was referring particularly to the nonsecular aspects of men's lives, but the same sort of selectivity has occurred in our notions of proper socio-political boundaries. Certain boundaries — those delimiting the nation-state — have been considered functional, so the pertinent questions political scientists seek to answer are mainly those defined by the needs of nations. My proposition in the following chapters is that the nation may be the logical unit for development, but the matter is open to question. Development questions are wider ranging than nation-building questions. Political development, at bottom, means men's cultivation of forms for public power and authority that enable them to meet external challenges and internal needs. Ethnic groups are proving that nations do not have a monopoly on political development. In the end, a current of ambivalence runs throughout this study. Approaching political development through ethnic groups makes us more aware than ever of the political imagination and inventiveness resident in men of all cultures. At the same time, however, this approach makes the observer acutely conscious of the extent to which political leaders depend on artificial contrivance and coercion to realize their goals.

[12] Gabriel A. Almond, "Historical Perspectives on Political Development," in *Political Development: Essays in Heuristic Theory* (Boston: Little, Brown, 1970), p. 330.

CHAPTER II

Varieties of Ethnicity

OF ALL THE GROUPS that men attach themselves to, ethnic groups seem the most encompassing and enduring. Their capacity to survive amid radical change and even under direct attack has attracted the attention of modernizing elites as well as social scientists.

Ethnicity has both a communal and a personal dimension. It refers to a peculiar bond among persons that causes them to consider themselves a group distinguishable from others. The content of the bond is shared culture. Culture, in turn, is a pattern of fundamental beliefs and values differentiating right from wrong, defining rules for interaction, setting priorities, expectations, and goals. Cultural bonds grow out of men's recognition of the distinctiveness of their own standards of behavior and prizing of those standards to the extent that they feel most comfortable and secure when among persons sharing them. On the personal level, ethnicity equips an individual with a sense of belonging; it positions him in society. As social relations become complex and impersonal, ethnic identity may be grasped tenaciously. It is a familiar and reassuring anchor in a climate of turbulence and uncertainty.

CHARACTERISTICS OF ETHNIC GROUPS

All men are cultural beings; not all men, however, consider themselves members of an ethnic group. Ethnicity is only one kind of link between individuals. Alternatives include ties of occupation, geographic region, social class, religion, sex, age, race, and ideology. Each takes on varying degrees of importance as conditions for development change. It is tempting for outside observers to list cultural similarities among people and then categorize individuals according to shared attributes. But ethnicity depends on self-identification, not on objective categorization, although the way an individual defines himself is partly a response to other people's perception of him.

Michael Moerman, an American anthropologist working with the Lue, a minority in northern Thailand, has issued a useful caveat. He considers the Lue to be a distinct ethnic entity "because they successfully present themselves as one." The Lue present themselves as a group ethnically separate from other lowland Thai and hill tribes by their *own* use of ethnic labels when referring to people of other villages. In other words, it is not the anthropologist's taxonomic skill that determines whether the Lue are a genuine ethnic community but the Lue's own expressions of communal distinctiveness.[1] An ethnic group must have reality in the minds of its members, not just in the eye of the beholder. This is why the modern proclivity toward communication and mobilization has such import for ethnic leaders. On the one hand, expanded communication and intensified mobilization break down ancient parochialisms; on the other hand, they can raise ethnic self-consciousness among persons who hold similar values but previously were cut off from one another.

1 Michael Moerman, "Being Lue: Uses and Abuses of Ethnic Identification," *Proceedings of the American Ethnological Society* (Spring 1967); reprinted by the Center for Southeast Asia Studies, Reprint No. 275, University of California, Berkeley, Calif. Moerman also warns the field researcher that if the people he is studying are aware of his interest they will go out of their way to make ethnic distinctions, thus distorting their real interest in this particular line of social cleavage.
American Indians' responses to the 1970 United States census illustrate the political importance of recognizing ethnicity's subjective quality. Due to changed classification procedures and increased pride among Indians, the 1970 census showed a dramatic increase in the number of Indians in the United States, amounting to 50 per cent over the 1960 figure of 523,591. Fewer Indians considered their origin to be a stigma in 1970 and so made no attempt to hide their Indianness from census reporters. *New York Times,* August 25, 1971.

An ethnic group is largely biologically self-perpetuating. Marriage, for instance, has significant implications for the survival of an ethnic group but not for the survival of an economic interest group. However, the social ramifications of marriage, not its genetic consequences, affect an ethnic group. The important question about marriage across ethnic lines is whether the bride or groom breaks ethnic ties and patterns of behavior as a result of marriage. American Jews, for example, have been anxious about rising rates of intermarriage and a resultant dilution of the ethnic community. An estimated 10 to 15 per cent of all American marriages involving a Jewish person are between Jews and non-Jews.[2] Individualism and its encouragement of extracommunal marriage is a primary risk taken by ethnic groups seeking integration within a modern society.

A second characteristic of ethnic groups is that they share *clusters* of beliefs and values. One value held in common by a number of persons is insufficient to sustain an ethnic community. Catholics in the United States are a religious group, with some political importance in voting and issue conflict. But American Catholics do not comprise an ethnic group. In the United States as well as in Belgium, Catholicism is professed by persons of several ethnic communities. The Belgian Catholic party until recently united Walloons and Flemings. In 1968 it broke into communal factions. By contrast, the Catholics of Northern Ireland *do* constitute an ethnic group because there Catholicism is interwoven with a community's historic past. It separates native Irish from Protestants of Scottish and English ancestry; it shapes national allegiances, associations, and expectations.

Value clusters find expression through associational forms. Ethnic groups possess communal institutions that parallel those of the larger society: they care for individuals' welfare, train leaders, articulate interests, and even provide police protection. Ethnic groups generate political organizations more readily than other sorts of groups do. However, their posses-

[2] *New York Times*, November 8, 1970, reporting on statistics published in the *American Jewish Yearbook*, 1970 edition.

sion of parallel institutions makes them a formidable threat
to insecure nation-builders. Ethnic institutions seem to pose
an explicit and intolerable challenge to the authority of the
national government. They perform functions that should belong exclusively to the state.

Finally, ethnic groups have internal differentiations. The
width of the gap between intracommunal status groups affects
the community's political capacity to deal with outside pressures. Over time, degrees of differentiation can change within
a single ethnic group. Widening or narrowing of status distinctions can be caused by developments altering the larger
society or by changes emanating from community members
themselves. As we will see, class tensions within an ethnic
group can frustrate its own political development and that of
the nation as well.

Like all human groups, ethnic communities are subject to
change. The fundamental nature of an ethnic group's common culture and its associational expression permit a surprising
degree of adaptation without surrender to complete assimilation. Several American political scientists have described the
tenacity of ethnic groups even in a country that puts heavy
stress on individual mobility and functional interest groups.
Michael Parenti chastises social scientists for stumbling into
the assimilationist pitfall, unwittingly or because of ideological bias. A group may be "Americanized" and yet remain an
identifiable subgroup with boundaries of social interaction
and individual perception based on ethnic identity.[3] Sometimes the survival of ethnic groups can be traced to the subtle
but enduring obstacles put up by the rest of society. In other
instances survival is the product of communal imagination
and adaptability.

Frequently an outsider sees a group's visible characteristics
disappearing. He predicts the group's demise: soon it will be
swallowed up in the mass society. Later he is puzzled as the
people who surrendered their traditional clubs, fashions, and
diets continue to label themselves ethnically, as well as occu-

[3] Michael Parenti, "Assimilation and Counter-Assimilation," in Philip
Green and Sanford Levinson, eds., *Power and Community: Dissenting
Essays in Political Science* (New York: Vintage Books, 1970), pp. 174–75.

pationally or nationally.[4] Maintaining the boundaries of subgroups may be a more subtle process than it appears at first
glance.

A good example is found in New York — not in the city,
where ethnic enclaves are celebrated, but in Southampton, a
partly suburban and partly resort town on Long Island. Southampton is the home of a Polish community that has sloughed
off its overt cultural peculiarities: "The delicatessen with the
herring and the pickle barrels has disappeared. Pulaski Hall
has become almost a village meeting place, the family unit
isn't as tightly knit as it once was, and few of the younger
generation speak their ancestral tongue." [5] Yet the Polish-
Americans in Southampton are not assimilated totally. They
are acculturated, but not assimilated. Like Moerman with the
Thai-Lue, we get a clue from the people's own expressions.
Some in Southampton still think of themselves as members of
a specific group and refer to non-Poles as "Yankees." They
cherish the memory of what families used to be and hold
their Polish heritage in high regard.[6] Yet Southampton's Pol-
ish-Americans at present do not take their ethnicity into politics in any clearly visible manner. Should their ethnic legacy
become politically salient, then surface manifestations might
be resurrected to assist in mobilization and organization.

An ethnic group is a network of regular communication
and interaction. Except in extremely remote communities,
ethnicity does not delineate the total field for members' relationships. A Bolivian Indian is stereotyped as parochial, but
he is likely to have frequent dealings with Spanish-speaking
mestizo landlords and merchants. In time of war and geographic expansion, even the most remote group is impinged
upon by outside contacts. Extra-ethnic transactions may even
reinforce a person's conviction that he belongs to a special
community. Governments that launch campaigns for national
consolidation stimulate communication across ethnic boundaries. Yet accelerated interethnic contact may intensify rather

[4] Fredrik Barth, "Introduction," in Barth, ed., *Ethnic Groups and
Boundaries* (Boston: Little, Brown, 1969), pp. 32–33.
[5] *New York Times*, September 1, 1970.
[6] Ibid.

than dilute ethnic pride and awareness. Escalation of group
tensions may be a sign of integration, not disintegration. Isolation or remoteness is not necessarily the strongest bastion of
ethnic communalism. As we will see in subsequent chapters,
modernizers who penetrate social barriers inadvertently generate interethnic conflict and ethnically based mobilization. To
understand the impact of ethnicity on politics we therefore
have to analyze the quality of communal bonds and look
closely at rates and ranges of contacts between members and
outsiders.

VARIETIES OF ETHNIC PLURALISM

Ethnic pluralism can be considered in terms of its intensity
and its quality. Intensity refers to the cultural distinctiveness
of the ethnic groups in a given country. How far apart are
their beliefs and values? To what extent are their cultures
mutually exclusive? Do they converge at important points, for
instance in common language or religion? Ethnic pluralism
poses especially difficult problems for nation-builders when
several groups hold the same element of culture in high esteem.
For example, religion is critical to ethnic identity for both
Catholics and Protestants in Northern Ireland. If the Ulster
regime favors one religion over another, it implicitly favors
one ethnic group over the other and thus sows communal distrust. On the other hand, Malays and Chinese in Malaysia do
not give equal weight to religion in their respective definitions
of ethnicity. Malays hold Islam to be an integral part of their
communal identity, but the religiously eclectic Chinese care
more about their nonreligious cultural traditions. This discrepancy permitted Malaysian politicians to make concessions
to Islam without seriously alienating Chinese citizens.

Sometimes lines of cultural differentiation are so vague
that debate centers on whether ethnic pluralism exists at all.
Formosan nationalists on Taiwan, for example, have asserted
that indigenous Formosans are distinct from mainland Chinese, whether those mainlanders are backers of Mao Tse-tung
or Chiang Kai-shek. Perhaps one explanation for the movement's apparent inability to gain widespread support on
Taiwan lies in the inseparability of mainland Chinese and For-

mosan ethnicity. A recent survey of attitudes held by Taiwanese youths concludes that, "except perhaps for the small aboriginal population, the people of Taiwan are essentially Chinese in their social and political outlooks as well as their ancestry." [7] It is hard to mobilize a political movement on the basis of ethnic pride when ethnic plurality is not clearly visible to the average citizen.

In countries containing numerous ethnic communities there may be a whole spectrum of ethnic differentiations, ranging from barely noticeable to strikingly apparent. Such a situation creates not one but several systems of interethnic relations. In the Soviet Union the spectrum — measured by cultural proximity to the dominant Great Russians — might have the Ukrainians on one end, the Asian Muslims on the other end, and the Jews in the middle. A similar spectrum in the United States, measured again by proximity to the dominant community, would have Scots and Indians at opposite ends. Nowhere is disparateness of ethnic distinctions more notable and politically important today than in Israel. At one end of the spectrum are the Eastern European Jews, whose attitudes have set the pattern for Israeli culture. Not far away culturally are Jewish immigrants from Western Europe and the United States. Considerably more distinct and thus more difficult to integrate are Jews born and reared in neighboring Arab countries. Despite the fact that these so-called Oriental Jews hold Judaism in common with their fellow Israelis, they possess cultural attributes that earlier Western immigrants consider alien. There is still, however, a group more culturally distant: the Arabs. Some 330,000 Muslim Arabs (plus a few Christian Arabs) stayed behind in 1948 when Israel won independence. Today they present a problem for Israeli leaders quite different from that posed by the Oriental Jews. The Arab minority is closer ethnically to Israel's enemies than to its own citizenry. The government energetically tries to assimilate the Oriental Jews, but it is not at all sure what to do with the

[7] Seldon Appleton, "Taiwanese and Mainlanders on Taiwan: A Survey of Student Attitudes," *China Quarterly*, no. 44 (October–December 1970), p. 56. For a critique and discussion of Appleton's findings, see *China Quarterly*, no. 46 (April–June 1971), pp. 353–57.

Arabs. For the time being, they are allowed to follow their own way of life. But the other side of this coin is minimal integration into Israel's political life.[8] The Israeli government, like the governments of the Soviet Union and the United States, must formulate several ethnic policies to meet the several degrees of pluralist intensity within its borders.

One dimension of intensity, therefore, is the cultural distinctiveness between a country's ethnic groups. Another relates to the amount of communal expression given to these cultural distinctions. Some groups are slow to create rituals, symbols, and institutions to externalize their beliefs and values. They are politically underdeveloped when it comes to fending off manipulation by nationalizing elites. By contrast, other ethnic communities are fully equipped with associations and formal processes with which to express collectively their cultural separateness. British colonial administrators, for example, were so impressed by the high level of communal organization among Malayan Chinese that they left them virtually alone to manage their own affairs.[9] Likewise, the sophisticated hierarchy of the Catholic Church insulated French Quebeckers from English-Canadian interference for generations. As long as a country's several communities do not need each other, ethnic pluralism fosters stability. But as soon as independence or foreign economic pressures make interdependence and pooling of scarce resources imperative, institutional expressions of cultural separateness become threats to stability, instead of the assurances of social harmony they once were.

The second aspect of ethnic pluralism is its quality. A great deal of confusion about ethnicity stems from its variety. Even when we use the criteria spelled out earlier — that is, cultural bond, communal association, self-identification, location within some larger political unit — "ethnic group" remains a slippery

---

[8] The problem of the Arab minority could become more politically acute if the current coalition of Premier Golda Meir lost the parliamentary support of the Orthodox Jews. Although they hold very few seats in the Knesset, Arab representatives conceivably could hold the balance of power in such an event. *New York Times*, January 29, 1971.

[9] The British official held responsible for the immigrant Chinese was the protector of Chinese. For a fascinating account of British-Chinese relations in Malaya at the end of the nineteenth century, see R. N. Jackson, *Pickering: Protector of Chinese* (Kuala Lumpur: Oxford University Press, 1965).

term. One solution would be to narrow its definition arbitrarily so that it is precise in meaning and manageable in analysis. The notion is attractive, but it would reduce considerably the utility of ethnicity as a concept for unraveling political development. Furthermore, who is to say which criterion is valid? Despite its dangers, a more inclusive definition seems desirable.

We can minimize analytical problems by at least making clear the different sorts of ethnic groups that exist and the political significance of their differences. Ethnic groups differ according to the origins of their separate identities. Three types of ethnic groups are most prevalent: (1) tribal, (2) nationality, and (3) racial.

Tribal ethnicity is characterized by cultural and communal boundaries derived from bonds of kinship. Tribes are more exclusive than other sorts of ethnic groups because membership in them is formal and the group is highly integrated. Tribes possess no strong political organization but are regulated by a variety of social institutions. A tribe is essentially egalitarian, with little in the way of an elaborate hierarchy intervening between the chief and family households. The tribe is larger than a band or clan. As it grows in numbers exact kinship relations may be blurred, but the myth of kinship ties among members remains central to tribal identity.[10]

> Tribal society is of such a nature that one must experience it from the inside. It is holistic. . . . Being inside a tribal universe is so comfortable and reasonable that it acts like a narcotic. When you are forced outside the tribal context you become alienated, irritable, and lonely.[11]

[10] American Indian tribes disagree over the criteria for legal membership. The Crow require one quarter Crow blood and possession of tribal membership as of July 23, 1953. Pine Ridge Sioux call for members to have been born on the reservation and have one parent a tribal member. To qualify as a Chippewa one must have an ancestor on the 1889 tribal roll. Regardless of criteria, however, a person must be the member of some tribe to claim legal status as an American Indian. Shirley Hill Witt, "Nationalistic Trends Among American Indians," in Stuart Livine and Nancy Oestreich Lurie, eds. *The American Indian Today* (Baltimore: Penguin Books, 1968), p. 109.

[11] Vine Deloria, *We Talk, You Listen: New Tribes, New Turf* (New York: Macmillan, 1970), p. 12.

Tribes are likely to have their own languages and customs; this is what makes them ethnic groups, not merely extended families. Their high levels of integration together with their kinship bond make their ethnicity especially hard to break down. Though "detribalization" has been a primary goal of many African nationalists, success has been sporadic. Several tribes within a country will usually share the same racial characteristics and be able to lay equal claim to legitimacy as national citizens. National unity in multi-tribal societies may have to be built on top of, not at the expense of, tribal ethnic groups.

Nationality ethnicity is characterized by communal identity having its roots in association with a foreign country. Ethnic groups referred to as "nationalities" usually are made up of relative newcomers. Although the alleged "indigenous" people of the country may in fact have been migrants centuries earlier (for example, Vietnamese, Malays, Thais), nationality ethnic groups entered the country within recent memory and came from a recognized political entity abroad. Their ethnic peculiarities may undergo modification, but basically they reflect the linguistic-religious-moral culture of their previous homeland. A nationality may be closely integrated. Rarely does a person have formal membership. One "belongs" to a national ethnic group by secondary associations or simply subjective affiliation.

Exceptions to this usage of "nationality" are found in Communist nations, where the term refers to tribal and racial ethnic groups as well as ethnic groups that used to belong to other polities. The Communists may see "nationality" as a term conferring political worth and dignity on an ethnic group.

During political integration national ethnic groups are likely to be looked upon as alien, having less right to the rewards of national sovereignty than indigenous groups. For this reason nationality ethnic problems often revolve around guarantees of citizenship. National ethnic groups become significant when political development is most immediately affected by relations with foreign governments.

Racial ethnicity is characterized by values and bonds stemming from physical and biological distinctions. More than either tribal or nationality groups, racial ethnic groups are the result of someone else's prejudice. Had it not been for whites' narrow beliefs about physical acceptability, Negroes in the United States, the Republic of South Africa, Trinidad, and Guyana might be not a single ethnic group but a multitude of tribal ethnic groups. The experience of exclusion, however, led certain racial groups to create a cultural system of their own suited to the social conditions they faced wherever they were.

Because of its physical base, racial ethnicity is perpetuated by visual memory. Its explicit, concrete quality burdens racial ethnic relations with symbol and myth. A large quotient of irrationality together with biological determinism makes racially defined ethnic tensions among the most troublesome for nation-builders to resolve. Race is not particularly malleable or subject to legislative tinkering. It is particularly open to demagogic exploitation.[12]

Even for the excluded race, integration may have drawbacks. If racial ostracism has led a people to cultivate a subculture of their own and if that subculture and its communal ties have positive value, then desertion of it for the sake of assimilation may in time lose its desirability.

What is true of ranges of intensity is also true of qualitative differences: one society can contain several kinds of ethnic pluralism. Governments in such complex societies must devise development strategies appropriate to two or three qualities of ethnic communalism. For their part, ethnic groups them-

---

[12] The question of whether races are differentiated by *intelligence* as well as by physical traits has surfaced again, causing heated argument among geneticists, statisticians, and social scientists. A persuasive case is made by two geneticists for being wary of any I.Q. tests purporting to show differentiation between whites and blacks. They directly attack the reliability of statistical analyses done by educational psychologist Arthur R. Jensen and doubt that at present it is even possible to separate socioeconomic factors from purely genetic factors in comparisons of white and black intelligence. Walter F. Brodmer and Luigi Luca Cavalli-Sforza, "Intelligence and Race," *Scientific American* 223, no. 4 (October 1970): 19–29. See also Arthur R. Jensen, "How Much Can We Boost I.Q. and Scholastic Achievement?" *Harvard Educational Review* 39, no. 1 (Winter 1969): 1–123.

selves work out various sorts of relationships with groups whose boundaries are defined by different criteria. Language will be of little consequence for Englishmen when they deal with immigrant Trinidadians but will pose tremendous problems when they try to reach an accommodation with immigrant Pakistanis. Racial stereotypes will shape the Englishmen's reactions in both situations, whereas it will have no impact in their relations with Welsh and Scottish nationalists. Not only nations but subnational communities continually seek ways to harmonize their existence with the complex and heterogeneous environments around them. The task before an ethnic community living in a simple racial ethnic pluralistic society is easier than the task facing a community in a racial tribal pluralistic society.

For the past two decades the government of Kenya has dealt with all three major kinds of ethnic diversity: tribal, nationality, and racial. Each kind has been prominent and has shaped development priorities at different times. Racial ethnic tensions were highest when the issue was national independence, because race was basic to the British colonialists' claim to rule Kenya. The Kenyan nationalist movement, conversely, was propelled by a desire to topple the white race from its position of superiority. Relations between British settlers and administrators on the one hand and black Africans on the other were dictated largely by racial perceptions. Once sovereignty was achieved, the white settlers' problems had a low profile and demanded little attention from African policy-makers. The emergent ethnic problems were tribalism and "alien" economic domination — that is, relations between indigenous Africans, regardless of tribe, and immigrant Asians, who controlled much of Kenya's commerce.

Despite racial differences, African-Asian ethnic relations focused on nationality. How loyal were Kenyan Asians? Were they merely opportunistic transients who still identified with their homeland or with Britain, or were they genuine Kenyan citizens eager to accept the responsibilities that that status required? Nationality ethnic groups are particularly vulnerable to exportation because they hold no claim to citizenship. Thousands of Asians were compelled to leave Kenya. Tribal ethnic groups, however, usually have full legal rights; their members are indigenous to the country and have heritages intimately connected with its history. Kenya's two major tribes, the Luo and Kikuyu, must find some way not only to coexist but to cooperate and must trust one another if the nation is to meet the challenges of modernization. The assassination of Tom Mboya, a Luo and possible successor to president Kenyatta, heightened intertribal conflict. With racial ethnic problems resolved by decolonization, and nationality tensions lessened by stringent citizenship requirements, the Kenyan government is left confronting the most stubborn and subtle of its ethnic dilemmas: tribalism.

From the point of view of national policy-makers what is most important to determine is, first, How likely is any ethnic combination to polarize? Is the pluralism a kind that will merely retard development, or is it likely to set off a civil war? Second, how malleable are the kinds of ethnicity dividing the citizenry? Can communal parochialisms be penetrated by educational reform, national language requirements, secularization of political authority? If kinship and race are central to ethnic identities, perhaps nation-builders will have to exercise restraint and patience, realizing that laws will have little impact. Original plans to make national mobilization the path to modernization may be modified to allow for greater decentralization or a communally fragmented party system.

CLASS AND ETHNICITY

Socio-economic classes and ethnic groups are analytically separate, though in practice they continually intertwine. Some ethnic communities include a full catalog of class distinctions. In other instances the majority of a community's members fall into a single class category.

Modern development takes a heavy toll on the solidarity and autonomy of ethnic groups. Homogenization of cultures — often labeled "Westernization" — plus pressures for centralized nation status undermine associations dependent on cultural separateness. Simultaneously, mass communication, complex organization, specialization, urban growth, and industrialism uproot people from established patterns. The uncertainties of transitional society provoke a self-consciousness about identity that was superfluous in the past. One of the ironies of modernization is that it combats ethnic loyalty while it stimulates ethnic awareness.

Ethnic groups participate unevenly in modernization. Development disparities in a pluralist society transform some ethnic communities into socio-economic classes. In other instances, gaps are reflected within communities as well as between them. A distinction can be made between vertical and horizontal ethnic differentiation. In a vertical system, social stratification is synonymous with ethnicity. Mobility upward necessitates a change in ethnic identity. When vertical ethnic differentiations are overladen with racial criteria, upward mobility is virtually impossible except from generation to generation through intermarriage.[13] Arthur A. Fletcher, United States assistant secretary of labor in the Nixon administration, is one of the handful of black Republicans. He graphically described his experience of vertical ethnic differentiation: "It was a damned bitter experience," Fletcher recalled:

> The same whites I had gone to college with were beginning to move into middle-management positions and I was still washing windows — when I could find the work. I couldn't change my color. Education couldn't change my color. The same thing was happening to me that happened to my mother. A college degree [in nursing and teaching] didn't help her.[14]

Even ambitious men cannot simply cast off values, language, and associations without psychic cost. Still, if opportunities and rewards depend on changing identities, many persons will pay the price. In Oklahoma today some people refer to

13 Donald L. Horowitz suggests that "color" — that is, race — is a stronger factor in vertical ethnic differentiation than in horizontal. Even where groups are racial ethnic, if class stratification is horizontal, non-physical criteria will be most salient. Donald L. Horowitz, "Three Dimensions of Ethnic Politics," *World Politics* 23, no. 2 (January 1971): 244.

14 William W. Prochnau, "Arthur A. Fletcher, Who Has a Degree from Malcolm X College, Is a Rare Bureaucrat," *Potomac Magazine, Washington Post,* February 7, 1971, p. 14. Fletcher's principal interest as assistant secretary was to break vertical stratification by compelling labor unions to accept more black members. His vehicle was the Philadelphia Plan.

"white" Cherokees; Liberian tribesmen move up in Monrovian society by adopting Americo-Liberian life styles; Bolivian miners are "de-Indianized" as they migrate from peasant villages to mining towns; French Canadians become bilingual in order to compete for high-salaried jobs with English and American firms. Vertically stratified societies are threatened by modernization because it demands maximization of skills and rational deployment of resources. If pressures for modernization are blocked too long by ethnic barriers, a society ultimately confronts two unpleasant alternatives: either it will have to sacrifice economic growth and social development for the sake of maintaining the communal status quo, or it will have to alter ethnic relations radically. Whatever the decision, the country will undergo a profound transformation. If authorized policy-makers refuse to face their choices, they court revolution. The Republic of South Africa currently has this problem.

Horizontal ethnic differentiation is less prone to revolution under the strains of modernization. In horizontal systems parallel ethnic structures exist. One community may hold power disproportionate to that of others, but all have their class stratification hierarchies. At least a minority within each ethnic group enjoys prestige and perhaps wealth. Socio-economic tensions are not translated so immediately into communal tensions. Pluralism under such a stratification system appears more stable because of overlapping interests. Elites of several communities have a stake in preserving the social order. The danger lies less in interethnic conflict than in *intra-ethnic* unrest. As mass media and urbanization disperse information, the expectations of the poor rise. Lower classes in each of the country's ethnic groups are more keenly aware of the disparities between their own reasonable expectations and those of their elites. As they become familiar with the ways of the city and factory, persons at the bottom of the social ladder gain self-confidence and begin to challenge the natural perpetuation of intracommunal inequalities. Established communal spokesmen continue to represent their groups at the national bargaining table, but they cannot be sure now that their compromises will be accepted by their own rank and file.

While an ethnic lower class questions the credibility of its own elite, it perceives its new aspirations rivaled by the desires of mobile persons in other communities. Rebellions or riots break out as intracommunal stratification disintegrates. But revolution remains beyond reach as long as the lower classes of various ethnic groups remain as hostile to each other as they are to their own leaders. Tensions generated by horizontal ethnic differentiation are often obscured by the discontinuity of class cleavages and ethnic cleavages. If not modified to fit changing perceptions, a horizontal system can produce as much political instability as the more blatant vertical system.

Many multi-ethnic nations house the components — and risks — of both vertical and horizontal stratification. For instance, in pre–Civil War United States and in prerevolutionary Mexico some ethnic groups were virtually coterminous with social classes, while other groups had members distributed among several classes. Governmental economic strategies will affect these two sorts of ethnic class systems differently. Stratification systems can be altered by political action. Abolishing slavery, outlawing caste denominations, demolishing feudal estates — these are all acts that undermine vertical differentiation, even if they do not eliminate it altogether. National policies that provide more school openings, encourage bilingualism, or promote geographic dispersal of industry also affect class relations within and between ethnic groups. On occasion a regime follows one or more of these policies with little awareness of the ethnic consequences. Thus the regime may be caught unprepared when popular expectations outstrip the possibilities of entrenched pluralist relationships.

Is the evolutionary process irreversible? Once a little mobility is permitted for members of all ethnic groups, are communal boundaries too fragile to contain forces that would widen opportunities further? Theories of modern development generally imply that ethnicity is an irrelevant criterion for evaluating performance and distributing rewards. Modern nations are not free from class distinctions, but class positions presumably are based on functional skills rather than on communal association. If the majority of any ethnic group falls into a single class status, one suspects that its members are being deprived of a chance for education or job training. Today ethnic conflict allegedly is due to abortive modernization or represents class conflict in disguise.

Sociologist and former presidential adviser Daniel Moynihan argues that we have become too enamored of class as an explanatory tool. In relying so heavily on class analysis, we have overlooked the peculiarly ethnic factors that shape stratification systems and frustrate development policies. Part of our confusion between class and ethnicity is due to the origins of sociological theory. The great social scientists of the 19th century came from France, Germany, and England, countries unusual in their cultural homogeneity at the time. To them ethnicity was a peripheral problem compared to the widening gaps between rich and poor, proletariat and bourgeoisie. Moynihan writes: "To be sure, there are class realities but ethnic realities are there as well. Increasingly they are the *dominant* realities. Social science needs to become much more sensitive to them." [15]

A current academic debate compounds the difficulty of disentangling class and ethnicity. The controversy grows out of the stubbornness of poverty in the United States. Despite public programs to eliminate poverty, it persists. To get at the root of this persistence, social scientists have come up with new theories. American blacks and Puerto Ricans have been the objects of most investigations, and this may explain why the current controversy takes the shape it does: social scientists are divided over whether the poor are a class or a subculture. In other words, what is the central fact about poor people — the fact with the greatest explanatory power? That they have less money than the majority, or that they live according to peculiar beliefs? Anthropologist Oscar Lewis is credited with the expression "culture of poverty," which sums up the second hypothesis. Lewis' critics, led by Charles A. Valentine, lean toward an economic explanation.[16] Elements of ethnicity such

---

[15] Daniel P. Moynihan, "Eliteland," *Psychology Today* 4, no. 4 (September 1970): 70.

[16] Oscar Lewis, "The Culture of Poverty," *Man Against Poverty: World War III* (New York: Knopf, 1968), pp. 260–74. Charles A. Valentine, *Cul-*

as family structure and morals are weighed by both sides, but
ethnic groups per se get lost in the shuffle. "Culture of poverty" studies make an ethnic group out of the poor themselves,
so that the condition of being impoverished supersedes the
usual communal bonds of language, race, and religion. Edward Banfield, also responding to widespread disillusionment
with the war on poverty, argues that programs stressing that
blacks are black, rather than that blacks are poor, are doomed
to failure. Removing the discrimination that confines a ghetto,
for example, will leave its residents still unable to reap the advantages of modern America. Racial ethnic factors do exist,
but — according to Banfield — they are secondary to debilitating self-perceptions.[17]

Those who detract from the "culture of poverty" thesis likewise look beyond the ethnic group to explain the dynamics of
poverty in an affluent society. They emphasize class and socio-
economic status, rather than value system. If policy-makers
want to make inroads into rural and urban slums, they should
worry less about the behavior of the poor and more about the
inequities of the nation's economic and political systems. Mexican Americans in Los Angeles and Puerto Ricans in Spanish
Harlem do have peculiar problems, but the cause does not lie
in cultural deviations. To the contrary, their troubles derive
from the fact that they *share* many of the middle-class aspirations of the American majority.

At bottom, the controversy concerns who is to blame for the
underdevelopment of the United States. Is the national political system incapable of adapting public resources to pressing
public needs? Alternatively, should the blame be placed at the
doorsteps of the poor themselves? Are certain subgroups underdeveloped and ill equipped to cope with urbanization and
technology?

Running through much of the literature on poverty in the

---

ture and Poverty (Chicago: University of Chicago Press, 1968). A lengthy
discussion of Valentine's critique by several social scientists, including
Lewis, appears in "Culture and Poverty: Critique and Counter-Proposals,"
Current Anthropology 10, no. 2–3 (April–June 1971): 181–201.

17 Edward C. Banfield, *The Unheavenly City* (Boston: Little, Brown,
1970), pp. 73–87.

United States and in other countries as well is the implication that being "ethnic" is a handicap in the modern world. Part of the "culture of poverty" is an emotional attachment to an ethnic community, *any* ethnic community (as long as one does not feel that white Anglo-Saxons comprise an ethnic community).[18] To be "ethnic" is to be parochial, limited in one's horizons and contacts. Because affluence in modern societies requires men to maximize their mobility, ethnic communalism is a hindrance. Consequently, assimilation into a cosmopolitan society is urged not only for the sake of political stability, but also because it enhances the opportunities of individuals to advance in a competitive society. To resist "detribalization" or secularization, or to cherish a language unsuitable for international communication, is to deliberately obstruct development.

Much of the material in subsequent chapters challenges this assumption of the dysfunctional nature of ethnic loyalty. There are instances in which individual progress toward self-confidence and efficacy depends on an ethnic group's development as a community. Since this is so, then one way to reduce class discrepancies is to foster ethnic pride and communal activism. Analyses based on "culture of poverty" and economic class both may be off the target. Heightened ethnic differentiation could be the price for overcoming poverty in a plural society.

When interethnic contact is governed by stable rules and expectations that serve the interests of all actors without diminishing their respective ethnic distinctiveness, we say that a "plural society" exists. The very notion of a plural society rests on a certain degree of stability. Most countries are plural societies, their diversity being due to colonial manipulation, ancient boundary disputes, or popular migrations. But development connotes transition. All kinds of social ground rules, including those governing interethnic relations, are unsettled

---

[18] A study of poor ethnic group members in New York City presents an opposite finding. It concludes that persons struggling amid poverty abandon their ethnic peculiarities. Chinese, Italians, and Puerto Ricans adopted many common traits as a result of poverty. The American Dream, stood on its head: poverty, not affluence, is the fire under the melting pot! Stanley E. Jones (Paper presented at the fifty-fifth annual meeting of the Speech Association of America, New York, December 29, 1969).

or discredited. Technological advances, demographic shifts, ideological conversions, decolonization, and foreign interventions call into question the wisdom of established modes of behavior. They alter lines of dependency and communication; they require new definitions of identity. Development does not automatically herald the demise of ethnicity. It does introduce a period of flux, cultural and social. The story of development is not just a nation's story; it is the story of numerous subnational communities trying to cope with profound change.

CHAPTER III

Ideology and the Reality
of Ethnic Identity

It is in country unfamiliar emotionally and topographically that one needs poems and roadmaps.

Clifford Geertz [1]

The Duiker antelope does not try to prove his Duikertude. You will know him by his elegant leap.

Wole Soyinka [2]

Is IDEOLOGY "DEAD"? Are we entering an era of development when ideology will be obsolete? The answers so far are inconclusive.[3] But the questioning has aroused interest in the nature and function of ideology. People speaking on both sides of the argument do agree that ethnicity's influence on the rise or fall of ideology is peripheral. In this respect social scientists are similar to the propagators of ideology, for both pay little attention to the existence of ethnic groups and ethnic identities.

[1] Clifford Geertz, "Ideology as a Cultural System," in David Apter, ed., *Ideology and Discontent* (New York: Free Press, 1964), p. 63.
[2] Wole Soyinka, African playwright, quoted in *New York Times*, April 24, 1966.
[3] See, for example, Chaim T. Waxman, ed., *The End of Ideology Debate* (New York: Simon and Schuster, 1969).

Ideology is a coherent view of reality and its potential, and most people concerned with ideology rate ethnicity as either unreal or irrelevant. This attitude is particularly characteristic of *modernizing* ideologies. Ethnicity is assigned significance mainly in those few ideologies that express skepticism about modern life. Ideology's typical avoidance of ethnic reality reflects the nature of both as they affect modernization.

FUNCTIONS OF IDEOLOGIES

The concept of ideology originated during the Enlightenment among the eighteenth-century French philosophes. This intellectual vanguard was eager for men to exploit their capacities for rational thought and action, thus expanding human beings' control of their own lives and of nature. Chief among the obstacles to such fulfillment were the irrational, subjective myths and superstitions onto which men held so firmly. "Ideologues" were men who sought to promote a "science of ideology" devoted to unmasking prejudice and maximizing objectivity.[4]

Ideology was an alternative to subconscious belief and mindless emotion, as well as a tool for action. Since Voltaire's time ideologues have proliferated, each professing an objective view of the world and man's place in it. To nonbelievers a given ideology appears little more than a new mask replacing an older mask, with reality just as far out of reach as ever. Consequently, many people — particularly those naively oblivious of their own ideological premises — reverse the original meaning of the term "ideology." It becomes synonymous with contrived and deceptive orthodoxy. In the decades following World War II, a time of intense rivalry among superpowers and powerful pressure for rationally planned change, one man's truth came to be another man's ideology.

"Erroneous" ideologies veil reality rather than expose it. But, theoretically, ideology is neither true nor false. It is a form of thought with a special relationship to action. Simply put, ideology is an explicit, logical system of ideas that explains how the world works; it provides reason and meaning together

4 David Minar, "Ideology and Political Behavior," *Midwest Journal of Political Science* 5, no. 4 (November 1961): 317–31.

with a set of goals and guides for behavior. Whether it takes the shape of African socialism, Western democracy, or Marxism, ideology is remarkable for its wedding of abstract reason to concrete action. Rare is the ideologue who is not also an activist.

Recently "ideology" has served as an umbrella for several quite different political phenomena. Studies in the United States by Robert Lane and in Malaysia by James Scott have sought to uncover *latent* ideologies in men not ordinarily described as ideologues: blue collar workers in Lane's case, federal civil servants in Scott's.[5] In their context ideology refers to the obscured, unconscious logic of individual beliefs. For Lane and Scott, ideology exists chiefly in the mind of the interviewer. Strictly speaking, the men of Bridgeport, Connecticut, and Kuala Lumpur are not ideological, but they have the potential for being so should conditions become so intense that latent beliefs are forced to the surface. Ideologization also can be the product of deliberate government policies that encourage citizens to articulate their beliefs and justify their actions. The Communist regime of China probably has gone further in this regard than any other contemporary government. The result is an unusually high level of political self-consciousness among Chinese citizens.[6] More commonly, a nation's citizens are compelled to think systematically about public affairs only sporadically, in times of great stress. Thus ideology is a distinctly public, rather than private, mode of thought. To an ideologue, however, everything is significant because it is explicitly and integrally related to the whole human experience. The way a father treats his son or a worker regards his job reflects in a small way the nature of society.

Despite frequent characterizations of ideology as somehow pathological — myths dressed up in the trappings of science — it performs positive functions for men, particularly during periods of crisis and change. Perhaps this is why people com-

[5] Robert Lane, *Political Ideology* (New York: Free Press), 1962. James Scott, *Political Ideology in Malaysia* (New Haven: Yale University Press, 1968).

[6] See Franz Schurmann, *Ideology and Organization in Communist China*, 2d ed. (Berkeley: University of California Press, 1968), pp. 17–104, 506–31. Also see Robert Jay Lifton, *Thought Reform and the Psychology of Totalism* (New York: Norton, 1963), pp. 243–399.

pelled to modernize rapidly are so subject to ideologization.

Men always require meaning, but only occasionally do they need public systems of beliefs. Meaning we may define as an understanding of the relationships between identifiable objects and events, and the consequences of those relationships. But meaning can derive from custom, religion, and firsthand experience. Most men rely on these sources to make sense of the world they must cope with daily. But at times traditions prove inadequate or unreliable. Life begins to seem unpredictable, empty, worthless. Events appear arbitrary, and the ramifications of even the most mundane acts are uncertain. In a minor way every person experiences this disjointedness as he matures and struggles to establish his own identity. But when large numbers of men face these traumas simultaneously, the time is ripe for ideology. Whereas heretofore it had been sufficient to follow well-worn paths of behavior with minimal conscious deliberation, now each action demands public explanation. What earlier could be taken for granted now must be explicitly defined.

Sometimes the burden of conscious redefinition falls disproportionately on a single subgroup in society. But ideologization is the same. Before they parted ways politically, black writer Eldridge Cleaver described admiringly how Stokely Carmichael drove home the importance of self-definition:

> Each time he gave a talk, Stokely would cite *Alice in Wonderland*. "When I use a word," Humpty Dumpty said in rather a scornful tone, "it means just what I choose it to mean, neither more nor less."
>
> "The question is," said Alice, "whether you *can* make words mean so many different things."
>
> "The question is," said Humpty Dumpty, "who is to be master, that's all." [7]

According to Cleaver, Carmichael went on to stress how critical it was for black people to do their own defining: *black power was the power to define*. In Cleaver's words, "By re-

[7] Eldridge Cleaver, "My Father and Stokely Carmichael," in Robert Sheer, ed., *Post-Prison Writings and Speeches* (New York: Vintage Books, 1969), p. 54.

acting to white America's definitions, blacks allowed themselves to be put in a bag which white America controlled." [8]
If whites defined black as evil, blacks should define it as good; if whites interpreted integration to mean blacks want to marry white girls, blacks should not react defensively. They should stick to their own definition of integration, which includes jobs, housing, and representation.[9] The problem of meaning for an ethnic community, in other words, is not simply a "language problem." American blacks speak the same language as whites. The problem is one of definition: who is the master of interpretation?

Except in a few fortunate Western nations, modernization has necessitated rapid transformation of the most fundamental aspects of society and culture. Moreover, "modern" implies a special kind of intellectual approach to comprehending that transformation. It presumes that man is rational, that affairs are open to secular analysis. Armed with this conviction, men respond to the unsettling advances of urbanization and industrialization by pursuing new modes of explanation. Even ideologies critical of modern life share the presumption of human rationality.

MODERNIZING IDEOLOGIES AND
ETHNIC IDENTITY

The basic function of ethnicity is to bind individuals to a group. It informs a person where he belongs and whom he can trust. Its foundation is a sense of common manners, rituals, and values, and the limits of that commonness set boundaries for group interaction. Ethnic groups are not irrational, but they do grow out of sentiment, custom, and familiarity rather than out of deliberate calculation. In this regard they are unlike labor unions, peasant syndicates, corporations, and other functional interest groups. Ethnic groups by their very defini-

---

[8] Ibid.

[9] Ibid., pp. 55–56. Carmichael was not comfortable with ideology in a vacuum, however. He advised a Chicago audience to "Organize! That is the only thing that counts. . . . And don't worry about ideology. I always say that my work is my ideology. You will find that after you get going, your ideology will develop out of your struggle." Ibid., p. 50.

tion have boundaries separating insiders from outsiders. Membership is ascriptive. An ethnic group that became universal — if such a thing is imaginable — would lose its ethnic quality.

To most ideologues of all political shadings, ethnicity is to be cast off in the process of rationalization because ethnic identity is too dense and inarticulate to be a product of reason. It confines men within parochial networks of relations. Historically, individuals have become less "ethnic" as they moved closer to self-conscious ideology. Look at the personal careers of Karl Marx, Joseph Stalin, Che Guevara, and Rosa Luxemburg: ideologization was their path out of ethnic communalism. Ideology can also serve as a vehicle not for denying ethnic identity altogether but for subsuming it under a universal movement not limited by ethnic criteria. Chinese-Malaysian Communist leader Chen Ping, Ukrainian Nikita Khrushchev, Yugoslavia's Tito, and Black Panther leader Huey Newton all came close to following this second route.

MARXISM AND NATIONALISM

Ideologies have excluded ethnic reality in different ways. Marxism, for instance, bases its world view on a presumption of materialism: relationships to the conditions of material production are the only real relationships. Property, capital, machines, labor, and the social stratification resulting from their unequal distribution are the stuff of reality for the Marxist. Karl Marx was all too aware of religion, nationalism, and other sorts of sentiment, but to him they were chimeras, concealing the real world and restricting men's ability to alter reality. Men marched off on religious crusades when they should have been fighting for land reform. Men died in foreign wars for the sake of their country's alleged honor when they should have been battling for control of their work places back home. Until people realized that economic class comprises their most significant association, they would devote their lives to tilting at windmills, and social orders would survive unchanged.[10]

10 Marx did recognize ethnic heterogeneity as an obstacle to class mobilization and singled out ethnic diversity as a factor undermining solidarity in the abortive revolution of 1848. Likewise, Frederick Engels, Marx's alter

Marxism has undergone numerous modifications since Marx sat on his bench in the British Museum. Even today Marxist ideology is plagued — or perhaps vitalized — by persistent debate about class, the conditions of revolution, the goals of a communist society. Who is a revisionist, Mao or Khrushchev? Is guerrilla strategist Regis Debray a heretic? Are experiments in Yugoslavia and Czechoslovakia to be welcomed or feared? What should a Marxist do when faced with Japanese and Indian Communist parties split between Maoists and Muscovites?

One of the persistent controversies among Marxists concerns nationalism. Both theory and practice demand at least temporary resolution of the argument, for nationality affects the theoretical concept of class as well as the strategic problems of alliances and party programs. The Western world Marx sought to understand was one in which both class and nationality provoked conflict. But in the middle 1800's socialists and nationalists frequently found themselves on the same side of the barricades. Workers and bourgeoisie were natural allies in the struggle against nineteenth-century autocracy. Most political conflict took place among the major ethnic groups within states. It would take another half-century or so before more remote ethnic communities were drawn into the political arena. Thus in the nineteenth century nationalism and ethnic mobilization were almost coterminous.

With the beginning of the twentieth century, nationalists and socialists moved farther apart. Nationalism, earlier considered a progressive force, increasingly was viewed by Marxists as a weapon of the propertied class. Nationalist fervor prevented workers from recognizing their true political allies. The nation-state was an artificial contrivance; the capitalist economic system was what men should be trying to understand.

Lenin, even more acutely than Marx, perceived the dangers

---

ego, cited ethnic divisiveness as one of the "very great peculiar difficulties for a steady development of a workers' party. . . . The bourgeoisie need only wait, passively, and the dissimilar elements of the working class fall apart again." Engels to Friedrich A. Sorge, London, December 2, 1893, quoted in Maurice Zeitlin, *Revolutionary Politics and the Cuban Working Class* (New York: Harper Torchbooks, 1970), p. 67.

inherent in nationalism for the international socialist movement. Lenin was the organization man, the practical revolutionary. He had to decide who was trustworthy, what appeals
could best cement the party, how broad a coalition was needed
to ensure revolutionary success. Each strategic decision brought
Lenin face to face with the problem of national allegiance.
During most of his political career he dealt with mainstream
nationalism—national movements led by dominant ethnic
communities in Germany, Austria, Poland, and Russia. Only
after 1917 did Lenin come to grips with the political aspirations of minority ethnic groups, particularly those within the
former czarist empire. Lenin's views on mainstream ethnic nationalities developed out of his arguments with other Marxists. The Austrian socialists Karl Renner and Otto Bauer
believed that nationalism was progressive because it had the
same enemy as socialism — the aristocracy of the decaying
Austro-Hungarian empire. Rosa Luxemburg sharply disagreed.
She displayed "radical impatience" with nationalist spokesmen, branding them totally irrelevant.[11] Lenin himself, a master of political strategy and a genius at assessing the potentials
of existing situations, took a stance somewhere in between
Renner, Bauer, Russia nationalists from the Ukraine, Georgia,
and Armenia on the one hand, and the supporters of Rosa
Luxemburg on the other. His position was strategically practical though ideologically ambivalent: nationalism was a force
to be harnessed even if it was generated by misconception.
Vietnamese and Chinese Communist leaders have wrestled
with similar discrepancies between strategy and ideology. Uneasy marriages of nationalism and Marxism become increasingly strained *after* such a communist revolution took place.[12]
When nationalism is a popular movement against imperial
autocrats, it is functional; when it takes the form of ethnic
communalism resisting central Communist party control, it is
intolerable.

Marxists acknowledge the short-term utility of ethnic identity but not its legitimacy. Moreover, nationalism, a political

11 Alfred G. Meyer, *Leninism* (New York: Praeger, 1957), pp. 147–48.
12 See Chapter IX, pp. 248–55.

allegiance, is useful. Communal bonds derived from cultural tradition are not. Ethnicity is least bothersome ideologically when it is coterminous with economic class, as in slave-holding and colonized countries.

Two beliefs lie behind Marxist abhorrence of nationalism and its ethnic content. First, Marxists hold that nationalist movements are commonly promoted by the middle class and ultimately serve its interests. If workers ally with bourgeois nationalists unconditionally, there is scant hope for class revolution. National security will take precedence over social reform, and workers' energies will be siphoned off in foreign wars. Second is the fact that minority communities fighting to retain their ethnic uniqueness usually turn out to be socially and economically "backward." If the Uzbeks of Soviet Central Asia or the Turkish Muslims of northwest China were permitted to preserve their distinctive life styles, this would mean granting portions of society immunity from history. Such communities, along with the Montagnard tribesmen of Vietnam and the Indians of Bolivia and Peru, are simply preindustrial and "feudal," according to Marxism. It is not their identity that is distinctive but their place in history. Though one or two steps behind, they are on the same road as everyone else. The solution to ethnic conflict therefore is to hasten the historical development of retarded groups. As they are liberated from feudal backwardness they will lose their uniqueness and come to share the proletarian class interests represented by the Communist party. Pampering ethnic communalism delays development and liberation. According to his Soviet interpreters, Lenin realized that in Central Asia the new economic relationships could not be established at once: "There had to be first created the necessary objective and subjective conditions for the transition of the peoples of Soviet East from precapitalist relations to socialism." [13] To this end, "there must be rapid industrial development in Central Asia which would provide the material basis for the transition of socialism." To ensure that subjective transformation accompanied objective develop-

[13] B. Lunin, *Lenin and the Peoples of the East* (Moscow: Novosti, 1970), p. 28.

ment, Great Russians, the most proletarian of Russia's peoples, were resettled in "feudal" minority regions. In addition, political education was introduced to guarantee the "deliverance of the Central Asian peoples from age-old religious and nationalist prejudices." [14]

The People's Republic of China has struggled for more than two decades to match ideological precepts with development requisites in minority affairs. Its experience underscores the dynamism of ideology in practice and reminds us of the changes that occur in ethnic relations as countries pursue modernization. The principal ethnic group in China is the Han Chinese, distinguished by its use of the Chinese system of character writing and a Confucian-Taoist tradition. Han Chinese, however, are by no means homogeneous, and cultural differences between Han Chinese of various regions can be almost as great as those separating Han and non-Han groups in China.[15] The lack of precision in defining Han Chinese is due to China's history of popular migrations to the south and to the north. However, the base point of a unified Chinese state is the empire of the Han dynasty (206 B.C.– A.D. 221), from which the current ethnic majority derives its label.

The principal non-Han groups are the Mongols and Uighur Turks of Sinkiang in the north and the Tibetans and Chuangs in the south. The Manchus, founders of the last dynasty, have virtually disappeared. Manchuria is settled now by Chinese who began migrating northward in the last century, despite Manchu prohibitions.[16] Today non-Han Chinese number be-

---

14 Ibid., p. 29.

15 Regional stereotypes still influence the way Han Chinese of northern, central, and southern China view each other. Stereotyping takes account of the characteristics of individual provinces as well. For instance, Chinese perceive people of Fukien province to be "narrow-minded, petty-minded, stick[ing] together, suave," whereas persons from Hunan (Mao's home) are "hot temper[ed], emotional, militaristic, heroic, upright, unyielding." Wolfram Eberhard, "Chinese Regional Stereotypes," *Asian Survey* 5, no. 12 (December 1965); 604–05.

16 During most of its reign the Ch'ing (Manchu) dynasty followed a laissez-faire policy toward the sparsely inhabited Manchurian region. Local tribes were granted wide-ranging autonomy in return for tribute. But the old policy of isolating the frontier from the rest of the empire and upholding traditional ethnic institutions lost its utility as Russia began pressing southward and Chinese migrants moved northward in

tween 35 million and 45 million, merely 6 per cent of the total population. But those relatively few people have an importance that the regime's ideologues cannot ignore. They occupy more than 50 per cent of the land, much of it rich in natural resources and along China's borders. Since the middle of the nineteenth century, political development for any Chinese government has involved exploiting natural resources and guaranteeing frontiers against foreign invasion. For the Communists the minorities take on further significance. The Communist party looks upon minority regions as showcases exemplifying the relevance of the Chinese revolutionary model for non-Han peoples, though minority persons are excluded from top posts in the vanguard of the revolution of the party, even in their own home regions.[17]

In policy as well as ideology, Peking's treatment of minorities has wavered between a "soft" approach permitting considerable ethnic freedom and a "hard line" stressing assimilation into Han Chinese society. The most influential factor determining which way the pendulum swings is how urgent modernization appears to the central government: the greater the felt urgency, the more assimilationist the approach. Mao Tse-tung's formulation of Marxist-Leninist doctrine recognizes two sorts of societal discontinuity. "Antagonistic" contradictions, such as exist between classes and between imperialists and the oppressed, must be eliminated if the revolution is to survive. "Nonantagonistic" contradictions, though they generate tension and warrant close surveillance, are tolerable; their existence will not subvert the revolution. Until about 1956 differences between Han and non-Han peoples were classified

---

search of arable land. In the end, Peking allowed Chinese migration only to stave off foreign intrusion and reorganized the administration to augment central control. Robert H. G. Lee, *The Manchurian Frontier in Ch'ing History* (Cambridge, Mass.: Harvard University Press, 1970), pp. 116–27.

17 June Dreyer, "China's Minority Nationalities in the Cultural Revolution," *China Quarterly*, no. 35 (July–September 1968), p. 96. For data on the relative exclusion of non-Han persons from top party posts, see Henry G. Schwartz, *Leadership Patterns in Chinese Frontier Regions*, External Research Paper No. 149 (Washington, D.C.: External Research Staff, Department of State, May 1964), pp. 82–86.

as "nonantagonistic." Mao and his colleagues could tolerate minority autonomy so long as they were convinced that, at bottom, China's lower classes shared a common interest. Admittedly, the Mongols, Uighurs, Chuangs, and Tibetans lagged far behind the Han people in socio-economic development. Still, they did share with them a common experience — oppression — and a common foe — imperialism.[18]

For the first several years the Chinese Communists were willing to permit some cultural differentiation by the minorities, for central policy-makers were preoccupied with consolidating power among the Han majority. This policy was justified ideologically by modifying the Soviet orthodoxy regarding criteria for nationhood. Stalin had set down four criteria for defining genuine nations: common language, territory, economic life, and psychological makeup. Furthermore, according to Marxism-Leninism, nations arise only at the time feudalism collapses and capitalism emerges. In other words, strictly speaking, a "nation" is a product of modernization. The Han Chinese could qualify under these ideological conditions, but the tribal and "feudal" peoples in the frontier regions could not. However, in accordance with the early "soft" approach, Chinese Communist theoreticians modified the Stalinist formula so that unqualified minorities — especially small tribal groups — could be recognized as "nationalities." After all, the argument went, these ethnic groups might well have progressed more rapidly had it not been for imperialistic oppression. Minorities had to follow Peking's direction to accelerate their development, but as "nationalities" they could modify practices to fit their own cultural traditions.[19] In the period directly following their 1949 victory, Communist leaders were anxious not to alienate or frighten the minorities or to leave

[18] Writing in the early 1950's, one of Communist China's most authoritative officials in minority affairs, Chang Chih'i, noted that this anti-imperialist bond uniting minorities and majority in China was absent in Russia, for there the imperialist oppressor of minorities had not been a foreigner but the Russian czar himself. As a result, minority alienation from Great Russians did not disappear with the Soviet revolution. In China, the Han-led revolution was seen as a liberation for all peoples. George Mosley, ed., *The Party and the National Question in China* (Cambridge, Mass.: M.I.T. Press, 1966), pp. 70–71.

[19] Ibid., pp. 36–37.

themselves open to outside charges of "Chinese chauvinism."

In the middle 1950's a major shift took place in Peking's outlook. The Chinese confrontation with American military might in Korea had been a traumatic experience. Khrushchev's discrediting of Stalin in his 1956 "secret speech" provoked profound anxiety in Peking. The leadership grew increasingly impatient with the slowness of development and began looking for alternatives to the Soviet model. Many contradictions that initially had seemed nonantagonistic were perceived now to be antagonistic and thus intolerable. Climaxing the growing sense of urgency was the Great Leap Forward. This grandiose plan for economic and political mobilization had as its symbol the commune. Mao, with his tremendous faith in manpower, hoped to speed up the Marxist historical process by leaping over the capitalist period into socialism. This policy shift diminished the regime's tolerance of all deviations, of anything that would hamper total mobilization. Consequently the Great Leap was accompanied by a new minorities policy, one that pressed for unswerving compliance with central directives. There was greater ideological emphasis on the minorities as historically backward, rather than as culturally distinct. Their retardation made full acceptance of Peking instruction all the more imperative. Any ethnic leader who resisted or tried to stir up his people was obviously a feudalist seeking to maintain his superiority under the cloak of nationalism. Chinese fear of being labeled "chauvinists" had been replaced by devotion to carrying "the Han man's burden." [20]

Nationalities Solidarity, a Chinese communist publication, described how minorities were progressing under this new policy. The only way for non-Han peoples to achieve liberation was to discard traditional myths and turn a deaf ear to the seductions of false "nationalists." Superstition and nationalism only delayed the day when men would gain proletarian class consciousness. The following quotation celebrates the contribution of minority women to their people's revolutionary progress:

> Nurtured by Mao Tse-tung's thought, broad laboring masses
> of minority women have shown a new attitude of struggle in

[20] Dreyer, "China's Minority Nationalities," pp. 98–99.

the three great revolutionary movements. Moreover, they have brought forth many, many revolutionary generals. These generals . . . have one outstanding point in common: they dared to struggle against feudal superstitions and against the forces of the old society that are hindering socialist progress. They dared to break completely with all the old customs and old conceptions, to do things that have never been done before.[21]

The editor warns against recognition of any people's "special characteristics." The only reality is class:

Feudal superstition, all old customs, and old points of view are component parts of the superstructure that served the reactionary ruling class. In the old society they were tools used by the landlords, serf owners and slave owners, or other [segments of] the exploiting classes to oppress and exploit the laboring people of their own nationality. In the new society, these reactionary classes were unwilling to die and they tried in a thousand and one ways to use [feudal superstition and old custom] to numb the class consciousness of the laboring people. . . . It is not difficult to see that feudal superstition, the clan concept, and all other backward customs and habits bearing the brand of [the exploiting] class are certainly not any "special characteristics," but are tricks on the pretext of which the reactionary classes seek to prevent the thorough liberation of the workers. . . . We should use the method of class analysis in order to clarify our class viewpoint.[22]

The American escalation of the war in Vietnam caused Peking to worry about the chronically unstable southern provinces with their several ethnic minorities. China's break with the Soviet Union reinforced Peking's desire to ensure the security of the minority regions along its northern borders, especially Sinkiang, the location of Chinese nuclear research.[23]

21 "A Female General in the Three Great Revolutions," *Nationalities Solidarity* (March 1966), pp. 37–39, reported in *Chinese Sociology and Anthropology* 1, no. 1 (Fall 1968): 71.

22 Ibid., pp. 71–72.

23 Peking did an about-face to sanction a nationalist resurgence among Mongols in Inner Mongolia, perhaps with the hope that Mongol nationalism would restrict Russia's influence in Outer Mongolia, a sovereign state but a satellite of Moscow. Paul Hyer, "The Reevaluation of Chinggis-Khan: Its Role in the Sino-Soviet Dispute," *Asian Survey* 6, no. 12 (December 1966); 696–705. Then in 1972, apparently anxious over border security,

In mid-1970 Chinese communist authorities expressed concern over Soviet-directed subversion in Sinkiang. The Sinkiang revolutionary committee (replacing the regular party machinery during the Cultural Revolution) called the Soviet appeal to Sinkiang's minority peoples "social-imperialism" and advocated greater efforts "to promote the great revolutionary unity of people of all nationalities." Within Sinkiang's six hundred thousand square miles are uranium and oil as well as a Uighur Turkic ethnic group, Kazakhs, Mongols, and some 2 million Chinese. Soviet broadcasts from over the border in Soviet Kazakhstan played on non-Han unrest. They declared that the situation in Sinkiang was "extremely bad" and that the Chinese had "forced the people of Sinkiang to endure political suppression and economic exploitation." Furthermore, the Soviet broadcast said, the Chinese had destroyed the "traditional culture of minority peoples." Sinkiang's revolutionary committee retorted that class enemies were cooperating with the Russians in "undermining our national unity." [24]

On top of the Sino-Soviet split came the Cultural Revolution of 1967–1969 with its intensification of ideological consciousness. The Red Guards, an extraparty force, were standard-bearers of this campaign to purify the Communist party of revisionists and reaffirm the ideals of the revolution. Many young leftists in Europe and the United States admired the youthful Red Guards for their attacks on bureaucratization, but on the question of minority rights the two groups diverged. During the Cultural Revolution Red Guards and other backers of Mao Tse-tung demanded that party administrators in the minority regions be purged. Though Han Chinese, these

---

Peking took drastic steps to curtail Mongol nationalism. It detached a large section of Inner Mongolia's western territory and placed it under the authority of Kansu province and the Ninghsia Hui Autonomous Region, where Peking had tighter control. Native Mongols were thus further dispersed. Gene Gregory, "China: The Troubled Grasslands," *Far Eastern Economic Review* 85, no. 4 (January 22, 1972), p. 15.

24 *New York Times*, August 16, 1970. See also Harrison E. Salisbury, "Marco Polo Would Recognize Mao's Sinkiang," *New York Times Magazine* (November 23, 1969), pp. 14–41; and Harrison E. Salisbury, *War Between Russia and China* (New York: Bantam Books, 1970), pp. 37–44, 101–15.

veterans had learned from experience that it was best to allow cultural variations in the implementation of Peking's policies. The failure of the Great Leap added to their caution. From the vantage point of the ideologically zealous Maoists' however, bureaucratic pragmatism only camouflaged persistent "decadence" within feudal societies. They published pamphlets accusing the old party of creating a "national schism" by overemphasizing the rights of national minorities. A reformed party should stress the Maoist dictum "National struggle is in the final analysis a question of class." [25]

The ethnic and ideological power situation was especially complicated in the southeastern province of Kwangsi, technically an autonomous region because of its large population of Chuangs. At the height of the Cultural Revolution violent conflict in Kwangsi involved numerous Red Guard factions, each claiming to be most loyal to Mao, as well as Red Army elements and old party bureaucrats. Most of the political infighting was done by ethnic Han Chinese. Out of a provincial population of twenty-three million there were eight million Chuang farmers, clustered mainly in the mountainous western part of the province. In the turmoil of 1965–1969 they remained on the sideline. Peking named Wei Kuo-ching, a Han-assimilated Chuang, to head a group to reestablish Kwangsi's administration. Red Guards protested Wei's appointment, calling him anti-Maoist. Traditionally there had been friction between Hans and Chuangs, and the Cultural Revolution acerbated ethnic relations. Despite his assimilation, Wei was thought to have Chuang supporters. Thus, though he was linked with the old party bureaucracy, Peking was hesitant to oust him and anger Chuangs. Minority sensitivity outweighed Red Guard protests in Kwangsi.[26] Kwangsi's political disorder was all the more worrisome to the central leadership because of its strategic relationship to the war in Vietnam. The main rail lines between Peking and Hanoi ran through Kwangsi, and the violence of the Cultural Revolution delayed trains carrying Soviet and Chinese materials to North Vietnam. In

25 Dreyer, "China's Minority Nationalities," p. 109.
26 *New York Times,* July 14, 1968.

mid-1968 Chou En-lai sent a personal telegram to Kwangsi insisting that disorder be ended and a revolutionary committee established under Wei's direction.[27]

Fluctuations in Chinese Communist ideology represent more than attempts simply to justify policy changes. Ideology is supposed to endow the chaos of everyday life with meaning and direction. If that life is as dynamic as China's has been for the last seventy years, a rigid ideological catechism is useless. Chinese Communists owe success thus far to their willingness to experiment and to revise doctrine when it clearly does not match reality. Maoist thought has never deserted the basic tenets of Marxism-Leninism, but it has recognized that British and Russian conditions are not timeless or universal in each detail. As for the place of minority peoples in the revolutionary scheme, they remain most secure in their class identification. Even China's "soft" line started from this point. The question was how rapidly peoples outside the mainstream of modernization could catch up. The one price that Chinese Communists were most hesitant to pay was opening themselves to charges of imperialism. They had just overthrown a system accused of bowing before imperialists, and they were denouncing Moscow as imperialistic for its refusal to surrender frontier territory sliced off from China by the Russian czars.[28]

Here is the core of the Marxist ideological dilemma in multiethnic states: all peoples are essentially members of socioeconomic classes, but imposing class consciousness on a group

[27] Harold Hinton, "Vietnam Policy, Domestic Factionalism, Regionalism, and Plotting a Coup," in Lucian W. Pye, ed., *Cases in Comparative Politics: Asia* (Boston: Little, Brown, 1970), pp. 145–58. See confirmation of Wei's survival in *New York Times,* February 22, 1971.

[28] George Lichtheim finds that Lenin linked his theory of imperialism too closely to private capitalism. Lenin naively assumed that as countries revolted and adopted socialism, imperialism would disappear, The Chinese communists, in Lichtheim's opinion, are poor Marxist theoreticians, but they have made a significant contribution to Marxist thought. They, far better than the Russians, recognize the possibility of *socialist imperialism.* Revising Lenin, the Chinese see imperialism not as a partner of one kind of economic system (for example, capitalism) but as the product of *development gaps* between socialist or capitalist countries and underdeveloped countries. George Lichtheim, *Imperialism* (New York: Praeger, 1971).

whose traditions obscure class divisions leads to oppression from above. How can Marxism-Leninism-Maoism be true both to class analysis and to anti-imperialism? Added to the dilemma is Communism's promise of modernization to underdeveloped countries. Communist doctrine is a blueprint for development, but it calls for centralization and a high level of popular mobilization. With a revolutionary war still sharply etched on their memory, the Chinese Communists place special emphasis on the potential of mobilized manpower to accomplish what technology and investment capital accomplished in advanced nations. Coupled with the presumption of proletarian class cohesion, a modernizing strategy dependent on human mobilization made minority autonomy and claims of "special characteristics" unacceptable. The "winding down" of the Cultural Revolution and the cooling of Sino-Soviet hostilities relieved some of the immediate pressure. But the existence of ethnic groups taking pride in their distinctiveness from the Han Chinese continues to pose policy problems and ideological embarrassment.

The adequacy of any ideology is judged from at least two different perspectives. One is that of the Soviet and Chinese cases, where majority communities are looking for means of coopting minorities into inclusive movements. The other perspective is that of the minority community torn between broadly-based alliances and protection of its own "special characteristics." Marxism-Leninism has attracted numerous minorities searching for an explanation as well as an escape from their oppressed status, though recruitment of minority peoples by the Communist party is not necessarily proof of the appeal of Marxist ideology. For instance, Chinese Malaysians who joined the mainly Chinese Communist party insurgency during the 1940's and 1950's were found to be motivated primarily by ethnic grievances and had little ideological comprehension.[29] A small sampling of ethnic Cambodians who

[29] These findings, and those for South Vietnam, were gathered from interviews with defectors. It could be that these men were among the more weakly committed and thus less ideological of rebels. Lucian W. Pye, *Guerrilla Communism in Malaya* (Princeton: Princeton University Press, 1956), pp. 222–26.

joined the Viet Cong in South Vietnam demonstrated a similar disinterest in formal communist ideas.[30]

THE AMERICAN BLACK AND MARXISM

American blacks have had a long history of ambivalence toward Marxism. Generally, blacks who believed their deprivations resulted from the materialism of industrial capitalism have found Marxist doctrine most satisfactory. The oppressiveness of the black condition may be more severe and blatant than that suffered by other sectors of the lower class, but it too sprang from capitalism's need to exploit human labor. Marxist concepts have less relevance for American blacks who think of their condition in terms of cultural deprivation — a denial of cultural heritage and pride robbing black men of self-confidence.

Harold Cruse, critic and historian, is perhaps the most eminent black to break publically with Marxism. Cruse wonders whether any radical social theory is applicable to both whites and blacks in the United States. The gap between their social perceptions is a *cultural* gap:

> There can be no new social theory of radical nature developed in America until this gulf in perception is breached with the aid of a new cultural theory. But the most difficult concept for the white radical mind in America to understand and accept will be precisely such a cultural theory.[31]

Cruse directs this comment to all radicals, but especially to American Marxists, who he believes are either unable or unwilling to acknowledge the need of blacks for cultural nationalism. Since American blacks do not command property or the tools of production, they are more reliant than ever on communal unity. That solidarity, in turn, will emerge only in tandem with cultural revival.[32] Cruse questions the sincerity of white Marxists who court American blacks and twist their

---

[30] Jeffrey Record, "Viet Cong: Image and Flesh," *Trans-action* 8, no. 3 (January 1971): 49–51.

[31] Harold Cruse, *Rebellion or Revolution* (New York: Morrow, Apollo Editions, 1968), p. 27.

[32] Ibid., pp. 66–67.

ideological framework to fit black experience. Negro reality is not the white laborer's reality. Thus the relationship of black oppression to modern capitalism is unique, fitting only awkwardly into the dialectic of international Marxism. In Cruse's view:

> the Negro movement has its spiritual affinities not with the white working class of America whose status vis-a-vis American capitalism is qualitatively different from Negroes. White labor's heyday is behind them in the history of the 1930's. The American Negro movement is currently a semi-colonial revolt that is more inspired by events outside America than within it.[33]

Harold Cruse maintains that blacks need cultural nationalism to overcome American colonial imperialist domination. This need was the basis of his rejection of Marxist ideology. However, other black militants today stress the same condition in order to support the validity of Marxism in the black struggle. The Black Panthers and others define the black community as an "internal colony." This analysis, focusing on colonization, restores the relevance of Marxism. Classical Marxist interest in industrial production and the proletarian class is not attracting these radicals. Imperialism, rather, draws their attention. In other words, whereas Cruse dismisses Marxism, the Black Panthers find meaning in Marxism-*Leninism*. Cruse sees American blacks linked to other black peoples through cultural and racial identity. The Panthers, by contrast, have doubts about black studies programs and other activities stressing cultural identity because colonization is above all a *political* condition. They tie their cause to that of all Third World peoples who suffer under colonialism or the more subtle neo-colonialism. In the words of Black Panther Eldridge Cleaver:

> The first thing that has to be realized is that it is a reality when people say that there is a "black colony" and a "white

---

[33] Ibid., pp. 151–52. Cruse's article "Marxism and the Negro" is reprinted together with retorts and criticisms by the Socialist Workers party (Trotskyist), in Harold Cruse, George Breitman, and Clifton Deberry, *Marxism and the Negro Struggle* (New York: Merit, 1965).

mother country." Only if this distinction is borne in mind is it possible to understand that there are two different sets of political dynamics now functioning in America.[34]

The white liberals' campaign for racial integration is interpreted as simply a neo-colonialist strategy for exercising control through socialization. The "internal colony" is not liberated through integration; it is just harder to locate.

Even federal programs combining integration with community control are called neo-colonial. A black student of economics at Columbia University attacks the Model Cities Program:

> The Model Cities program of the City of Chicago is a neo-colonial program, seeking as its primary objective not to better the living conditions of black people, but rather to entice them into a position of servitude within that urban center. . . . Rather than see its empire crumble, the United States throws a few crumbs from its table to the minority groups living within its boundaries.[35]

The author draws an analogy between the situation of American blacks and that of African blacks since the departure of European colonialists. An "internal colony" and "neo-colonial imperialism" are subtler forms of domination than Sir Stamford Raffles or Rudyard Kipling ever imagined:

> A neo-colony is a colony that is no longer needed as such. In the African situation, this meant that the colonizer had completed his work of industrializing the territory. He had disrupted the indigenous way of life of its inhabitants, replacing traditional values with those of the West. . . . All that remained was to establish the indigenous bourgeoisie, sympathetic to the Western culture which had created it, at the political helm, and the country would then be granted "independence." The colonizers could then withdraw their forces back home. They sit comfortably in their living rooms, reaping economic gains from all over the world.[36]

[34] Eldridge Cleaver, "The Land Question and Black Liberation," in Speer, *Post-Prison Writings and Speeches*, p. 57.

[35] Ralph H. Metcalf, Jr., "Chicago Model and Neo-colonization," *Black Scholar* 1, no. 6 (April 1970): 24.

[36] Ibid., p. 25.

Black militants who have adopted the Leninist explanation fail to see much difference between Senegal and the Model Cities district of Chicago.

Analysis of black reality in a framework of colonialism and nationalism induces broad and highly political programs. Initiation of new modes of drama and dress is not sufficient, nor is the mere replacement of white officeholders with black officeholders. A case study of politics in Gary, Indiana, before and after the election of its first black mayor, Richard Hatcher, employs concepts of colonization and nationalism to clarify the depth of transformation necessary if the city's black citizens are to be active participants rather than passive spectators in civic affairs. Prior to Hatcher's 1967 campaign and 1968 inauguration, Gary was the "colonized" corporate company town par excellence. Gary was designed by the United States Steel Corporation in 1905 to suit its own industrial needs. Even the town's demographic design mirrored company needs. Initially it brought cheap white labor over from Europe. Later, as immigration quotas tightened, the company recruited black laborers from the South. By 1967 Gary was a three-tiered society: corporate management at the top, white "ethnics" holding skilled labor positions and municipal offices in the middle, and the numerically superior blacks outside the spheres of power and opportunity at the bottom. Many blacks saw Hatcher's remarkable electoral victory as the dawn of a new age. Hatcher had run on a broad platform, evidence that he knew how much had to be altered if Gary was to be modernized and its black citizens given equality of service and influence.[37]

To date Gary's political dawn has been overcast. The problem lies, according to an observer who worked in the Hatcher administration, not in the new mayor's performance but in the institutional barriers to change. As the Hatcher administration was frustrated by bureaucratic resistance, its black constituents lost enthusiasm and hope. A new face in city hall had not improved their lives. The new mayor confronted a

37 Edward Greer, "The 'Liberation' of Gary, Indiana," *Trans-action* 8, no. 3 (January 1971): 30–36.

situation not unlike that facing a nationalist regime taking office as the Tricolor or Union Jack is lowered:

> When the new administration took over City Hall in January 1968 it found itself without keys to offices, with many vital records missing (for example, the file on the United States Steel Corporation in the controller's office) and with a large part of the city government's moveable equipment stolen. The police force, for example, had so scavenged the patrol cars for tires and batteries that about 90 per cent of them were inoperable. This sort of thing is hardly what one thinks of as a normal process of American government. It seems appropriate to a bitter ex-colonial power. It is, in fact, exactly what happened as the French left Sekou Touré's Guinea.[38]

The "liberation" of Gary's black community does not require secession, but it was not won simply by victory at the polls. In the context of colonial-nationalist analysis, liberation means an end to "neo-colonialist" interference from Washington and sustained black nationalist mobilization locally.[39]

The usual response to colonialism is nationalism, and presently within the American black community is a spirited debate about the practicality and character of black nationalism. There are at least three different positions, not in absolute contradiction but overlapping at certain points. They appear more mutually contradictory when set out ideologically than when black men and women personally sort out their beliefs and hopes.

One position is nationalism based on Leninist concepts of capitalist imperialism. Associated with the Black Panthers, this is an interracial, internationalist definition emphasizing the

[38] Ibid., p. 36. Analyses of Hatcher's 1967 election are also in Jeffrey K. Hadden, Louis H. Massotti, Victor H. Thiessen, "The Making of the Negro Mayors, 1967," in August Meier, ed., *Black Experience: The Transformation of Activism* (Chicago: Aldine, 1970), pp. 112–19; Chuck Stone, *Black Political Power in America* (New York: Dell, 1970), pp. 220–24.

[39] Since Gary had been placed in bankruptcy by preceding administrations, which underassessed United States Steel and collaborated with organized crime, Mayor Hatcher had to depend on the federal government for funds for innovations. This relationship made Gary vulnerable to pressure from Washington. Stone, *Black Political Power in America*, pp. 39, 63.

common plight of all Third World peoples, whether they be American Indians, Chicanos, and Puerto Ricans, or foreigners in Nigeria and Vietnam. It is not essentially ethnic nationalism but more inclusive political nationalism. There is even room for white middle-class radicals in this Leninist nationalist movement. Drawing from Marxism-Leninism, Panther spokesmen such as Huey Newton insist that genuine decolonization of an "internal colony" must include restructuring of the entire American society. Black nationalism can be attained without emigration if the society in which blacks reside is rid of its exploitative mechanisms.[40]

A second nationalist program proposes physical separation and the creation of a new territorial base in which American blacks can exercise control of their own destinies. Sometimes this state is said to be in Africa, where blacks by cultural heritage are most at home. Current leaders such as Stokely Carmichael are frequently associated with an earlier black leader, Marcus Garvey, when they suggest such a separation for achieving nationalist liberation. Other separatists look less toward Africa and more toward the continental United States when they search for territory.

Finally, there is a nationalism that envisions not territorial sovereignty but cultural liberation for black citizens within the United States. This is more an ethnic than a political program and comes close to the aims spelled out by Cruse.

The three definitions of nationalism are grounded on different notions of the relationship between black ethnicity and class, and between culture and self-determination. Newton's, Carmichael's, and Cruse's varieties of nationalism also differ in their politicalness and extra-ethnic inclusiveness.[41] Lenin's

40 Huey P. Newton, "Letter to the R.N.A. [Republic of New Africa]," in Philip S. Foner, ed., *The Black Panthers Speak* (Philadelphia: Lippincott, 1970), pp. 71–72.

41 Despite important disagreements, blacks from a wide range of political positions have expressed indignation over an admittedly "sympathetic" white analyst's conclusion that black nationalism is only a "fantasy" and the colonial metaphor mistaken. The book is Theodore Draper, *The Rediscovery of Black Nationalism* (New York: Viking, 1970). Critiques include those by Eric Foner, "In Search of Black History," *New York Review of Books* (October 22, 1970), pp. 11–14; Eric Foner and Theodore Draper, "Exchange on Black Nationalism," *New York Review of Books*

concept of imperialism is causing unease among the Han Chinese and Great Russian Communists intent upon modernizing their multi-ethnic countries. But for militant ethnic leaders in the United States, such as the Black Panthers and the Puerto Rican Young Lords, Marxism without Lenin's anti-imperialism would offer little.

THE DILEMMA OF DEMOCRATIC IDEOLOGY

As the French ideologues implied, becoming ideological is a purging process. Marxism is not alone in pressing men to purge themselves of ethnic sentiment. Western democracy also favors deethnicization. However, while Marxists point to class membership as the cornerstone of objectivity and reasonable behavior, students of Locke and Jefferson instruct men that they are, first and last, individuals: it is as individuals that men are born into this world to inherit rights and obligations.

Every ideology seeks to define the basic unit of society, the entity most salient in shaping relations of power, trust, and cooperation. Marxism points to class, collective entity. Democratic thought picks out individual human beings apart from any collective body with which they may associate. Democrats acknowledge that groups form and have an impact on social conditions but deny that a group is organic. It is simply the summation of its members' interests, and has no reality apart from the individuals who belong to it. In efforts to explain and predict governmental or economic behavior a democrat returns repeatedly to individual men and women. Since ideologies are action oriented, what is empirically true is normatively proper. Any realistic political system must cope with individuals; likewise, individual opportunity and fulfillment are the legitimate ends of the good polity. Cooperation and public spirit stem from individual interests and actions. People are treated as a class, tribe, or sexual group in certain societies, but these are aberrations to be remedied.

(December 3, 1970), pp. 49–53; Harold Cruse, "A Fantasy in Black and White," *Book World* (July 26, 1970), p. 7; Earl Ofari, "Book Reviews," *Black Scholar* 2, no. 2 (October 1970): 47–52.

In a democratic context, schools and bureaucracies that seek efficiency as well as justice promote people according to their own merit. It is realistic and right (though the norm is frequently breached) that political candidates appeal to constituents as individuals, not as groups. Citizens, in turn, maximize their political influence when they evaluate officeholders as individual actors, not as vessels of some particular culture. Yet democratic ideology runs into trouble when serving as a guide for citizens and their governments. Thomas Jefferson and John Dewey share with Lenin and Mao the dilemma of denying ethnic groups theoretically while being preoccupied with ethnic conflict strategically. Standing on a platform and pronouncing ethnic loyalty to be an anomaly will not make it disappear.

Currently democratic believers on both right and left are uneasy about ethnicity's ideological nonconformity. The uneasiness is apparent in British, Canadian, and American debates over education, representation, and job training. In each case, the established ideological presumption is that each person should move ahead according to his own skills and worth. Self-conscious democracies cannot tolerate anything that smacks of vertical ethnic differentiation. But what should be done about the striking imbalances between ethnic groups? Should ethnic quotas be sanctioned? Should prospective employees put their photographs on their job applications? Should a person be put on a government committee *because* he is French or Puerto Rican or Pakistani? There is a new attitude toward racially segregated schools and communities. Desegregation and voting rights guarantees fit nicely into the democratic credo. But what should a democrat think of a largely black school that resists desegregation in order to retain communal cohesion?

Democratic ideology goes undisturbed as long as ethnic communities are intent upon assimilation or as long as they are too politically underdeveloped to make their existence forcefully known to the oblivious majority. While this blissful condition lasts, democrats can sing the praises of individualism and pluralism simultaneously. The conceptual trick is to acknowledge diversity of cultures within the society but assume that culture deals mainly with styles and cooking recipes and has relatively little impact on ambitions, moral judgments, and public goals. If ethnicity is this shallow, then things that really matter to individuals will hardly be affected, and it will not impinge on important national decisions. In other words, the discrepancy between democratic ideology and ethnic reality is resolved by reducing ethnicity to style. However, as ethnicized individuals begin to question the benefits of assimilation, and as ethnic communities engage in their own political development, this comfortable premise is harder to maintain.

Theoretically, the democratic state is inescapably pluralistic because it consists of individuals and is legitimized by popular participation. James Madison, chief engineer in the construction of American federalism, went so far as to say (in No. 10 of the *Federalist Papers*) that men were so ornery that they would manufacture conflicts of interest if none naturally existed. However, for the most part, differences among individuals or groups of individuals reflected differences in interests, which in turn arose from dissimilar social perspectives. Because men in a truly democratic polity would be free to work out their own destinies, they were likely to be socially and geographically mobile. Alexis de Tocqueville, French aristocrat and social analyst traveling through Jacksonian America in the 1830's, was the first of a long line of observers to be impressed by the restlessness and fragility of associational bonds among this country's citizens. Tocqueville predicted that as the democratic ethos spread to Europe men there would experience a similar mobility and dilution of human ties. A century or so later writers are struck by the applicability of the Frenchman's prophesy, not only for Germany and Britain but for Japan and Singapore. Tocqueville scrutinized the dark as well as the light side of democratic society and observed that in America, "the bond of human affection is extended, but it is relaxed." [42]

The mobile democrat did not wander about in a vacuum,

---

[42] Alexis de Tocqueville, *Democracy in America* (New York: New American Library, 1956), p. 193.

however. Quite the contrary: he had more and more diverse associations than ever due to his freedom to pursue opportunities according to his merits, unhindered by his family or status at birth. Democratic pluralism allows for a multitude of organized interests, but the danger of uncontrollable conflict is mitigated by the fact that every citizen has numerous interests and group affiliations that cut across each other. The individual citizen is the sole consistency. No group envelops the entirety of its members' lives; therefore none can claim total allegiance. In any public dispute citizens will have mixed feelings or be distracted by other matters.

Though the political system in a pluralist democracy has coercive powers, they are used sparingly because legitimacy rests on popular consensus. Minorities oppose governmental policies from time to time but, because morality and religion are kept outside the government's purview, opposition is never so intense that it cannot be mollified. It follows that public authority is limited, many activities being conducted by private or semi-public organizations. Political processes are fractured just enough to permit accommodation, compromise, and veto at certain steps. And, at least in the United States, there are multiple centers of power.[43]

Believers in pluralistic and individualistic democracy are not alarmed by the persistence of ethnic groups so long as their members are attached to other interest associations as well. If the country is genuinely democratic, men inevitably will be too because, after all, five Italian-Americans and five French Canadians remain ten individuals differentiated by aspirations and talents. In fact, ethnic groups that are not stubbornly exclusive can be functional because they cut across and thus mute socio-economic class conflict.[44]

43 Robert A. Dahl, *Pluralist Democracy in the United States: Conflict and Consent* (Chicago: Rand McNally, 1967), p. 23.
44 Raymond E. Wolfinger, "Some Consequences of Ethnic Politics," in Kent Jennings and L. Harmon Zeigler, eds., *The Electoral Process* (Englewood Cliffs, N.J.: Prentice-Hall, 1966), p. 52.
According to one of the newer spokesmen for American Jewish radicalism, "during its period of credibility, the melting pot served as the contractual mechanism for buying into American democracy and affluence and was rarely recognized as a device for fragmentation and mass control.

When ethnic groups *do* appear personally undifferentiated and thus politically unassimilable, immigration restrictions may be imposed for the alleged welfare of democracy. Australia, Britain, Malaysia, and the United States all have immigration laws intended in part to ensure that pluralism encourages individual separateness. Modern democracies nonetheless feel more comfortable if quotas can be defined in terms of the functional and skill needs of the nation. Outright ethnic categories are harder to reconcile ideologically.

The British government has been under pressure to revise its imperial concept of immigration, which permitted entry to persons from all over the globe who held British passports. General unemployment in the West Indies, African nationalism in Kenya, and professional unemployment in India all contributed to a rise in nonwhite immigrants. Neither the Labour nor the Conservative party was eager to author a law clearly discriminating against particular ethnic communities. The Conservative solution was revealed finally in February 1971. It did not go so far as urged by Conservative Enoch Powell, spokesman for Britons who would like to have seen forced "repatriation" of all "coloured" immigrants, but it went far enough to arouse criticisms of civil rights advocates. Under the proposed law, an Indian, an Australian or a Kenyan who wanted to come to Britain to work would need a permit for a specific job. On the surface, the requirement is rational, modern, and functional, not ascriptive. But there are exceptions. The immigration bill gives great advantages to Commonwealth persons with ancestral — and thus implicitly racial ethnic — connections with Britain. These exceptions, called "patrials," are defined as persons born or naturalized in Britain or having a parent or grandparent who was. Patrials will

---

Just enough ethnic and cultural variety was permitted to disarm the wary, to separate us into mutually hostile, competitive groups and so keep us vulnerable to collective blackmail. Not nearly enough identity was allowed to remain to serve as a source of moral inspiration or political strength and unity, capable of providing motivation, energy and power for progressive action." Robert Greenblatt, "Out of the Melting Pot into the Fire," in James A. Sleeper and Alan L. Mintz, eds., *The New Jews* (New York: Vintage Books, 1971), p. 40.

be allowed to enter without restriction. Civil rights oganizations and Asian and West Indian representatives were quick to note that this gave an unfair advantage to the Kenyan white settler over the Kenyan African or Asian.[45] It takes legal and ideological adroitness to draft a *democratic* immigration bill.

The democrat trusts in the rationality of the average man. Rationality involves dissection of one's condition, separating needs from one another, and calculating priorities. Few conditions are immune from rational political inspection. Those that are, like religion, should be beyond politics. Men naturally have emotions, but they can be put into perspective and subjected to the light of reason. Nations progress only if interests are rationally articulated and conflicts of interest are weighed against requisites for growth. Ethnic identity is treated with the same clear-eyed rationality as occupational or regional concerns. Any claims by ethnic groups for special status or undissected treatment must be dismissed because such groups will compete for members' attention and public rewards on an equal footing with labor unions and gun clubs. Thus, for example, president Nixon for several months refused to meet with twelve black congressmen, saying that he did not want to acknowledge them as ethnic group delegates — although they represented interests of constituencies as disparate as Los Angeles and Brooklyn and were elected by numerical majorities.[46] The sum of individual votes, not an ethnic mandate, invests them with authority — according to the democrat.

A representative's duty is to ensure that institutions treat citizens as equals, follow publicly sanctioned procedures in making decisions, and abide by limits set down in law. Substantively, public actions should foster popular participation and encourage men to exploit their own potentials. If the law is fair, the economy productive, the performance prized, all citizens will reap satisfaction and have reason to remain loyal.

Democratic liberals are puzzled when their efforts to pro-

---

45 *New York Times*, February 25, 1971. For a profile of the controversial Enoch Powell and his immigration proposal see Paul Foot, *The Rise of Enoch Powell* (Baltimore: Penguin Books), 1969.
46 *New York Times*, February 14, 1971.

mote representation and widen avenues of individual mobility elicit contempt from newly self-conscious ethnic communities. To the leaders of a mobilized ethnic group liberal programs look like attempts to fragment the group's hard-won cohesion. Individual mobility threatens to accentuate class differences, opportunism, and nonethnic values within the community. This is especially so when the broadened social avenues are still defined by criteria foreign to the ethnic group's distinctive value system. Even representation in state and national bodies seems to undermine communal unity, for democrats demand that leaders be elected by quantitative processes, even though electoral contests may strain internal ethnic consensus. Again, the democrat may accept as spokesmen group members who approximate the style and mode of negotiation valued by the rest of society. Finally, by agreeing to democratic representational procedures, the ethnic community may be creating a new elite whose prestige depends not on constituent support but on the majority group's evaluation.

Liberals are eager to define advancement in individual terms not just to break up the dangerous solidarity of ethnic communities. They usually also act out of a sincere ideological belief that individual fulfillment can be enjoyed only when man is free, unburdened by collective attachments or the past. To maximize potentials the democrat must define his identity in terms of personal goals and perhaps suprahuman ideals. All other affiliations are transient and mutable. Americans' progression from immigrant generation to less-ethnic second generation to fully individualized third generation is analogous to the move westward. Both are journeys away from the confines of the past and toward expansive opportunities. Many European and North American democrats believe ethnicity clings to men who should be allowed to go free. Assimilationist members of ethnic groups also believe this. Their complaint is only that theory is violated in practice; they are willing to drop their ethnicity, but other people keep categorizing them ethnically. The member of a mobilized ethnic community intent on preserving group distinctiveness disagrees with the liberal at a fundamental level. He is likely to assert that what is freedom for the liberal is to him alienation: sloughing off ethnic attachments leaves him not free, but alone.

Democracy in Europe and the United States is characterized by a political system with a high degree of mobilization and ease of communication. It requires rationalism and desecularization. Because the basic unit is the individual citizen and his influence is presumed equal to that of others, mandates must be quantitative majorities and groups should be considered collections of men. These peculiar traits affect the ways different sorts of ethnic groups adjust to democratic pluralism. Democracy's premium on communication puts a linguistically distinctive community at a great disadvantage. American blacks have a head start in political integration relative to, say, Puerto Ricans and Mexican Americans. Secularization puts at a disadvantage groups defining their ethnicity in religious terms. Pakistanis and Indians are more likely than Jamaicans to find religion "interfering" with their political participation in the British system. Numerically sizable communities, such as the French in Canada and the Walloons in Belgium, are usually not compelled to argue "special status" to defend their interests, but Canadian Indians, for example, are powerless in strict numerical contests and thus try to seek out extrademocratic procedures in policy-making affecting them.

Democratic ideology is not steadfastly hostile to ethnicity, but it diminishes its reality in two ways. First, democracy assumes that in the final analysis society is composed of individuals, not groups, and thus ethnic identifications are real in the sense that myths are real in the minds of untutored men. Second, ethnicity that intrudes into political affairs is interpreted shallowly as style and symbol.

ANTI-MODERN IDEOLOGIES AND ETHNIC IDENTITY

For an alternative to culturally sterile Marxism, Harold Cruse turned to the poet Leopold Senghor, who is also president of the African nation of Senegal. Senghor has been the most politically authoritative enunciator of the idea of Negritude:

> A third revolution is taking place, as a reaction against capitalistic and communistic materialism . . . which will integrate moral, if not religious values, with the political and economic

contributions of the two great revolutions [Soviet and American]. In this revolution, the colored peoples, including Negro Africans, must play their part, they must bring their contribution to the construction of the new planetary civilization.[47]

What Senghor propounded was an ideology that stressed moral quality and ethnic identity. It was also a scheme of thought and guide to action that voiced serious reservations about the alleged rewards of modernization.

The ideologies that consider ethnicity to be a central factor in historical development tend to be ambivalent, if not outright hostile, toward modern society. Their major objection to modernity is its impersonalization and atomization of society. They consider unrestrained modernization to be contrary to men's natural need for spiritual harmony and collective sentiment. Modernity's commitment to abstract science and its promotion of materialism, together with its furtherance of automation and urban sprawl, lead to the destruction of the natural qualities of human society. Ideological systems skeptical of modernization are likely to reject both Marxist socialism and Jeffersonian democracy. Their common concern with social harmony, cooperation, and men's spiritual lives induces anti-modern ideologies to grant ethnicity more significance. Ethnicity, after all, implies affection based on intangible bonds and a belief in collective sustenance. While the modernizing ideologies relegate these characteristics, and thus ethnicity itself, to the trash heap of "tradition," anti-modern ideologues find the same qualities to be proof of ethnic reality.

The two most significant schools of thought casting doubt on modernity and asserting ethnic reality are African socialism and fascism. Of course, these two ideologies are at odds on many points, the most important being their unequal tendencies toward chauvinism and racial scapegoating. Ultimately, they even part ways over the implications of ethnic allegiance. Their serious differences notwithstanding, African socialism and fascism contain similar evaluations of modern society and ethnic communalism. Each was born out of disillu-

---

[47] Leopold Sedar Senghor, *African Socialism*, quoted in Cruse, *Rebellion or Revolution*, p. 152.

sionment with Marxist and democratic concepts of rational man and the secularized community. Each shies away from the notion that development requires assimilation.

Three other ideologies also give more weight to ethnic identity: Zionism, South African apartheid, and American southern agrarianism. All focus on communal cohesion and challenge modern progress when it appears to subvert that cohesion.

FASCISM

Fascist ideology, like all ideologies, is a result of men's search for meaning and direction in the midst of wide-ranging change and disintegration. In the aftermath of World War I Europe was shaken by both. The "Great War" had shattered the international order pieced together by diplomats at the end of the Napoleonic era. Old empires crumbled, royal families were forced into exile, and nationalism ran rampant, politicizing dozens of ethnic minorities. Added to this was the inflation of the 1920's followed by the depression of the 1930's. Wild economic fluctuations were made all the more disastrous by the interdependence industrialism had engendered. Finally, Europe was being shaken by a new militancy among the working class, fanned by communism and the Russian victory of the Bolsheviks in 1917.

Fascism grew out of bourgeois anxieties resulting from these traumatic changes. It offered the middle classes of Europe a way of explaining such disturbing events and perhaps a program for reversing them. Although in Germany, for instance, fascists called themselves "national socialists," they were not copying a socialism of the "soft cap" laborers who were the concern of the Fabian movement in Britain and the social democrats on the Continent. Rather, they pitched their appeal to persons caught between the militant proletariat on the one side and the arrogant aristocracy and capitalists on the other. Fascism's perception of Europe's troubles made most sense to farmers, artisans, and small businessmen. Germans call this sector of society the *Mittlestand.*

Spokesmen for fascism argued that the cause of Europe's malaise was fragmentation. Marxist predictions of inevitable class conflict and liberals' faith in human rationality had subverted society's organic unity, fascists said. Cities destroyed the closely-knit family, a key entity in a healthy society. Industrial manufacture isolated men from one another and turned them into depersonalized cogs in a machine. Men no longer trusted their colleagues or their own handiwork.

Ideologies offer remedies as well as diagnoses. The fascist solution was a social model, a normative blueprint, which stressed unity and consensus in place of modernism's conflict and individualism. To realize their goal, German fascists designed policies reaffirming the integrity of the skilled laborer (versus the unskilled worker or capitalist investor). They encouraged migration out of cities to small towns and elevated the middle class to a favored status.[48]

The element of economic class was treated differently from country to country. It was most central to the fascism of modernized Western societies such as Germany and Italy. It played a lesser role in the fascist thought of the agrarian East European countries, where industrialism had not made sufficiently deep inroads to produce large proletariats and urban middle classes. In such situations, fascism soft-pedaled its middle-class bias and found common cause with the conservative aristocracies by promoting nationalism.[49] Where modernization was less of a social irritant, racial interpretations of history were particularly prominent. Thus it may be that while the Nazis carried out the most extreme racial program, German fascism *as a formal ideology* was less dependent on the factor of race than the Hungarian or Rumanian brands of fascism.

Fascists' acknowledgment of ethnicity stems from two fundamental tenets. The first is that the *nation* is the primary arena for human action; a strong state depends on a strong nation. The nation is more than just a political community; it is a *volk*, a collection of men bound to one another by history and blood. The biological aspect of nationhood is rationalized by pseudo-scientific Darwinist logic and derives from fascism's persistent concern for race. Going a step further, fascism

[48] Nazi social programs are discussed in A. J. Nicholls, "Germany," in Stuart J. Woolf, ed., *European Fascism* (New York: Vintage Books, 1969), pp. 63–82. See also Arthur Schweitzer, *Big Business in the Third Reich* (Bloomington: Indiana University Press, 1965), pp. 200–06.

[49] Stuart J. Woolf, "Introduction," in Woolf, *European Fascism*, pp. 5–9.

mistakenly equates race with ethnicity. "Jew" becomes a racial label rather than an ethnic category. Jews and other foreigners are deemed impurities, diluting the strength of a genuine nation.

But racial theories alone cannot be blamed for fascist aberrations. A second tenet holds that modernity causes degeneration and threatens a potentially great nation or *volk*. Because it is antithetical to national welfare, modernity must be basically "alien." Fascists in West European countries looked at large business firms, cosmopolitan urban culture, and internationalists in the Communist movement as symbolic of modernity and its corrupting influence. They considered foreigners, especially Jews, to be promoters of business. As so often happens, ideology became a clouded filter instead of an accurate telescope. Fascists asserted that Jews dominated the modern sphere and were thus responsible for its defects. In actuality, the influence of Jews in Europe before World War II varied greatly from country to country. In Germany, Jewish politicians were prominent directly after the 1918 armistice, but not for long: "In the whole history of the [Weimar] Republic only five Jews held cabinet office." Moreover, industry was largely controlled by Gentiles, and there was "plenty of Gentile competition even in banking and newspaper ownership." [50] Jews, nevertheless, were able to gain entry into German administrative and judicial structures. Austria, by contrast, had a less developed middle class; there the Jewish community thus was correspondingly more influential. As fascist ideology worked out in practice, the difference in ethnic minority status meant that anti-Semitism became most virulent in Germany. Where Jews were indeed the backbone of the middle class, as in Austria, the *Mittlestand*-oriented fascists were disinclined to stress their ideology's anti-Semitic tenets, though the ideology was emotionally nationalistic. In neighboring Germany, with its far smaller "Jewish problem," fascist anti-Semitism met little resistance. [51]

---

[50] Peter G. J. Pulzer, *The Rise of Political Anti-Semitism in Germany and Austria* (New York: Wiley, 1964), p. 38.
[51] Ibid.

Memories of the horrors of World War II and Nazi rule make it tempting to think of fascism as essentially a racist ideology, an explanation of events based solely on the supposed consequences of racial differentiation. It may well be that racism, particularly the portrayal of Jews as the prime source of modern ills, provided the fuel for turning European fascism into a popular platform rather than the litany of an ignored political sect. Certainly, anti-Semitism was not *created* by the ascendancy of Hitler and his Brown Shirts. The term "anti-Semitism" allegedly was coined by the nineteenth-century writer Wilhelm Marr, and it became attached to a group of ardent nationalists.[52] This devotion to nationalism and its rationalization gave ethnic racial factors their relevance. Both Marxism and democracy have been employed to promote nationalism, but each was concerned formally with aspects of modernization that superseded national unity. Fascism co-opted many of the earlier ideas about the nature and value of national unity and presented them in a more universal, action-oriented system of explanation. The convergence of nationalism with economic crisis made this possible. Fritz Stern writes:

> Paradoxically, this anti-modern element in anti-Semitism modernized the ancient prejudice and gave it renewed impetus in industrial Germany. Old charges about ritual murders and other crimes of religion were not particularly persuasive in a secular society, but the identification of Jew and modernity became an immensely powerful component of anti-Semitism, though one that has often been overlooked.[53]

Eventually even in those countries where anti-modern sentiment originally was central to volkish nationalism, race became one of the few remaining ideological consistencies. Analysis of the societal defects of modernity were much more difficult for quasi-political citizens to understand than was racial symbolism. The economic foundations of fascist ideology also proved ambiguous, further weakening its drawing power. Nostalgia for the values of an agrarian-artisan community and the

[52] Ibid., p. 49.
[53] Fritz Stern, *The Politics of Social Despair* (New York: Anchor Books, 1965), p. 94.

concomitant hostility toward big industry were sacrificed for the sake of nationalism. By the middle of the 1930's it was apparent that a defeated European nation, still intent upon glory and empire, had to rearm — no matter what the treaties said. Rearmament in Nazi Germany meant support from industrialists and financiers. Thus, between 1936 and 1939, restrictions meant to stave off modern ills gradually were revoked in Germany. Curbs on urban migration were lifted, and the dispersal of labor was halted. Hitler's ministers gave wartime manufacturing top priority.[54] Yet the formal ideology legitimizing the regime remained unaltered.

While policy veered toward modernization, fascist ideologues went on trumpeting the values of agrarian society. The discrepancy between policy and theory was not simply hypocritical: "That the Third Reich, or important elements of it, wanted an agrarian state while, at the same time, accelerating industrialization, was not a misunderstanding or a feat of propaganda. Like anti-Semitism, it was one of the few consistent premises of Nazi life." [55] This inability to close the conceptual gap between the imperatives of national expansionism and the values of agrarian society meant that although the Nazis finally promoted modern change, they gave the German people no way of making sense of it or reconciling themselves to it. German citizens were left with the worst of both worlds: modernization programs and an anti-modern ideology. National ethnic communalism was the thin thread holding them together. As modernity was pursued unrelentingly during the late 1930's, the ethnic dimension of fascist ideology was exposed. What began as an ideology ended as merely a biological myth.

Even Fascism's nationalist rationale proved ambiguous, for an ideology claims to be more than an opportunistic program for a single adventurist polity. Fascist hopes for empire faltered on the ideological proclivity toward universalism. Fascists in one country would almost certainly move quickly from expedient Axis alignment to animosity against all foreigners.

54 Schweitzer, *Big Business in the Third Reich*, p. 206.

55 David Schoenbaum, *Hitler's Social Revolution: Class and Status in Nazi Germany* (New York: Anchor Books, 1967), p. 153.

This was most likely to occur where the foreigners a country allied with were ethnically related to a domestic minority. Hungary, for example, contained a significant German minority when it allied with the Axis, and Hungarian fascists finally splintered over ideological inconsistency. One Hungarian group supported the Axis, while another faction advocated anti-German policies at home and abroad.[56] The ideology that held consensus and community to be man's ultimate goals finally led to history's most destructive conflict.[57] Moreover World War II did as much as any event in the twentieth century to elevate modernization to a global commitment.

AFRICAN SOCIALISM

African socialism shares with fascism a wary attitude toward modernity and a positive evaluation of ethnic distinctions. However, African socialism leads logically to universalist values, whereas fascism headed toward narrow exclusivism.

African socialism embraces several streams of thought: monistic, pluralist, and individualist. The appeal of each has varied with the nature of social cleavage threatening a given country. The monistic variety, commonly linked to Kwame Nkrumah and Sekou Touré, has prevailed where ethnic divisions have been relatively mild. It advocates a high level of political mobilization and relies on personal charisma and a dominant political party. The pluralist variant of African socialism had its most notable trial in Nigeria before the civil war there. It is especially attractive to tribally multi-ethnic societies and is more tolerant of intergroup and interparty conflict. The individualist mode has been relevant to Africans in countries with profound cleavages — usually black versus white — such as South Africa, Zambia (formerly Northern Rhodesia), and Kenya.[58] South Africa's Nobel Peace laureate, Arthur Luthuli, for example, has spoken out against programs

---

[56] J. Eros, "Hungary," in Woolf, *European Fascism*, pp. 139–43.

[57] Today Italy is experiencing a minor revival of fascism. It seems to be tied to law and order and a desire for the return to Mussolini's "corporatism," a system of state-dominated organizations. Anti-Semitism appears to have little impact. *New York Times*, January 28, 1971.

[58] Charles F. Andrain, "Democracy and Socialism: Ideologies of African Leaders," in Apter, *Ideology and Discontent*, p. 171.

of "black government" and tribalism. His goal is a democratic socialist system that ignores race and judges men according to individual merit. But today militant Africans in South Africa dismiss Luthuli's individualist ideology as unrealistic and undesirable. They instead are anxious to mobilize a revolutionary movement based on black solidarity.[59]

Running through all three streams of African socialism is the conviction that African native tradition has something unique to contribute to socialist ideology and to modern life. In a sense, African socialists use the traditions of tribal society to overcome the tensions of ethnic tribalism and to generate a new feeling of African national self-confidence. Culturally, they draw values from the precolonial village, the cornerstone of the tribe. Their presumption is that, however dissimilar they may be from one another, native Africans have a basic cultural commonality. The culture of African tribal villages is portrayed as consensual and cooperative. Personal relations are more important than formal and institutional linkages. Religion played a central role in sustaining harmony. Thus African socialism, unlike its European counterpart, is not wedded to secularism and legalism in politics. Likewise it rejects the Marxist and Western socialist belief that class conflict between rich and poor is inevitable. Tribal culture developed ways of dealing with the differences and prevented irreparable breaks. Central to socialism, in the eyes of its African adherents, is cooperation and sharing in the name of public welfare. Conflict and secular rationalism seem less functional.

The style of modern life developed in Europe and America is considered sterile and alienating for all men but above all for Africans, because of their cultural and social heritage. African socialism underscores the dysfunctional consequences of simplistic emulation of Western development and offers a congenial alternative. The advantages of this alternative ideology are twofold. First, it enables African nations to avoid the tensions and impersonalization that afflict Western countries. Second, it provides a bridge between old and new, soft-

[59] Ibid.

ening the shock of rapid transition from traditional to modern life. African socialism presents a model for modernization that preserves a modernizing people's sense of their own distinct ethnic origins. Modernity itself is modified. Whereas orthodox democracy, Marxism, and socialism all imply that successful development in the twentieth century requires persons to purge themselves of ethnic uniqueness, the African formula perceives ethnic heritage to be a useful aid in development. The liberated African need not eschew science and technology, but he must not surrender his own identity and culture in their name.

There is one difficulty, however — an ideological oversimplification. The "African" culture that is presented as common to all Africans is a minimal one. It is a rock-bottom common denominator overlaid with a multitude of cultural variants — religious, linguistic, and social. To get down to this purely "African" base, national leaders must convince their constituents that different tribal ethnic traditions are inconsequential. In other words, while African socialists do assign more weight to fundamental ethnic identity, they, like Western elites, urge citizens to slough off secondary identities. Even African socialism involves loosening certain cultural bonds. It praises the qualities of tribal society while it condemns tribalism. It seeks pan-African unity while legitimizing strong national regimes.

The supratribal, racial connotation of African socialism is most explicit in its variant called "Negritude." First articulated by French West Indian writer Aimé Césaire, Negritude has won wide followings in Africa and, more recently, in the United States. Leopold Senghor is its best-known spokesman. Although Frantz Fanon died before "black power" came into full bloom, his books are among the most frequently quoted by contemporary black leaders. Interestingly, Césaire, Senghor, and Fanon — Fanon is an advocate of black pride, though a critic of Negritude — all grew up in French colonies and had close contacts with intellectual circles in France. African artists from former British colonies, by contrast, were less prone to abstract and more likely to express themselves as novelists than as poets and aestheticians. It is ironic that France, the European colonial power proudest of its racial tolerance

and cultural assimilation, should spawn men devoted to blackness as a source of artistic inspiration and political solidarity.
Yet an integrationist policy can raise men's hopes and expectations to the point that, when frustrated, the response is ideological. Acute disillusionment robs life of its meaning, and so
a new system of explanation and rationale for action must be
created self-consciously. For blacks in French territories, acceptance was blocked by racism and colonialism. Western-
educated men, who felt their exclusion most bitterly, began
searching for an identity and a world view independent of integration and whiteness. The psychological and cultural cost
was greatest for Fanon, Senghor, and other blacks who considered themselves part of French intellectual traditions. According to Fanon, born on the French Caribbean island of
Martinique:

> The Martinician is a Frenchman, he wants to remain part
> of the French Union, he asks only one thing, he wants the
> idiots and the exploiters to give him the chance to live like
> a human being. I can imagine myself lost in a white flood com-
> posed of men like Sartre or Aragon; I should like nothing
> better.[60]

Assimilation into French society initially was believed to be
the road to achievement, security, and modernization. Fanon's
early years were taken up with these pursuits, though they led
down an illusory road. He volunteered for the French army
and served in Europe after 1944. Subsequently he studied
medicine and psychiatry at Lyons. On the threshold of acceptance, his medical exams, the illusion was destroyed. The
white French professor examining him thought it appropriate to address Fanon with the patronizingly familiar *tu*. Still,
dreams die hard, and Fanon persisted in his attempt to "belong." He married a Frenchwoman and in 1953 was appointed
head of the psychiatric department of a hospital in Algeria.
Social stratification in colonial Algeria made it hard for him
to believe that rewards come with performance. While he was
visiting neighboring Tunisia, "the eyes that turned to watch

[60] Frantz Fanon, *Black Skins, White Masks* (New York: Grove Press,
1967), p. 202.

him in the street never let him forget the color of his skin." [61] Eventually Fanon branded the pursuit of whiteness, mentally and physically, a false pursuit. The objective was not as desirable as it first appeared, and the journey was psychologically destructive. Fanon later attacked Negritude for its mysticism; still his career shared with Senghor's a dedication to black self-confidence and a rejection of whiteness as inherently good.

Much that is written about the ideas of Negritude concerns literature and the arts. Of all the ideologies seeking to cope with the pressures of development, Negritude is the most aesthetic. Its ideological impact has been greatest among black writers and artists. Ideologies always carry implications for creative expression, but Negritude's special force comes out of its overwhelming concern with the problem of identity. In this concern the poet and the psychiatrist converge. While most contemporary ideologies treat identity as a secondary matter, a by-product of something else, proponents of Negritude consider it the starting point in any search for meaning and direction. Such a preoccupation with identity makes ethnicity more relevant than it is for Marxists and democrats.

During the first World Festival of the Arts, hosted in Senegal by President Senghor in 1966, American poet Langston Hughes translated "Negritude" into the vernacular of American blacks. In Hughes' words, "Negritude had its roots deep in the beauty of the black people — in what younger American writers and musicians call 'soul.' " Soul, in turn is

> the essence of Negro folk art redistilled — particularly the old music and its flavor, the ancient basic beat out of Africa, the folk rhymes and Ashanti stories — all expressed in contemporary ways so emotionally colored with the old that it gives a distinctly Negro flavor to today's music, painting or writing.

In short, explained Hughes, "soul is contemporary Harlem's 'Negritude.' " [62]

---

61 David Caute, *Frantz Fanon* (New York: Viking, 1970), p. 4.

62 *New York Times,* April 24, 1966. American blacks' migration to Northern cities has complicated the meaning of "soul." Many blacks remaining in the South prize their Southernness and share with white "new agrarians" a fondness for the South's less industrialized, more personalized culture. Differences between Northern and Southern blacks surface not

On the surface, race is the ground for identity and the key to Negritude's world view. In practice racial characteristics symbolized by "blackness" are translated into African cultural inheritance. It is not black skin that has to be rediscovered. The values and traditions that men of black skin created before colonization and industrialization must be recaptured if Africans are to be spiritually whole. Thus Negritude places its emphasis on racial symbolism, while joining with the broader African socialist movement in the synthesis of African native culture and Western development. Senghor has had sharp disputes with Nkrumah and Touré, but all three stress the similarities and gloss over the differences among black African peoples. Proper understanding of their common traits, it is argued, will carry forward newly independent African nations. Neither Negritude nor African socialism treasures nostalgia for its own sake; both are guidelines for development. Senghor makes this clear:

> The problem which now faces us, Negroes of 1959, is to know how we can integrate Negro-African values into the world of 1959. There is no question of reviving the past, of living in a Negro-African museum; the question is to inspire this world, here and now, with the values of our past.[63]

As Senghor suggests, African socialism and Negritude are universal ideologies. Africa's legacy of village and tribal culture has something to offer to all contemporary societies wracked by conflict and unsettled by scientific, rational abstractions. Not all blacks, however, agree with Senghor on the long-range compatibility of symbolic blackness and development. The first Pan-African Cultural Festival, held in Algiers in 1969, revealed Africans' and American blacks' conflicting opinions about the utility of Negritude's stress on identity and spiritual awareness. Is it a hindrance to economic development? Is eco-

---

only in discussions of "black identity." See Joyce Ladner, "What Black Power Means to Negroes in Mississippi," in Meier, *Black Experience*, pp. 131–55; Ulf Hunnerz, *Soulside* (New York: Columbia University Press, 1971), pp. 144–58; Taylor Branch, "The New Agrarians," *Washington Monthly* (September 1970), pp. 22–26.
[63] Senghor quoted in P. C. Lloyd, *Africa in Social Change* (Baltimore: Penguin Books, 1967), p. 282.

nomic development a requisite for lasting national development? The revolutionary participants of the conference, together with Arabic African delegates, denounced proponents of Negritude for their sentimentality and parochialness, both of which only play into the hands of white neo-colonialists. Negritude's backers stressed the overriding need to secure cultural identities, and politicized militants retorted that development lay in technical and economic progress. The militants argued that even Fanon saw Negritude as serviceable only at an intermediary stage; to move beyond that to revolutionary action meant to move beyond Negritude.[64] It meant that preoccupation with *culture* must be replaced by attention to *politics*. The split between two of America's most prominent black leaders, Stokely Carmichael, the pan-Africanist, and Eldridge Cleaver, the revolutionary, dates to the Algiers arguments.[65] Both remain in exile from the United States, but their places of refuge reflect their differing opinions concerning the central quality of blackness in a functional ideology for blacks: Carmichael resides in Guinea; Cleaver lives in Algeria. The division among blacks over the best way to sustain development is a microcosm of the splits one finds in all politicized, ideologized ethnic communities. Should communal development be defined in terms of modernization and thus in terms of secular, universal, and material values? Or does the best hope for the community lie in creating ethnic self-consciousness and measuring progress by the group's distinctive cultural norms?

[64] Nathan Hare, "Algiers, 1969," *Black Scholar* 1, no. 1 (November 1969): 4–8. See also Sekou Touré, "A Dialectical Approach to Culture," Ibid., esp. pp. 15–21; also, Stanislas Adotevi, "The Strategy of Culture," Ibid., pp. 27–35.

[65] Stokely Carmichael, "Pan-Africanism — Land and Power," in Sheer, *Post-Prison Writings and Speeches*, pp. 36–43; Eldridge Cleaver, "Education and Revolution," ibid., pp. 44–53. Three years after Algiers the rift was just as wide. Carmichael told an interviewer in Conakry, Guinea, that the Black Panthers used rhetoric to state positions they cannot defend, and he doubted the reliability of white radicals as allies: "To develop a revolutionary movement you need to develop a base, hold it and move out. You can't do that in the States today. . . . The transformation of America should not be the primary concern. Our concern is Mother Africa." Interview with English journalist Jonathan Power in *New York Times*, February 6, 1971.

COPING WITH ETHNIC IDENTITY

Ideologies characteristically neglect ethnic identity because, as spinoffs from Enlightenment rationalism, they incline naturally toward universal application and objectivity. Parochial boundaries, as well as dependence on intangible bonds of sentiment, make ethnic groups irrelevant to most ideologues. Ideology, moreover, came of age as a tool of modernization. A primary obstacle to modernity has been primordial group loyalties that inhibit centralized planning and nationwide mobilization of resources. Ethnic identity and rational ideology have been cast as competitors for men's minds.

Not all ideologies handle ethnicity in the same fashion. Those going farthest toward rejecting or overlooking ethnicity are Marxism, Western democracy, and European socialism. Each makes material progress and impersonalized justice its goals. Objectivity, secularism, and instrumental evaluation are the means to those ends. Myth, sentiment, and parochial fragmentation are the enemies. On the other hand, ideologies operate in concrete situations, and they frequently undergo modifications. Marxism, for instance, acknowledges that societies move through historical stages at different speeds and thus some minority cultures may still be "feudal" while the rest of their country is entering into capitalism or is already in its throes. With the grafting of Lenin's pragmatic actions onto orthodox Marxism, there is even more leeway for cultural differences, for some societies are believed to suffer from capitalist imperialism, which slows their progress. Colonized peoples may only be able to throw off imperialism by mobilizing under the banner of nationalism; true class consciousness will have to come later. European socialism has been modified in Africa. Cooperation is common to both schools, but in African socialism cooperation takes priority over economic class conflict by drawing on black people's tribal heritage. The individualism of Western democracy is blunted somewhat by its merger with pluralism. Democratic pluralists make ethnic groups legitimate, but only as long as ethnic sentiments are not intense and members associate with nonethnic interest groups as well. These expedient adjustments notwithstanding, Marxism, socialism, and democracy remain hostile to ethnicity. All three cope with ethnic identity by either diluting its meaning or assuming that it is transitory and at a higher stage of development will disappear.

Other ideologies are fundamentally ambivalent in their stands on modernization and thus allow more room for ethnic reality. Supporters of these schools of thought equate modernization with selfishness, conflict, abstraction, and alienation. But rather than surrender the benefits of modern life altogether, they soften its harshness with strong doses of communal sentiment. The community is often defined by ethnicity — German, Jewish, African, Afrikaner, Southern white Anglo-Saxon. When pushed to their logical extremes, as can happen in periods of great stress, these ideologies lean toward agrarian reaction and communal exclusiveness. Hence, if *anti-ethnic* modernizing ideologies can leave the individual alienated and alone, *anti-modern* ethnic ideologies can leave groups isolated and fearful.

Many multi-ethnic countries are not notably ideological. Their politics eschew abstract reasoning and concentrate on meeting short-range objectives and avoiding immediate conflagration. In these polities ethnic conflict remains confined, at least conceptually. But the practice of focusing on the present and frowning upon generalized schemes tends to conceal the essence of national discontinuities; governments and citizens are thus deluded. This was the case in the Federation of Malaysia prior to the traumatic communal riots of 1969. The Malaysian regime and many in the opposition put their faith in "pragmatism" to the point that they ignored the depths of hostility between and within the three major ethnic groups. The riots so shook the foundations of the political system that Malaysians were compelled to think in systematic, long-range terms about their society and its goals.[66] Malaysians' genuine reluctance to think ideologically about their political choices

[66] Cynthia H. Enloe, *Multi-Ethnic Politics: The Case of Malaysia* (Berkeley: Center for South and Southeast Asia Studies, 1970). See also R. S. Milne, " 'National Ideology' and Nation-Building in Malaysia," *Asian Survey* 10, no. 7 (July 1970): 563–73. The Malaysia leadership, especially the cosmopolitan Malay elite now controlling the federal government, apparently feels that open discussion of the country's ethnic problems is too risky. It introduced a constitutional amendment making it a crime even to talk about Malay-Chinese issues. *New York Times*, March 2, 1971.

sheds light on the paradox of ideologization: it assists in functional policy-making but sharpens conflict by clearly separating friends from enemies, good behavior from bad. When political actors are ideologically conscious, making compromises and introducing change through gradualism are difficult. The true meaning of all decisions appears to be blatantly exposed. On the other hand, in a nonideological political system the long-range ramifications of current decisions not only are rarely considered in debate, they are even hard to envision in private. It is easy to fool ourselves that "Band-aid" programs are preserving social integration when we concentrate on the present and avoid relating discreet events to one another. The way out of ideology's paradox may be to argue that in multiethnic societies ideology does stimulate conflict in the short run, though it ensures a more clear-eyed approach to the future. Of course, the trouble is that many polities are not strong enough to withstand ideologized ethnic conflict in the short run and may not last to enjoy the clear-eyed future. The dilemma remains.[67]

We began this analysis with a reference to the "end of ideology" debate. The current resurgence of ethnic communalism around the world suggests that analysts prophesying the demise of ideology may be correct, but for reasons contrary to their own. According to those who see ideology on the wane, science and technology plus affluence make rigid orthodoxies impractical and unpalatable, and post-modernization will be the burying ground for ideologues of all schools, Superrationality, summed up in the computer, makes ideological rationalism obsolete.

Technology is indeed on the way to becoming the single most important fact of development, but the spread of technological imperatives is being strangely paralleled by a revival

67 We need more empirical research on the process of ideologization among ethnic groups. A comparative study might consider groups strung out along two spectra: (1) degree of political ideologization and (2) degree of *ethnic* awareness central to a group's ideology. The first might have Peruvian Indians at one end, American blacks at the other, and Northern Ireland's Catholics and the Palestinians somewhere in the middle. The second might have white Anglo-Saxon Americans at one end and South African Afrikaners close to the opposite end.

of nonrational rational ethnic consciousness. If ideologies are hostile to ethnicity, then the challenge to ideology may be double-barreled: from anti-modern ethnic mobilization on the one side and from post-modern technology on the other. How these two trends interact is the major problem any new scheme of thought will have to unravel.

CHAPTER IV

Jurisdictions
to Match Identities

POLITICAL DEVELOPMENT requires jurisdictional units and compatible institutions, both serving functions expected of a state. Though institutions and jurisdictions are discussed separately, ethnic conflict illuminates their close relationship. The formula for political development and its relative success are influenced by the ways in which institutions and jurisdictional patterns foster national integration.

No nation-state deals with its populace — by definition "the common people" — en masse. Each devises administrative subdivisions appropriate to its geographical and social diversity. It is to be hoped that these logical subdivisions for participation will be reasonably workable administratively. Many nations, unfortunately, find that natural divisions for optimum participation do not create units capable of efficiently administering public policy. The discrepancy plagues multi-ethnic countries undergoing modernization. Functional modernity demands administrative centralization and nationalization of policy priorities to maximize the use of deficient resources and assure coordination of necessary "national" activities. However, unification of a multi-ethnic society often is achieved by acquiescing to entrenched communal desires; sometimes this price is demanded by ethnic integrity and it has to be paid.

Confronted by the discrepancy between conditions of unity and requisites for modernization, nation-builders may follow one of several courses. First, they can declare minimal integration and internal security the nation's first task. They accede to certain demands by ethnic groups, granting them territorial identity within the larger polity in return for loyalty. Ethnic groups are prone to connect their survival with a physical territory within which they can exercise social control, but one of the continuing areas of debate within ethnic groups and among state authorities concerns just how crucial land is to ethnic preservation. Usually land is deemed least essential to ethnic communities unlikely to acquire their own territory. A group already dominating a region is unlikely to surrender its territory without resistance.

If a territorial solution is too dangerous or unfeasible because the ethnic group is scattered, then a compromise may take the form of institutional recognition. In Czechoslovakia and Malaysia the dominant parties have ethnic group branches. In Burma and North Vietnam ethnic minorities are guaranteed representation in the national legislature. In Lebanon the top governmental posts are meticulously split among Christians and Muslims to perpetuate the image of a fifty-fifty population balance.

Countries that initially give top priority to integration probably will try to modify or reverse their priorities later when the nationalizing pressures of modern life intensify. When a government decides that administering programs in a piecemeal fashion is too inefficient, it may try to redefine jurisdictional and institutional boundaries regardless of communal resistance. Development crises do not always come at a nation's birth; they frequently come during a later phase as regimes try to reverse decisions made earlier. A delayed crisis can cripple a multi-ethnic political system as it shifts from integration-oriented to administration-oriented subdivisions. For instance, in mainland Southeast Asia the tribal peoples concentrated in the remote hill regions along the borders for a while encountered only sporadic government interference. When the war in Indochina jeopardized nations' security, tribal autonomy became less tolerable. Regimes that formerly measured their development by living standards in the capital city and lowland rice provinces began to worry that successful development would be impossible unless all peoples and resources within the nation's borders were mobilized. The new jurisdictional blueprints or institutional arrangements to accomplish this task remain vague. In Asia even the regimes' commitment to absorb the tribal communities is still ambiguous.

A second way of dealing with the tension between integrative demands and administrative requisites is to create structures to minimize the importance of ethnic communities. Regimes offer enticements — jobs, education, status, technology — to convince ethnic groups to sacrifice their communal integrity. This strategy calls for more political leverage than many underdeveloped countries possess. Even the American government, with all the resources at its disposal, has been unable to persuade Indians that territorial reserves are an obsolescent concept. Any government choosing this way must be equipped with coercive force. The Burmese military regime established by General Ne Win in a 1962 coup d'état accused its civilian predecessors of giving in to communal claims and thus weakening the nation. Yet General Ne Win has not mustered enough coercive might to suppress his country's various twenty-year-long rebellions.

A third strategy for solving the developmental puzzle is to permit jurisdictional boundaries to coincide with ethnic communities and simultaneously build institutions that cut across ethnic allegiances and thus undermine them. This solution is full of risks; it can lead to operational confusion and popular cynicism. Its success depends on the system's tolerance of constant tension and ambiguity. The strategy probably works best when ethnically defined territorial units have common allegiance to an energetic, expansive political party. Such a power combination was employed by China and the Soviet Union. Chinese and Soviet ethnic minorities were granted their own territorial subunits, while a supra-ethnic political party exerted strong centralizing control. The Congress party performed the same function in India, cutting across linguistically distinct federal states. In the last few years, however, the Congress party has splintered and lost some of its traditional appeal. As it loses its hegemony, the disintegrative tendencies of the member states threaten India's unity. It remains to be seen whether Prime Minister Gandhi's sweeping victories in the March 1972 state elections will serve as a base for durable national unity.

Bureaucracies and armies may serve supra-ethnic functions similar to those of a strong national party. However, they are inclined to be centralized or closely identified with the dominant ethnic group and thus suspect in the eyes of minorities.

Ultimately the compatibility of ethnic districts and supra-ethnic institutions depends on the transitoriness of ethnic group concentrations. If other peoples gradually move into regions once ethnically distinct, or if ethnic group members become mobile and disperse, then tensions inherent in this strategy may not reach the point where the groups feel betrayed or the institutions bog down in role conflict. Moreover, nations with more than one ethnic community can employ several integrative strategies at the same time.

A government can deal with various ethnic groups in different ways. The appropriateness of any regime's jurisdictional strategy must be measured by the cohesiveness and political leverage of the community and the relevance of the group to modernization.

In Guyana, a former British colony on the coast of South America, the indigenous Amer-Indians (distinct from the country's large East Indian population) live a nomadic life deep in the interior. Most Guyanese consider Amer-Indians peripheral to the nation's progress. Consequently, they have enjoyed wide-ranging autonomy and, until recently, were scarcely incorporated into Guyana's political system. The insecurity of the nation's borders because of Venezuelan territorial claims and the current government's intense interest in developing the unexplored interior are now undermining that autonomy.

Guyana has never been able to afford such autonomy for its main ethnic groups, not just because of their size but because of their interdependence in socio-economic growth. Guyanese Negroes and East Indians, consequently, have been merged into a unitary system despite their mutual hostilities. Even in this unitary system, however, the political institutions of the two groups remain ethnically distinct. The two major parties draw their support overwhelmingly from one community or the other. Guyana's national civil service, army, and police force all are heavily Negro; Indians are most active in influential commercial organizations.

Differential treatment likewise marks the unitary system of Thailand, where the Chinese minority, clustered in the cities, is permitted less autonomy than the allegedly backward hill tribes. In both the United States and Australia, too, relatively weak and backward indigenous peoples are granted a degree of jurisdictional and institutional separatism denied to European immigrant groups.

Ethnic groups as well as nations are dynamic. Their economic and political characters can and do change, and changes within ethnic groups can transform "developed" jurisdictional and institutional systems — that is, systems capable of coping with demands placed upon the nation — into "underdeveloped" systems. No political structure has reached the end of development so long as parts of the nation still have the capacity to increase their political leverage.[1]

The needs of a national government also can change, another indication of the precariousness of "development." The lesson repeats itself: development may engender more development, but it may also be succeeded by relative underdevelopment. What happens when, in the midst of an American energy crisis, fossil fuels and mineral deposits are discovered on lands legally reserved for Indians and Eskimos? What will a Brazilian regime do when exploiting the largely unexplored hinterland left to its Indians becomes feasible? Can the Muslim peoples in China's sparsely populated northwest continue to enjoy autonomy when their region becomes vital to China's nuclear experiments? In each instance, a new need perceived by the central government poses a new problem in dealing with ethnic communities that in the past had hardly been within the political vision of the decision-makers. Integrative

[1] See Chapters VII and VIII for a discussion of the political development of ethnic groups.

strategies long considered satisfactory suddenly appear obsolete when a government's physical needs or national potentials change.

A myriad of jurisdictional patterns is possible, each with several institutional overlays; the number and variety are a tribute to the imagination of political man. We can discuss only a few combinations here and in subsequent chapters: federalism, autonomous regions, and unitary systems.

FEDERALISM AS A SOLUTION
TO ETHNIC FRAGMENTATION

The European Enlightenment of the eighteenth century gave the Western world new confidence in man's capacity to rationally arrange societies to satisfy human desires. After the seventeenth century, politicians thought of themselves as engineers. Their blueprints were constitutions setting forth lines of communication and authority. Complex societies, composed of numerous cultures and subcultures, were treated as engineering challenges: if the planetary system with its diverse bodies and movements could maintain a dynamic balance dictated by rational laws, so could plural societies. An enduring political by-product of this confident era was federalism — *e pluribus unum,* one made out of many, not organically, but mechanically. Federalism would replace cruder empires as a system for integrating diverse peoples into a single polity. A deliberate design of subunits with their own institutions and obligations was called for. Added to this would be dual citizenship and sufficient authority at the national level to maintain coordination and security. As later nation-builders were to find, however, terrestrial diversity is much more dynamic and unpredictable than its planetary model. A principal force for change in an apparently stable order has been the ethnic group.

When it became independent in 1960, the Federation of Nigeria, with its 40 million people, 250 distinct languages, and strong economy, was heralded as a model for African development.[2] Nigeria's federal system included three largely

---

[2] Anthropologist Stanley Diamond has said that the cherishing of the Nigerian model is an example of Western bias and illusion stemming from

autonomous regions, each tribally distinctive. They had experienced dissimilar forms of British colonial administration, ranging from classic indirect rule in the north to thorough administrative penetration in the east. Each region had its own parliament, police force, university, and budget derived from local revenues. Despite the existence of numerous small tribes, the northern region was dominated by the Muslim, traditional Hausa, the eastern region by the energetic Roman Catholic Ibo. The western region was tribally mixed but included most of the country's Yoruba tribesmen.[3] The Ibo were European educated and among the strongest of Nigeria's nationalists.[4] After independence they occupied administrative posts throughout the federation.[5]

Then came a series of coups and countercoups that pitted tribal groups against one another, and civil war broke out in

---

a gilded vision of colonialism's contribution to political maturity: "Nigeria has been a prime example of our denial of African realities. As an anchor of British sovereignty in 'West Africa, as the arena for the most comprehensive colonial experiment in indirect rule, as the most populous and heterogeneous of the emerging African nations. Nigeria was celebrated as the model of colonial success. . . . Nigeria's 'moderation,' the vaunted 'conservatism' of the Northern leadership, the well-publicized 'democratic character' of the coalition have all been political myths, sanctioned by legal and constitutional documents. For the fact is, that the majority of Nigerians did not participate effectively in their government. . . . In reality, Nigeria was the very model of a colonial failure; for Africa, the critical model." Stanley Diamond, *Nigeria: Model of a Colonial Failure* (New York: American Committee on Africa, 1967), pp. 5–6.

3 Nigeria's 1962 census was a source of much political conflict because it affected tribal-regional distribution of power. Census figures remain questionable. See Etienne van de Walle, "Who's Who and Where in Nigeria," *Africa Report* (January 1970), pp. 22–23. Census taking has become a political issue in other multi-ethnic nations: Malaysia, the Soviet Union, the United States, Britain.

4 For an analysis of Nigeria's move toward independence see James S. Coleman, *Nigeria: Background to Nationalism* (Berkeley: University of California Press, 1958).

5 David C. McClelland, the foremost student of achievement motivation, has characterized the Ibo as an "achievement people." He says about the Nigerian civil war: "The Biafra story occurs often in history; in its peaceful version, the tinker's son gets rich and marries the daughter of the landed aristocracy whose god is Apollo, representing established power." "To Know Why Men Do What They Do: A Conversation with David C. McClelland and T George Harris," *Psychology Today* 4, no. 8 (January 1971), p. 70.

1967. After the massacres in the north, the Ibo fled to their eastern region and claimed the right of secession. They named their new state Biafra. It was by no means a homogeneous area, but the Ibo overpowered the weaker Rivers tribes (which earlier had pressed Lagos for their own regional autonomy). It took two years of costly and internationally complicated warfare to crush the Biafran secessionists.[6]

One of the first steps taken by the victorious federal government was to implement a pattern of federal jurisdictions announced, but not effected, prior to the civil war. The reorganization divided Nigeria into twelve states. Ibo still are concentrated in a state of their own, the new East Central State, but now they are only one of twelve instead of one among three.[7] Furthermore, they have been deprived of their outlets to the sea. The federal regime hopes that a dozen small units will offer little resistance to central authority.

Because tribal animosities continue, merely carving up Nigeria in a new pattern is an insufficient guarantee of unity. Deterioration of the political party system, the functioning of the federal cabinet, and the whole electoral process led to the tragic intertribal hostilities in the first place. Even the most nationally oriented institutions — the army and the civil service — could not withstand the centrifugal strains. Nigeria's postwar reintegration requires an institutional revival if the new federal relationships are to endure. Ibo have been given the principal posts in the East Central administration and gradually are being brought back into the national bureaucracy, but the military remains an obstacle to institutional reintegration. The civil war expanded the Nigerian army into a fighting force of two hundred thousand men, the largest in black Africa.[8] Though they had considerable influence, only several hundred Ibo officers were in the small prewar army. Now, with the likelihood of military rule for the foreseeable future, the

---

[6] A detailed account of events leading to the creation of Biafra is Frederick Forsyth, *The Biafra Story* (Baltimore: Penguin Books, 1969).

[7] The new states are Lagos (capital Lagos), Western (Ibadan), Midwestern (Benin City), East Central (Enugu), Rivers (Port Harcourt), Southeastern (Calabar), Kwara (Sokoto), Benue-Plateau (Jos), Kano (Kano).

[8] *New York Times,* October 1, 1970.

Ibo feel they must gain a substantial voice within the new army.[9]

The Hausa-dominated military regime in Lagos considers economic administration the institutional tool for, enforcing twelve-state federalism and tribal peace. Economic policy-making machinery is replacing political parties and parliament as the federal integrator. Money and planning are the keys to the centralization scheme. In the past the autonomous regions competed for new industries and thus caused wasteful duplication. The 1970 development plan provides the central government with $3 billion plus power to set national priorities and resolve conflicting claims between states. The plan also puts all army and police spending under federal administrators and gives Lagos a decisive role in education and road construction, each critical to a nation's unification.[10] The economic development plan is the first test of Nigeria's revised federal formula. There is no assurance that it will succeed. The economic development commissioner of the Ibo-populated East Central State voiced his skepticism: "I think that they have put the cart before the horse. . . . They want a degree of centralization that is far in advance of the constitutional development in this country." [11]

The problem nagging at multi-ethnic, underdeveloped nations is this: underdevelopment in the modern era creates a need for centralized authority to offset communal fragmentation; yet centralization effective enough to control disintegrative forces requires resources beyond the reach of underdeveloped systems. When the dilemma is acute — that is, when intergroup animosity is strong and central authority is weak — countries are mired in apparently endless civil strife. We need only look at the conflicts in Chad, Sudan, Ethiopia, and Iraq to understand the dimensions of the problem.

9 *Washington Post,* December 6, 1970.

10 The development plan for 1970–1974 stipulates the following priorities in the public sector: (1) expansion of public transportation, (2) development and diversification of education, (3) modernization and expansion of agriculture in which 70 per cent of the national labor force is employed. *New York Times,* November 12, 1970.

11 *Washington Post,* December 20, 1970.

Federalism has been a popular vehicle for coping with this development dilemma. It is the least of evils in the opinion of nation-builders who face stubborn subnational loyalties and yet are determined to create a polity large enough to supply adequate manpower and resources for security and economic growth. Rarely are federalism's advocates men of romantic enthusiasm; usually they are pragmatic compromisers, and it is hard for men of this temperament to generate nationalistic fervor. Imbued with the spirit of the Enlightenment, they believe in the viability of communities artificially contrived to satisfy man-made laws and rational calculation. Federal polities, consequently, are qualitatively different from ethnic communities, which grow naturally out of implicitly shared values and historical interdependence. The seemingly natural and organic character of ethnic groups makes them appear difficult to overcome. Nation-builders find it easier to skirt such groups, accommodating the national structure to them in the hope that eventually they will be dispersed by nonethnic attachments. Pragmatic federalists who have shaped multi-ethnic nations include Tunku Abdul Rahman (Malaysia), Mohammed Hatta (Indonesia), Lenin (Soviet Union), James Madison (United States), and Pierre Trudeau (Canada). Marshall McLuhan's observations about Trudeau may be applicable to many contemporary and future federalists:

> The TV generation has neither identity nor goals. Its instinct is to plunge into tragic violence as a means of creating a new identity or image. Trudeau suggests federalism in place of this tragic strategy; and federalism is the cool, causal interface of numerous components minus the old drives for goals and gains.[12]

The relationship among development, federalism, and ethnic distribution can be measured and compared within a single country or between different countries. Canada, the United States, Malaysia, Switzerland, and the Soviet Union all offer ample opportunities for comparative analysis. In member states in each, the political reinforcement of ethnicity varies.

[12] Marshall McLuhan, "Federalism and French Canadians," *New York Times Book Review*, November 17, 1968.

The Malaysian state of Kelantan, for example, is mostly Malay, economically underdeveloped, and governed by the nation's one Malay chauvinist opposition party. On the opposite side of the peninsula, the state of Selangor includes large numbers of Chinese, Indians, and Malays, as well as the federal capital; it is economically dynamic and has a strong branch of the government party plus a host of Malay and non-Malay opposition parties. Just as Mississippi and Oregon relate to the American federal system differently, so Kelantan and Selangor are affected in their federal relations by dissimilar ethnic political factors. In neither the United States nor Malaysia were state boundaries initially drawn along strictly ethnic lines.

Three potent variables determine the relationship of ethnic politics and development in a federal system: the extent to which ethnic clusters fit into man-made federal boundaries, the ability of constituent states to fend off federal penetration, and the extent to which national institutions, especially political parties, reinforce state-ethnic coterminality.

MOBILITY OF ETHNIC GROUPS
WITHIN FEDERAL SYSTEMS

The most visible of the three variables is the overlap between federal boundaries and ethnic settlement. Overlapping is not a fixed condition, however; immigration and domestic mobility can significantly alter the ethnic content of a federal state, regardless of the nation-builders' original intent. Shifting distributions of ethnic groups are accentuated when one part of a nation is developing faster than the rest, attracting citizens with an expanding labor market and better living conditions.

In 1940, 77 per cent of American blacks resided in the South. By 1968 only 53 per cent still could be found there; of the remaining, 40 per cent lived in the North and 8 per cent had migrated to the West.[13] Just before the 1970 census little

13 U.S. Bureau of the Census, *Current Population Reports,* Series P-23, no. 26, "Recent Trends in Social and Economic Conditions of Negroes in the U.S." (July 1968), p. 3. Figures have been rounded to the nearest percentage point. The 1970 United States census showed that Southern blacks moved north during the 1960's at the same rate as during the previous two decades. New York was the destination of most of the 1.4 million blacks

more than half of all American blacks still lived in the South, and the proportion was declining. The mechanization of Southern agriculture, the attraction of better wages in Northern industries, and the low and inadequate welfare benefits offered by Southern state governments have all encouraged migration. Politics in the North, South, and West reflected the changing migrational patterns by the 1960's. Blacks themselves discovered new political conditions, new opportunities, new and often subtle obstacles to their political participation. Black migration from the old Confederacy and border states is a sign of developmental imbalance in the United States and black citizens' tacit recognition of it. In the next decades, if the whole South, like Atlanta, makes rapid social and economic progress, the imbalance may be offset and the black population stabilized geographically.

Population shifts altering relations between ethnic groups and a federal government are not always left to chance or haphazard developments but can result from deliberate policy. The movements of Han Chinese to minority regions along the Sino-Soviet border is an example. The forced migration in 1838 of the Cherokee Indians from North Carolina to Oklahoma is another illustration of ethnic federal transformation by means of public policy.

Since the Bolshevik revolution the central government of the Soviet Union has encouraged Great Russians to resettle in non–Great Russian federal republics. The purpose of the move is to dilute the ethnic homogeneity of the republics and ensure their compliance with centralized authority.[14] This demographic strategy does not seem to have been entirely successful.

---

migrating from the South to the North. California, New Jersey, Illinois, and Michigan had the next largest gains in black population. See *New York Times,* March 4, 1971. The implications of population shifts for the distribution of power between and within countries are analyzed in Neil W. Chamberlain, *Beyond Malthus: Population and Power* (New York: Basic Books, 1970).

[14] Ukrainian nationalists have argued that Moscow has undermined their cause by resettling Ukrainians in the "virgin land" territories of the east. Tibor Szamuely, "The Resurgence of Ukrainian Nationalism," *The Reporter* (May 30, 1968), p. 16. For a description of Russian resettlement in an Asian republic, see Rupert A. Rupen, "Tuva," *Asian Survey* 5, no. 12 (December 1965): 613.

At one point it appeared that the 1970 census of the Soviet Union would show non–Great Russians outnumbering Great Russians for the first time, and Soviet authorities were reluctant to publicize the figures. Early tabulations, however, showed ethnic Great Russians holding on to their majority, though by a slim 53 per cent, a 2 per cent decline since the 1959 census. Thus, despite a large influx of Russians to Muslim republics, the indigenous peoples accounted for a growing proportion of the population. However, a heavy influx of ethnic Russians to the Baltic republics reduced the Baltic people's percentage of the population, especially in Estonia and Latvia.[15]

Just before the release of preliminary 1970 Soviet census figures, demographer Murray Feshback predicted that nationality questions would be among those most carefully tabulated. Census lists included 122 nationalities in the Soviet Union. For several years the population of Central Asia, which is mostly Muslim, has been growing 2.5 times faster than the Great Russian population. Western demographers refer to situations like the one now worrying Russian leaders as "the 50 per cent problem." Feshback described the Soviets' discomfort: "Soviet demographers in Moscow in September 1969 . . . emphatically denied the existence of this problem, but they obviously did not want to pursue the subject." [16]

15 Shortly after the census figures were released, two articles appeared in the weekly *Literaturnaya Gazeta* denouncing bachelors, particularly Russian bachelors. Reflecting a widespread concern over ethnic Russians' slow rate of national increase (only 13 per cent compared to Muslim Asian increases as high as 52 per cent), the two writers urged Russian men to marry earlier and produce more children. Not to do so was termed neurotic if not traitorous. The Soviet government, in turn, was pressed to supply sanctions and incentives to reduce Russian bachelorhood. *New York Times*, April 25, 1971.

16 Murray Feshback, "Observations on the Soviet Census," *Problems of Communism* 19 (May–June 1970): 61. When census figures were published, one ethnic group was notable for its absence. Although Soviet officials estimate that there are 1.85 million ethnic Germans in the Soviet Union, all data on them were omitted from regional statistical tables. The omission may be due to the regime's reluctance to publicize its geographical dispersal of Germans, despite their formal political rehabilitation in 1964. Since their Volga republic was obliterated in World War II, Germans have been the Soviet Union's largest minority without an autonomous region. *New York Times*, June 7, 1971.

If Great Russians lost their numerical superiority, the government might lean increasingly on urbanization and modernization of the Central Asian republics in order to control birth rates and foster cultural and political consolidation. Alternatively, Moscow could officially impose birth control on Central Asia. Such a policy would have two drawbacks: first, it would be resented by Third World peoples outside the Soviet Union; second, as long as Moscow and Peking are at odds, the Soviet Union needs an *increasing* population along its border with China.[17] As the Soviet dilemma suggests, development in the context of ethnic pluralism and federalism involves more than political engineering skills; it entails adjustment to unplanned ethnic change.

Swiss integration is often cited as the success story of modern pluralist development. The Swiss, like the Russians, must reconcile their extraintegrative goals (border security, Third World prestige, economic growth) with perceived integrative demands. But the ability of the Swiss to cope with diversity depends on strict decentralization — to a degree most modernizing nations cannot afford. The centralized authority of Switzerland's political system is drastically curtailed; adjustment to changes in ethnic patterns was entrusted not to government elites but to a national referendum. Infrequent movement between ethnic districts and the relative stability of ethnic numerical proportions create a safety cushion.

Prosperity and growing European interdependence are upsetting the integrative conditions in Switzerland by attracting new immigrants across the frontiers. Until the adoption of the 1848 constitution, movement from one canton to another was prohibited and cultural-territorial autonomy was preserved. As modernization's priorities gave primacy to the maximum use of human resources, the legal position became untenable. Yet intercantonal mobility still is infrequent in comparison to interstate movement in the United States, Canada, and Malaysia. Persons moving to a new canton are obliged to use its local language for the transaction of official business. French, German, and Italian linguistic frontiers within Switzerland

[17] Ibid.

remain sharply defined, even after a century of legalized mobility. The 1960 census indicated that in all German-speaking cantons, from 94 to 99 per cent of the Swiss citizens (excluding foreign residents) had the principal language of the canton as their mother tongue. In French-speaking cantons the percentages of citizens for whom French was the mother tongue were 82 in Geneva, 86 in Neuchâtel, and 87 in Vaud. In Ticino 88 per cent of the citizenry claimed Italian as their mother tongue.[18] Therefore, although Switzerland is one of the most dramatically pluralistic nations, each of its territorial subunits is remarkably homogeneous.[19] Economic growth, however, is altering this.

Economic progress has added a dimension to Switzerland's political development. A new element in Swiss politics (besides the introduction of female suffrage) is the influx of foreign workers, which is creating a new kind of ethnic pluralism, not too stable and with few roots in the country's historical territorial subunits. By 1970, Switzerland's population of 6 million included nearly 1 million foreign residents. Most were laborers with various skills — 600,000 Italians, Spaniards, Yugoslavs, and others, mostly from Mediterranean countries. By supplementing the limited supply of Swiss workers, foreign laborers fueled Switzerland's post–World War II prosperity.[20] According to economic statistics, at the beginning of 1971 there were only 59 unemployed people in Switzerland and 4,885 jobs vacant.[21] What would happen if the external labor pool dried up, as some employers fear? Wages would soar, setting

[18] Kenneth D. McRae, *Switzerland: Example of Cultural Coexistence* (Toronto: Canadian Institute of International Affairs, 1964), p. 12.

[19] An exception is the so-called Bern Question. Bern is Switzerland's German-speaking capital city, situated in a wholly German-speaking area of a bilingual canton. French-language citizens in the canton would like to break away from Bern. In a recent Bern cantonal election, voters agreed that its French Jura districts would be allowed to decide whether they want to separate. *New York Times*, March 2, 1970.

[20] Provisional figures of the 1970 Swiss census showed a total population increase of 15.2 per cent. But when the 970,000 foreigners are not counted, the size of the native population increases only 10 per cent over the 1960 figure. Five hundred thousand more foreigners were listed in 1970 than in 1960. A considerable number of these may not be "laborers" but high-income persons who claimed Swiss domicile to escape paying United States or British income taxes. *New York Times*, January 3, 1971.

[21] *New York Times*, January 15, 1971.

off an inflationary spiral.[22] Other Swiss are less alarmed about the economy than about what they considered a threat to Switzerland's delicately balanced federalism.

Two different interpretations of the relationship between ethnicity and development met head-on in a 1970 referendum. Swiss voters confronted a proposed constitutional amendment that would have opted for a traditional pluralist balance in preference to continued economic expansion. The amendment, if passed, would have expelled three hundred thousand foreign workers by limiting the number of foreigners in each canton (except Geneva) to 10 per cent of its population. Geneva would have been given a 25 per cent quota because of its international status. The amendment was defeated in the national referendum, but the popular vote was unexpectedly close: 654,588 in opposition to 557,714 in favor.

The negative vote cast in fifteen of the twenty-two Swiss cantons reflected the feelings of citizens who either had a cultural affinity with the Mediterranean foreigners or depended on Swiss industrial prosperity. They outpolled voters who were of German descent or who relied on rural or small-town commerce for their livelihoods.[23]

The substantial positive vote, to expel an enormous number of foreign workers, revealed a new Swiss ambivalence about the benefits of economic growth. Despite assurances that foreigners were "less disturbing to the ethnic cultural equilibrium of Switzerland than has been widely feared," many ordinary Swiss were afraid that their country's traditional stability was being upset.[24] The fact that big business strongly opposed the amendment aroused further anxiety among Swiss who thought

[22] *Wall Street Journal,* May 18, 1970.

[23] "Basically, the proposal was defeated by Zurich and the other big cities of German-speaking central and eastern Switzerland, together with the population of western Switzerland, most of whom speak French and Italian. These, being Latins themselves, are more tolerant of the foreign workers than German-speaking Switzerland." *New York Times,* June 8, 1970.

[24] Kurt B. Mayer, "Migration, Cultural Tensions, and Foreign Relations: Switzerland," *Journal of Conflict Resolution* 11, no. 2 (Spring, 1968) p. 151. Mayer bases his forecast of smooth assimilation on the likelihood of foreign workers' adopting the official language of the canton in which they reside. Since most foreigners work in German cantons, the long-range result will be to reinforce the current German superiority.

that banks and manufacturing firms were already too influential in national affairs.[25] Other supporters of the amendment were most bothered by the cultural alienism of Yugoslav, Italian, Spanish, and Greek immigrants.

In general, the two viewpoints converged in a shared concern about Switzerland's peculiar type of integrative politics. Historically, the Swiss political system has rested on decentralization, homogeneous and stable subunits, and male-citizen participation. (Women did not vote in Switzerland until 1971.) In other words, the Swiss tradition of popular democracy and ethnic tolerance has been sustained by a low level of national mobilization. Aside from the profit motive — Swiss businessmen have made money from both sides in European wars — this may explain why the Swiss have shunned involvement in war; modern warfare necessitates national mobilization.[26] But, though they have avoided the centralizing pressures of war, the Swiss have not been able to isolate themselves from the centralizing tendencies of industrialization. Even if the job market did not serve as a magnet for foreigners, urban and industrial growth would require modification of Switzerland's localized and personal democracy.[27] The controversy about foreign workers sharpened the country's developmental options. Swiss federalism may be entering a new and uncertain period of dynamism.[28]

---

[25] *Washington Post,* June 7, 1970.

[26] Switzerland does not have a standing national army. Army units are maintained only by the individual cantons. McRae, *Switzerland,* pp. 35, 37.

[27] For the Swiss village, the foundation of Swiss participatory democracy, survival will mean absorption into metropolitan complexes, which are "more diversified, more industrial, more centralized and more efficient. . . . Autonomy, full participation in public affairs, consensus on significant issues and communal collectivism are simply not compatible with modernization of this kind." Benjamin R. Barber, "Switzerland: Progress Against the Communes," *Trans-action* 8, no. 4 (February 1971): 50.

[28] In the 1971 federal elections for the national council, the lower house of the Swiss parliament, two new rightist parties campaigning with the slogan "Switzerland for the Swiss" won twelve seats and ran strongest in German-speaking cantons. *The Times* (London), November 2, 1971.

The ethnic content of Australia, another stable federal system, is also changing. The number of British immigrants has dropped, and newcomers from southern and eastern Europe are entering Australia as settlers. For the first time, there is a language problem among the white population. Australian shop-owners in one Sydney suburb must learn

RESOURCES AVAILABLE TO ETHNIC SUBUNITS

The second variable in the ethnic-federal equation involves the distribution of powers between member states and the federal government. The Soviets and the Swiss handle ethnic group mobility quite differently. Part of the difference results from dissimilar resource distribution between the federal center and the subunits. Soviet republics have minimal powers, whereas Swiss cantons are invested with significant authority. The degree of ethnic homogeneity in the constituent states does not appear to be the crucial consideration, for states in both countries are explicitly drawn to recognize communal group concentrations. Rather, the difference in the distribution of powers stems from the source of state authority and from the pervasiveness of nationwide institutions. Soviet republics rely for their authority on delegation from the federal center; the Swiss cantons originate much of their authority. Soviet republics are superseded by a highly centralized national Communist party, bureaucracy, and army; all institutions in Switzerland are decentralized.

Calculations of power mean little unless we take account of the kinds of power reserved to the central government and held by the subunits. Formal powers are only chimeras if jurisdictional units are ill equipped to back up their authority. One of the major resources for a subunit is social solidarity in the form of ethnic unity. A state with impressive legal authority may be impotent in practice if it must expend its energies preventing interethnic conflict. Outbreaks of civil unrest sparked by ethnic animosity can provide a central government looking for an excuse to intervene with just the excuse needed, and even when a central government's intervention in subunit affairs is markedly unenthusiastic, as it has been on occasion, the subunit's authority suffers nonetheless. The British gov-

---

Italian in order to communicate with their customers. By mid-1966, non-Britishers in the total population had reached 20 per cent. The 1971 census is expected to show a further increase. Richard Hughes, "Whiting a Wong," *Far Eastern Economic Review* 84, no. 50 (December 11, 1971): 11.

ernment's movement of troops into Northern Ireland in 1969, president Eisenhower's reluctant ordering of federal soldiers into Arkansas in 1957, prime minister Trudeau's imposition of emergency restrictions on Quebec in the wake of kidnapings in 1970 — all three decisions were made with grave misgivings, yet each severely damaged the integrity of subunit authority.

Federally granted jurisdiction does not guarantee an ethnic community that it will forever be the master of its own political destiny. When communal leaders bargain at the creation of a national system, they have to be farsighted enough to fight for the powers most essential to ethnic integrity. Most obvious are powers touching directly on the group's ethnic uniqueness — for example, responsibility for religious affairs and education. Nationally oriented politicians are most likely to give up the former. If, as in Malaysia, religious tradition hinges on the formal instruction of children, then a central government equipped with authority over education can even manipulate religious affairs. In the United States, Irish Catholic immigrants in Boston during the nineteenth century feared that their faith would suffer if their children were educated by Yankee Protestant teachers in the public schools.

Often the powers that determine the preservation or dilution of ethnic allegiances are least related to cultural policies. States that manage to secure authority over religion, public morality, and education may discover that, even if they wish, they cannot withstand assimilative pressures exerted from the federal centers of administration. If economic planning is monopolized by the federal government, movements of people in and out of various territories may be beyond state control, for people move to where they can find employment and employment opportunity is determined by federal priorities. If foreign affairs and defense policies are federal prerogatives, young men may be detached from their ethnic homelands by military draft. If a federal center sets universal criteria for professional licensing and civil service recruitment, then no amount of formal subunit authority over primary and secondary schooling is going to halt the trend toward nationally standardized higher education. States need their own revenues. Without independent taxing authority, subunits are at the mercy of federal ministries. None of these four policy areas is specifically "ethnic," though all affect the direction in which ethnic groups evolve. Ethnic groups are bound together by shared cultures, but values, identities, and associations all have to be relevant to men's everyday circumstances if they are to survive. The jurisdiction that has the strongest voice in determining those circumstances ultimately shapes a community's future.

The amount of authority a constituent state must possess to protect effectively its own communal interests may not be apparent while modernization is at a low level 'and social change is proceeding gradually. Under these conditions policy areas can be neatly segregated and thus legally divided between states and the federal center. Nor will ethnic integrity be so obviously dependent on technological and economic decisions. One of the hallmarks of modernization, however, is the increasing interdependence of various parts of society. "Everything becomes relevant" the motto of the modernist, is the bane of the ethnic federalist, for it means that defending state jurisdictions against central intrusion is almost impossible. The more apparent the interdependence of parts, the more insistent become federal policy-makers' claims of authority to affect and coordinate those interdependent parts. If modernization occurs, as it usually has, in a mood of impatience and anticipation, demands for coordinated decision are especially difficult to resist.

When negotiations for the creation of a multi-ethnic federal state are conducted during periods of rapid modernization, far-reaching interdependencies are visible and communal leaders demand broad authority for their jurisdictions. In quieter and less blatantly modern times, they might have been satisfied with responsibility for religious and cultural affairs, preservation of traditional ethnic institutions, and some concessions on language. However, once increases in mobility, industry, urban growth, and technology make it clear that communal integrity can be undermined by noncultural policy intervention, ethnic representatives will come to a constitutional congress with broad programs. Their demands for autonomy will be thrust before nationally oriented politicians who are more sensitive than ever to the fact that successful national development calls for an activist central government. The later in the modernizing process that a federal system is pieced together, the wider will be the gap between nationalists and ethnic communalists.

INSTITUTIONS IN MULTI-ETHNIC FEDERALISM

The third variable that effects the interaction of federalism and ethnic politics is the degree to which national institutions counter or affirm decentralization. Political parties are the most important institutions in this regard because of their capacity to instigate and channel collective mobilization. In an administrative polity, however, police, military, and bureaucratic institutions carry greater importance. Military coups in federal multi-ethnic nations — Pakistan, Burma, Nigeria — are reminders of the tenuousness of any institutional arrangement. Nevertheless, parties with finances and recruitment controlled at the national level can be an antidote to federalism's centrifugal tendencies. If parties are standard-bearers of ideologies that classify ethnicity as artificial or transitory, ethnic branches of federal parties will be ineffective servants of communal interests except as dispensers of patronage and symbolic gestures. If the federal distribution of powers requires crucial policy decisions to be made at the center, then, regardless of formal ideology, parties will seek to deethnicize themselves somewhat. They have to do this to capture the plurality needed to control parliament or the executive.

Communist parties, in theory, are centralized organizations based on class unity. In practice, however, numerous Communist parties have courted ethnic separatist movements. In Yugoslavia, Laos, South Vietnam, India, Guyana, Malaysia, Pakistan, and elsewhere, Communist parties have modified their structures and platforms to permit direct appeals to ethnic groups whose discontent they hope to channel into a wider political movement. In the Soviet Union the Communist party (CPSU) has made few concessions to ethnic communities and has been the chief instrument for counteracting the communal tendencies of federalism. Political parties do exist for the several non-Russian "nationalities," but they are token groups, outside the Communist organization and thus outside the real councils of power. Branches of the Communist party within the various Soviet republics have little autonomy and do not operate as ethnic advocates. The party's class doctrine militates against non-Russian interests because, with deference to the proletariat, CPSU members are recruited mainly from among town and city dwellers. As a result of the Soviet resettlement policy, many urban residents in non-Russian republics are Russian, and the native inhabitants remain rural peasants.

Various Soviet republics represent different sorts of ethnic political situations and are treated differently in the CPSU organization. There are four general patterns of ethnic composition in non-Russian areas:

1. Where the indigenous nationalities have consistently maintained clear predominance in the local party membership. Georgia and Armenia are probably the only examples of this pattern.

2. Where the indigenous nationalities, although in the past strongly underrepresented in "their" party organizations, have managed to maintain . . . a numerical majority. . . . This applies most notably to the Ukraine and Belorussia. It probably applies to Azerbaidzhan, and the Dagestan and Chuvash Autonomous Republics. The Baltic republics and Turkmenia evidently also conform to this pattern, but they have shown some signs of lapsing into Pattern 3.

3. Where the indigenous nationalities, though constituting a plurality or even an absolute majority of the population, now appear unlikely ever to attain (or regain) a numerical majority in party membership. This applies to Kirgizia and Moldavia, and probably also to the Kabardin-Balkar, North Ossetian, Tatae, Tuva and Yakut Autonomous Republics.

4. Where the indigenous nationalities are so heavily outnumbered in "their own" areas that their attainment of even a plurality in the local party membership seems out of the question — even in cases where their rate of party membership is relatively high. This applies in Kazakhstan, and in the Bashkir, Buryat, Kalmuck, Karelian, Komi, Mari Mordvin, Udmurt and Chechen-Ingush Autonomous Republics. The autonomous oblasts of the R.S.F.S.R. (the Russian Republic) probably all conform to patterns 3 or 4.[29]

[29] T. H. Rigby, *Communist Party Membership in the USSR, 1917–67* (Princeton: Princeton University Press, 1968), pp. 398–99. Rigby notes

The relations of Soviet Russia's 3 million Jews with the Communist party are affected by the fact that Jews are not concentrated in a single region as are most other nationalities. A Jewish autonomous region does exist, established in 1934 in the Soviet Far East. At present the region has approximately one hundred eighty thousand inhabitants, of whom at most twenty thousand are Jewish.[30] Thus Jews are recruited into the CPSU in a number of different republics. Rigby estimates that "Jews have continued to do well in the CPSU membership, in spite of the vicissitudes of the Soviet Jewish community." Still, perhaps as a reflection of the upsurge of anti-Semitism or, as it is officially labeled, "anti-Zionism," the proportion of Jews in the party to Jews in the total population has declined since the 1930's.[31] Neither Jews nor other non-Russian nationalities have done well in rising to positions of power in the Communist party. Deputy premier Veniamin Dymshits is currently the only Jewish member of the 190-member Central Committee of the CPSU.[32] Although in party representation and influence Soviet Jews may be more restricted than other national groups, the "Jewish problem" and the problems of other nationalities have much in common.

Andrei Amalrik, a young Russian intellectual and social critic, has written a short book in which he warns Soviet Communists that the Soviet Union is fragile indeed. Amalrik launched his critique at the height of the border conflict between the Soviet Union and China. This conflict had compelled Moscow to attend to its Asian republics in the east. Amalrik's book was published in the West at about the time demographers were speculating that the 1970 census would

---

(p. 376) that Great Russian overrepresentation was especially marked in the 1940's, though it moderated in the 1950's. On the other hand, Georgian and Armenian representation fell off in the 1950's.

[30] *Washington Post,* January 24, 1971. The 1970 census showed a decline in the total number of Jews in the Soviet Union. The official explanation for the decline, from 2.27 million Jews in 1959 to 2.15 million in 1970, was the assimilation of Jews into society. Some Soviet Jewish militants questioned this interpretation. *New York Times,* May 8, 1971.

[31] Rigby, *Communist Party Membership in the USSR, 1917–67,* pp. 386–87.

[32] *Washington Post,* January 24, 1971.

show the Great Russians losing their majority. Amalrik's predictions are significant not because they are based on scientific
data but because they were made by a leading member of
Russia's young intelligentsia and hint at general concern over
the durability of the Soviet federal-party integrative formula:

> I have no doubt that this great Eastern Slav empire, created
> by Germans, Byzantines and Mongols, has entered the last
> decades of its existence. . . . Marxist doctrine has delayed the
> break-up of the Russian Empire — the Third Rome — but it
> does not possess the power to prevent it.[33]

Amalrik pictures the final dissolution of the "empire" coming
amid strains of war with China:

> The unavoidable "deimperialization" will take place in an
> extremely painful way. Power will pass into the hands of
> extremist elements and groups and the country will begin to
> disintegrate into anarchy, violence and intense national [ethnic]
> hatred.
>
> The boundaries of the new states which will then begin to
> emerge on the territory of the former Soviet Union will be
> extremely hard to determine. . . .
>
> But it is also possible that the "middle class" will prove
> strong enough to keep control in its own hands. In that case,
> the granting of independence to the various Soviet nationalities
> will come about peacefully and some sort of federation will be
> created, similar to the British Commonwealth or the European
> Economic Community.[34]

Most prophecies, from Thomas More's to George Orwell's,
are unreliable guides to the future, but they do mirror contemporary hopes and anxieties. Andrei Amalrik's own version
of 1984 suggests that the strategy of overlaying ethnic subunits
with an allegedly supra-ethnic party structure is not foolproof.
Needless to say, this is the worst kind of heresy in the eyes of
CPSU dogmatists. Nevertheless, Soviet leaders, like the Swiss,
may be walking into a new era of ethnic political development.

---

[33] Andrei Amalrik, *Will the Soviet Union Survive Until 1984?* (New
York: Harper & Row, Perennial Library, 1971), p. 65.
[34] Ibid., pp. 64–65.

CHAPTER V

Systems in
Structural Transition

POLITICAL ANALYSIS would be easier if all nations followed the same path of development. However, various nations are moving away from, while others are moving closer to federalism. Furthermore, some of the nations reevaluating federalism's utility for their development are usually termed "Western" or "advanced." Yugoslavia has announced a plan for greater decentralization after the retirement of Marshal Tito. Belgium and Czechoslovakia are moving uncertainly toward a federal scheme, although the Soviet Union holds veto power over Czechoslovakia. In Britain, the textbook model of a unitary state, studies of the feasibility of a quasi-federal system are being made. Canada is pressing for greater centralization to overcome the frustrating problems of provincialism. The breakdown of Pakistan's federal system, which was hampered from the outset by geographical absurdities, led to open warfare with India in the autumn of 1971 and raised questions about the durability of federalism throughout the subcontinent. The United States appéars to be both moving away from and returning to federalism. In the midst of these rather confusing trends, the three basic variables that determine the relationship of ethnic politics and development in a federal system remain relevant — the extent to which territorial concentrations of ethnic populations and subunit boundaries overlap, the distribution of effective powers between constituent states and the central government, and the extent to which national institutions affirm or contradict ethnic autonomy.

PAKISTAN: THE LIMITS OF FEDERALISM

Pakistan was born of expediency. At the end of World War II, British colonialists were under pressure from their American allies to get out of India. The Muslim League, led by Mahomed Ali Jinnah, had worked with Hindu nationalists in the movement against Britain but sought a separate Islamic state; the leaders of India's Congress party, despite the Gandhian goal of Hindu-Muslim brotherhood, were anxious to achieve Indian independence. The product of these diverse motivations was independence for India and a Muslim nation of Pakistan, divided into two territories separated by more than a thousand miles of Indian land. People subject to the British were free to choose the country they preferred to make their political home. Although both countries remained religiously mixed, millions of Hindus moved into India and millions of Muslims migrated to East Pakistan or West Pakistan. As in Nigeria a decade later, the decolonization so shaped ethnic relations that future national development was fraught with risk.

Though most of the people in East Pakistan and West Pakistan were Muslim, the population, language, and levels of modernization in the two divisions contrasted sharply. The East — which later became the secessionist state of Bangla Desh — had a larger population but received less from national expenditures and less from foreign aid than the West. Generally, Easterners had a lower standard of living than their Muslim compatriots in the West, although the East generated a major proportion of Pakistan's foreign currency earnings.[1]

---

[1] Calculations indicate that the economic disparity between East Pakistan and West Pakistan worsened in the years after independence and partition: "East Pakistan, with 55 per cent of the population of the whole nation, has become poorer in per capita terms in relation to the less populous and richer western province. In 1951–52 the average per capita income in East Pakistan was 85 per cent of that in West Pakistan, but by

People of East Pakistan also considered themselves a distinct ethnic group, set apart by regional identity, cultural heritage, and language. They were mostly Bengali, whereas the dominant group in the West was Punjabi. Other Bengalis were just across the East's frontier in the Indian federal state of West Bengal. Bengali and Urdu were designated official Pakistani national languages, though only after stiff Punjabi opposition to Bengali had been overcome. Politically, West Pakistan was clearly the dominant political partner. The military regime of marshal Ayub Khan solidified the hegemony of the West as the federal center. Separatism has always had appeal among the Bengalis in the East, and an electoral reapportionment that assigned Easterners their rightful voting strength added new impetus to separatism. In October 1970 the pro-Bengali Awami League won an election in the East and a nationwide parliamentary majority. Its leaders came to the capital, Rawalpindi, with a six-point program for a new constitution. The revised federal system of Pakistan designed by the Awami League would have allowed East Pakistan far greater autonomy than it then enjoyed:

1. The constitution should provide for a Federation of Pakistan in its true sense on the basis of the Lahore Resolution and the parliamentary form of government with supremacy of a Legislature directly elected on the basis of universal adult franchise.

2. The federal Government should deal with only two subjects, Defense and Foreign Affairs, and all residuary subjects shall be vested in the federating states.

3. Two separate but freely convertible currencies for two wings should be introduced; or . . . one currency for the whole country, but with effective constitutional provisions, should be introduced to stop the flight of capital from East to West Pakistan. . . .

1967–68 the ratio had fallen to 62 per cent." Timothy and Leslie Nulty, "Pakistan: The Busy Bee Route to Development," *Trans-action* 8, no. 4 (February 1971): 19.

One reason for the West's vehement opposition to Bengali separatism was that the East was the biggest single market for the West's products. An estimated 40 per cent of the West's manufactured goods were sold in the East. *New York Times,* March 23, 1971.

4. The power of taxation and revenue collection shall be vested in the federating units and the federal center will have no such power.

5. There should be two separate accounts for the foreign exchange earnings of the two wings. . . .

6. East Pakistan should have a separate militia or paramilitary force.[2]

Little in the proposed federalist scheme was explicitly ethnic. Bengali representatives talked about currency, foreign exchange, and taxation. However, Zulfikar Ali Bhutto, leader of the People's party, West Pakistan's major party (and later appointed president of Pakistan in the wake of the country's military defeat), was both a Pakistani nationalist and a member of the West Pakistani establishment. As the constitutional assembly was preparing to convene, Bhutto declared that his party would accept only two of the Awami League's points — that Pakistan should be a "true federation" (left undefined) and that federating units should maintain paramilitary forces.[3] Reconstructing Pakistan's federal system, even in the absence of civil and international war, would have required more political skill than had patching it together in the first place. By 1971, political mobilization among the East's Bengali community was extensive, and the implications of interlocking developmental factors were clearer, thus strengthening the East Pakistanis' commitment to expanded autonomy and the West Pakistani elite's dedication to central control.

Ethnic polarization was total in March 1971, when negotiations between the central government and the Awami League broke down and West Pakistani troops descended upon the East to quash Bengali separatism. Estimates of the number of Bengalis killed ranged as high as five hundred thousand. Mil-

[2] M. Rashiduzzaman, "The Awami League in the Political Development of Pakistan," *Asian Survey* 10, no. 7 (July 1970): 583.

[3] *New York Times*, February 16, 1971. The military question was ethnically significant because of Punjabi (West Pakistani) dominance in the army. The East Bengal Regiment, the first regiment recruited from East Pakistan, had only four or five battalions, in comparison with the normal Pakistani regiment of from fifteen to twenty battalions. *New York Times*, March 27, 1971. When war broke out later in 1971, the East Bengal Regiment became the backbone of the rebel Bangla Desh army.

lions of Bengali refugees — many of them Hindu Bengalis —
fled into India, creating a massive problem for the already
overtaxed regime of prime minister Indira Gandhi. The refugee problem became the launching pad for the escalation of
Pakistan's interethnic conflict into a full-scale international
conflict. By the end of 1971, Indian troops and planes were
fighting West Pakistan's forces. The Soviet Union supported
India and the East, and the United States and China found
themselves backing West Pakistan.

With the help of India's victorious soldiers, Bengali nationalist leaders regained control of the East's capital, Dacca, and
declared Bangla Desh an independent nation. However, the
ethnic-political scene was more complicated than it had been
a year earlier. At the time of the Awami League's landslide
victory at the polls, its leaders were the acknowledged spokesmen for Bengali political aspirations. But as the new Bangla
Desh regime set about to consolidate its control in 1972, the
Awami League's generally middle-class and ideologically moderate leaders had to come to terms with the militant Mukti
Bahini guerrillas, who had provided the armed force for the
nationalist movement. At one point the Mukti Bahini reportedly had as many as seventy thousand men in the field.[4] In
addition, during the twelve months of turmoil the East's principal ethnic minority, the Biharis, had become estranged from
the Bengalis and were castigated for collaborating with the
soldiers of the West. Protecting the estimated half-million
Biharis living in Dacca from vendetta was an added burden
upon the new Bangla Desh regime.[5]

The interethnic conflict in South Asia does not neatly confine itself within national boundaries. One of the reasons Mrs.
Gandhi's regime took such an active interest in the Pakistani
dispute was that India has a large Bengali population and the
success of India's federalism depends on New Delhi's ability to
satisfy the demands of West Bengal. The state long has been
plagued by severe poverty and has given birth to both Maoist

4 T. J. S. George, "Mrs. Gandhi's Gamble," *Far Eastern Economic Review* 84, no. 48 (November 27, 1971): 5.

5 "India and Pakistan: After the Debacle," *The Economist* (January 1,
1972), p. 32.

and more orthodox Communist parties. The Communist party of India (Marxist) formally demanded "the right of self-determination for nationalities in India." The party's secretary general went on to say, "The time has come . . . for the people to start campaigning for their right to self-determination." He noted that West Bengal earned 20 per cent of India's total revenue but got back only 13 per cent. This and many other grievances voiced by West Bengal's dissidents were similar to those articulated by the Awami League in East Pakistan. India's central government in New Delhi found itself in the awkward position of supporting Bengali nationalism in Pakistan while trying to repress it in India.[6]

YUGOSLAVIA: ETHNIC POLITICS AFTER
THE CHARISMATIC LEADER

Since World War II, Yugoslavia's multi-ethnic federal system has been held together by the personal forcefulness of Marshal Tito and an official ideology, communism. The institution through which Tito has exercised his power and through which the ideology has been articulated has been the Yugoslav Communist League, which is not a single institution but a federation of ethnic parties. It has been observed that Yugoslav federalism derives from the "self-restraint" of the central Communist party.[7] This presumes that the national party could be as centralized as the Soviet model if it wanted to be. In fact, the nationalist prestige of marshal Tito cements the disparate parts together.[8] As he grew older, Tito began considering the problems Yugoslav integration would face after his departure, and in 1970 he unveiled a plan for securing Yugoslav unity. The plan did not resort to centralization; it

[6] "Dark Side of Freedom," *Far Eastern Economic Review* 84, no. 47 (November 20, 1971): 21.

[7] Carl J. Friedrich, *Trends of Federalism in Theory and Practice* (New York: Praeger, 1968), p. 168.

[8] Yugoslavia's 1961 census listed 8.3 million Serbs (including Montenegran Serbs), 4.2 million Croats, 1.6 million Slovenes, 1.0 million Macedonians, and 0.97 million Bosnian Muslims. They are divided ethnically into six republics. In addition, there were 914,760 Albanians, 504,368 Hungarians, and 182,964 Turks. U.S. Department of State, "Background Notes: Socialist Federal Republic of Yugoslavia" (1970), p. 1.

projected further decentralization of power and responsibility. In view of the peculiar history of Yugoslavia's development, the proposal was logical.

Tito's regime has its roots in the partisan guerrilla movement that fought German occupation forces so effectively during World War II. The partisans originated from fragmented prewar ethnic nationalist movements. Like all such movements, the guerrillas relied on popular support and effective grass-roots mobilization.[9] Tito, himself a Croat, consciously fashioned a movement that could withstand historic ethnic animosities and yet draw from the vitality of the various nationalisms. Soviet development gave primacy to centralized organization and planning; Yugoslav Communist development leaned heavily on local involvement, best symbolized by workers' councils. Robert Dahl, a student of American pluralist democracy, judiciously observes:

> the workers' councils are by no means autonomous; . . . in Yugoslavia organized party opposition is not permitted; strikes are rare and of doubtful legality; and the special influence of the party is important. Nonetheless, it seems clear that the councils elected by the workers are very much more than a facade behind which the party and state officials actually manage an enterprise.[10]

In a federal system commitment to local participation gives the states an expanded role. Where policy-makers have looked to local initiative to supply the driving force behind national development, ethnic attachments are not only tolerated but actually depended upon. Yugoslav federal development has moved toward creating elaborate devices for popular participation and taking explicit account of ethnic loyalties. Tito's

[9] Chalmers Johnson draws a parallel between the Yugoslav partisans and the Chinese Communists, both having successfully merged nationalism and communism during World War II. By contrast, Yugoslavia's Chetnik movement erred in identifying itself with just one ethnic group, the Serbs, thereby allowing Tito's partisans to capture the role of anti-German fighters. Chalmers Johnson, *Peasant Nationalism and Communist Power* (Stanford: Stanford University Press, 1962), p. 164.

[10] Robert Dahl, "Power to the Workers?" *New York Review of Books* (November 19, 1970), p. 20. See an expanded version of this discussion in Robert Dahl, *After the Revolution* (New Haven: Yale University Press, 1970), pp. 130–32.

1970 plan continued that trend, whereas in the United States "good government" reformers continued to link local ethnic politics with underdevelopment in an attempt to reduce the effect of ethnicity.[11]

In the American federal scheme ethnicity is not the basis of federal boundaries, yet ethnic groups continue to play a central part in party nominations and campaigning. Ethnic appeals and ticket-balancing are the prices paid for relying on local participation. The American hope is, however, that ethnicity will be confined to local and state politics and will have little impact on national policy decisions. As resources and issues are increasingly nationalized and state politics become subservient to national politics, the salience of ethnicity may wane. This could be one effect of an amendment to abolish the Electoral College and elect the president by direct national vote.[12]

The Yugoslav reorganization is grounded in an assumption contrary to American practice. It calls for the establishment of a presidium, a collective presidential body, to replace Tito. Composed of approximately twenty-five men, the presidium would be elected by the six ethnic republics and from the Communist party, business, youth groups, and war veterans. Chairmanship of the presidium would rotate among the six republics.[13] Belgrade would retain central jurisdiction only over defense, foreign affairs, aid to the country's underdeveloped areas, and regulation of the national common market. Primary responsibility for economic planning and financing

[11] Anti-machine campaigns, civil service reforms, regularization of welfare services, the institution of professional city managers, and nonpartisan city elections have all been aimed partly at diminishing ethnicity's role in local and state politics. There are indications, however, that these reforms have not caused the demise of ethnic politics at these levels. See Daniel N. Gordon, "Immigrants and Urban Governmental Forms in American Cities, 1933–60," in Brett W. Hawkins and Robert A. Lorinskas, eds., *The Ethnic Factor in American Politics* (Columbus, O.: Merrill, 1970), pp. 140–59.

[12] There is ample evidence to show that at the state level today politicians still use ethnic categories to formulate strategies and explain outcomes. For instance, Democratic Senate incumbent Ralph Yarborough was said to have lost the primary contest in Texas in 1970 because, although most black and Mexican American voters backed him, a significant number of Mexican Americans boycotted the primary and deprived him of needed liberal votes.

[13] *Washington Post*, October 11, 1970.

would devolve to the separate republics; however, their inequality is a potential problem. Together, Croatia and Slovenia
comprise just over 25 per cent of the Yugoslav population,
and — in stark contrast to the impoverished southern provinces — they account for almost 70 per cent of the country's
industrial production.[14]

In a federally divided multi-ethnic society achieving national development is easier than distributing it equally.
Eventually development gaps between states or republics acerbate ethnic animosities to the point that the nation's aggre-
gate development may be jeopardized. With Tito gone, will
the Communist party's ethnic branches be able to resolve their
differences and provide the integrative link in the newly decentralized system, or will the party's structure fracture along
ethnic lines and bring about national disintegration?

In the republic of Croatia nationalism is on the rise, and
Croatia is being asked to share its wealth with less fortunate
republics. Serbia is the main target of Croatian nationalists,
who feel that the Serbs' historical political dominance has not
been broken by Tito's brand of nationalist communism or by
the fact that Tito is a Croat. Belgrade, capital of the old Serbian royalist regime, remains the center of political and bureaucratic power in Yugoslavia. Croatian intellectuals and
Catholic spokesmen have protested a revision of the Serbo-
Croatian alphabet and a 1971 census questionnaire that would
underestimate Croatian numbers. In addition, they have urged
that the republic be allowed to establish its own banks, so
that the federal banks in Belgrade would not control foreign
currency earned by Croatian exports, Croatia's workers abroad
(including those in Switzerland), and local tourist resorts.[15]

At first the Croatian Communist party intervened to si-
lence such ethnic nationalism, but recently its leaders have
responded to obviously popular sentiments by either keeping
silent or speaking out in favor of Croatian demands. Jure

14 *New York Times,* February 5, 1970.
15 *New York Times,* February 10, 1971. Slovene and Serbian leaders have
backed Croatia in resisting central economic policies intended to divert
resources southward. *New York Times,* January 21, 1968; February 5, 1970;
July 8, 1970.

Juras — doctor of philosophy and medicine, Catholic, and active Croatian nationalist — objected to charges by Serbs and others that the Croats' nationalist revival is conservative and unhealthy: "The tendency to look on Croatian nationalism, Croatian culture and the Catholic Church as unhealthy is part of the old mechanism that always sought to put Croatia at a psychological disadvantage as a preliminary to suppression." [16]

Whether the party can reconcile Yugoslavia's traditional communal enmities without the commanding presence of marshal Tito and without fresh memories of the anti-German struggle will determine the fate of the proposed scheme of extended federalism. Paradoxically, strong-arm tactics from the federal center may be required to bring about the proposed decentralization. Angry over the strike of thirty thousand Croatian students and the involvement of party leaders in Croatia's nationalist movement, Tito in 1971 ordered a purge of the Croatian Communist party, labeling the expelled leaders "counter revolutionaries" and "class enemies." He also reminded the army, one of the most supra-ethnic Yugoslav institutions, of its responsibility for defending national unity and socialism.[17] The problem, however, is that in the participatory program that has distinguished Yugoslavia's political development, the Communist party in any republic is dependent on the support of the local populace as well as on authorization by Tito. The purged Communist officials in Croatia had popular backing, and their dismissals were followed by the voluntary resignations of numerous other party leaders in the republic. It will be difficult to carry out the new constitutional proposals without a legitimized party apparatus in so critical a republic.

Milovan Djilas, one-time partner of Tito, lately lamented:

> The League of Communists is not even a Yugoslav party any more. . . . It is six parties, in each of the six republics of our

16 Quoted in *New York Times,* February 10, 1971.

17 "If Czechs Applaud, We Should Tremble," *The Economist* (January 1, 1972), pp. 29–30. For an analysis of the role of the army in contemporary Yugoslavia, see Dan Morgan, "Yugoslavia Updates Its Partisans," *Washington Post,* October 31, 1971.

federation, each one looking out for the interests of its own state. The fact that there is no central idealism to hold them together has provoked a charged atmosphere throughout the country.

He added pessimistically, "Without Tito's authority, it is possible that they would all be at each other's throats again." [18]

BELGIUM: FEDERALISM TO REPLACE
A PARTY SYSTEM

Belgium's course of transition contains many elements of Yugoslavia's: ethnic territorial concentration, developmental inequalities, and ethnically torn political parties. But instead of hinging on the retirement or death of a central charismatic figure, decentralization in Belgium has been compelled by the rapid advancement of one of the nation's two communities and the inability of the current party system to absorb this change. In Belgium the partners are the Dutch-speaking Flemings — the traditional underdogs — and the French-speaking Walloons. Today advocates of Belgian federalization are in both communities.

Since the adoption of the constitution of 1831 and the achievement of independence from the Netherlands, Belgium has been a classic example of a unitary democracy. It has a

---

[18] Quoted in *Washington Post*, December 17, 1970. A. J. P. Taylor has questioned whether a softening of Soviet antagonism toward Yugoslavia would weaken the nation's cohesion by removing a common threat. A. J. P. Taylor, "The Independent Habit," *New York Review of Books* (February 11, 1971), p. 27. See also Wayne S. Vucinich, ed., *Contemporary Yugoslavia: Twenty Years of Socialist Experiment* (Berkeley: University of California Press, 1970).

Czechoslovakia is another Communist nation whose Communist party is divided ethnically. Its experiments with ethnic and territorial autonomy are even more vulnerable to Soviet interference than Yugoslavia's. During the short-lived "liberalization" under the leadership of Alexander Dubcek in 1968, a federal constitution was implemented. It would have granted the Slovaks, less developed than the Czechs, greater autonomy. Although there were ethnic motivations for the reform, it was part of Dubcek's plan for loosening the tightly centralized political system inherited from previous Stalinist regimes. Soviet intervention in August 1968, did not overturn the federal scheme but did make its actual working uncertain. A new era of centralized planning seemed to be initiated instead. *New York Times*, February 16, 17, 1970; February 19, 1971.

constitutional system headed by a "King of the Belgians" who is above ethnic communalism, a popularly elected parliament, and a multi-party system. For more than a century political cleavages that defined party contests and policy debates did not parallel communal boundaries; differences over the role of the Catholic Church and the value of secularized politics, plus conflicts over economic policy, cut across the Walloon and Flemish communities.[19] Since the end of World War II, however, ethnic issues increasingly have dictated electoral and parliamentary alignments, and in 1968 Belgians for the first time cast their ballots principally along communal lines. The three largest national parties were showing the strains. The Catholic Social Christian party, which traditionally had formed coalitions with either the Liberals or the Socialists, broke into Flemish and Walloon wings.[20] After the 1968 elections talk about revising the 1831 constitutional structure because it no longer was relevant to Belgium's ethnic relationships increased.

The progress of the Flemings in particular made the nineteenth-century jurisdictional system appear obsolete, "underdeveloped." Historically the Walloons had been more advanced than the Flemings. Deeply influenced by the industrializing and secularizing movements of neighboring France, urbanized mass society early was a fact of life in Wallonia, while the Flemings were still clerical and agricultural. Only in the second half of the twentieth century did the development balance begin to shift. As nationalization of Belgian politics finally began to take effect, democracy, education, and mass communication aroused the Flemings' awareness of their own communal identity. Industry and capital expanded in the Flemish provinces, particularly around the port of Antwerp. At the same time an accelerating birth rate increased the numbers of Flemings until they constituted more than 50 per cent of the Belgian population. By 1970, Flemings held a majority in parliament; both presidents of the two legislative chambers and the prime minister were Flemish, the governor of the

---

[19] Gordon L. Weil, *The Benelux Nations: The Politics of Small-Country Democracies* (New York: Holt, Rinehart and Winston, 1970), pp. 98–106, 120–21.

[20] *New York Times*, April 1, 1968.

national bank and the chairman of the developmentally crucial federation of industries were also Flemish. Only the foreign ministry remained in Walloon hands. "The emergence of Flanders from semi-colonial status is a striking fact of the twentieth century." [21]

The success of the democratization and industrialization ignited by post-Napoleonic development has caused the current crisis in the Belgian unitary system. Development is not a continuing spiral of success; it gives birth to new relationships, aspirations, and distributions of power, which a political system must be able to absorb. Unitary systems in multi-ethnic states may be sustained by the persistent underdevelopment of one of the country's major ethnic groups, but as the developmental disparity is diminished by economic and political mobilization, the attraction of federalism increases. Pragmatic synthesizers in Belgium are seeking solutions short of fragmentation, while the most mutually hostile Walloons and Flemings are calling for full federal separateness. As the influence of communalism continues to grow, politicians in the middle find their positions made untenable by polarization. The effect is apparent in the three established political parties. Three years after the Catholic Social Christian party broke into communal wings, the Socialist party did too. In 1971 Socialists appointed two presidents, one to represent Walloon members, the other to represent Flemish members.[22]

The monarchy is still a bulwark against outright fragmentation; additionally, there is a popular fear that a federal solution would mean the virtual disintegration of the Belgian nation. Just how far Belgium goes toward federalization will depend on how effectively the traditional Catholic and Socialist parties hold on to old constituencies and persuade the national public of the relevance of their proposed reforms, which stop short of federalism. The Belgian general elections of November 1971 cast doubt on the likelihood of both. The major parties' constitutional reforms were an important issue in the parliamentary elections; yet voters gave strong backing

21 George Armstrong Kelly, "Belgium: New Nationalism in an Old World," *Comparative Politics* 1, no. 3 (April 1969): 348.
22 *New York Times*, January 31, 1971.

to the nascent communal parties that opposed these reforms. Spectacular gains were made by the French-speaking parties. The Rassemblement Wallon in the south and the Front des Francophones in Brussels increased their combined number of seats from twelve to twenty-five. The Flemish ethnic party, Volksunie, likewise advanced, from twenty to twenty-two seats. The ruling Catholic and Socialist parties managed to retain their seats, but the Liberals suffered serious defeats. Consequently, in the 212-member lower house, Fleming and Walloon ethnic partisans commanded nearly one-fourth of the votes.[23] Commentators saw the electoral tallies as evidence of Belgians', especially Walloons', dissatisfaction with the constitutional plan that the traditional parties were trying to impose from above. The plan called for the Flemings, who hold a national majority, to concede parity to the French-speaking minority at the national level; in return, Flemings would get parity in Brussels, a city that is largely French speaking (though some French-speakers have Flemish origins, thus confusing the ethnic picture). Voters' backlash against these constitutional proposals not only could compel the "national" parties to move toward a more federalist reform but could usher in a new era of parliamentary instability in Belgium.[24]

Belgium's current national underdevelopment is the product of one of its constituent group's belated success at development. Political development occurs at two levels in a multiethnic society — the national and the communal. Increasing political consciousness, along with mobilization and economic modernization within the communities, can upset patterns of authority and cooperation in the nation as a whole.

CANADA AND BRITAIN: MODERN NATIONS WITH OPPOSITE TRENDS

Two additional countries deserve mention as we try to understand the factors encouraging the adoption of federalism as a solution to ethnic pluralism in the modern context. Canada and Britain are interesting because, although they have a similar cultural and ideological heritage and are modern nations,

[23] "Belgium: Le Backlash," *The Economist* (November 13, 1971), p. 30.
[24] Ibid., pp. 30–33.

they appear to be moving in opposite directions with regard to federalism. Canada, though beset with a mobilized French community, is considering reforms that would bolster the position of the central government. Britain, facing an explosive ethnic situation in Northern Ireland, plus Scottish and Welsh nationalist movements and an influx of Asian and West Indian immigrants, is toying with reforms that would modify its unitary system and introduce decentralization.

Canada's experience suggests that federalization can be an obstacle as well as a promoter of modern development. Unlike Belgium and Czechoslovakia, Canada has problems that have less to do with ineffective channels for popular participation than with the inability of a central government to fulfill its welfare and planning functions. Resistance to the expansion of Ottawa's powers, however, does not emanate solely from ethnic groups that comprise federal states. Certainly French Canadians in the province of Quebec would like more autonomy. However, additional objections to increased centralization are made by provincial regimes that jealously guard their extensive constitutional authority because of concerns that are regional rather than ethnic. There is a saying in British Columbia that Ottawa, the federal capital, is "3,000 miles away on the map and 30,000 miles away in the mind." [25] In many discussions of Canadian federalism, sectionalism does not get its due.

The British North American Act of 1867, Canada's basic charter, was designed to forestall sectional fragmentation. That it has not done so is due to economic differences generated by westward movement across the prairies, particularly by immigrants who were neither English nor French. A two-layer party system is the result. The first layer is comprised of the two national parties, Liberal and Conservative, which compete for control of the federal parliament and cabinet. Underneath them is a layer of parties interested in provincial problems and in capturing provincial premierships.[26] In

25 *New York Times*, October 24, 1970.
26 Steven Muller, "Federalism and the Party System in Canada," in Aaron Wildavsky, ed., *American Federalism in Perspective* (Boston: Little, Brown, 1967), pp. 149–51.

Quebec parties in the second layer are sensitive to French communalism; in other provinces they respond to economic regionalism. Provincial governments have enough resources — power, prestige, patronage — to make it possible for third parties to compete and survive even if they possess minimal national leverage. Provincial parties reflect the distinctiveness of their regions. For instance, the Prairie provinces — Manitoba, Saskatchewan, and Alberta — have a history of agrarian restlessness and discontent as well as a sense of being neglected by the central government. Farther west, British Columbia has evolved a strong trade unionist tradition, and unions have been active in politics outside the two major parties. The Social Credit party reflects both the vitality of the labor movement and Pacific Coast residents' feeling of remoteness from the federal capital.[27] Attitude surveys show residents of Quebec to be most consistently in favor of provincial rights, with westerners and citizens in the East Coast Maritime provinces close behind. Ontarians appeared to be the "least interested" in the exercise of provincial prerogatives.[28]

Overall, however, there is a growing recognition of Canada's need for federal involvement in economic planning. Prime minister Pierre Trudeau called a conference in 1969 to seek constitutional reforms enabling the federal government to meet its modern responsibilities with more money and more power. The ten provincial premiers were not persuaded. Interesting, though, was the similarity between the position of the ethnically preoccupied Quebec minister and the positions of his economically minded colleagues. With the exception of the leaders of Nova Scotia and New Brunswick, the premiers showed little enthusiasm for Trudeau's policy of vigorously enforcing bilingualism in the civil service and the army in order to mollify French Canadians. Most provincial representatives dismissed language rights as of "secondary importance to the issues of taxes and provincial powers." Even Quebec's

27 Edmund F. Ricketts and Herbert Waltzer, "Electoral Arrangements and Party System: The Case of Canada," *Western Political Quarterly* 23, no. 4 (December 1970): 713.
28 Mildred A. Schwartz, *Public Opinion and Canadian Identity* (Berkeley: University of California Press, 1967), p. 95.

premier argued that Canada "needed a charter of human rights less than it did a bill of provincial rights." [29]

Later in 1969 Trudeau called a second conference; again he made little headway. Provincial spokesmen still rejected his proposals as "too centralist." One leader asked, "What are we all doing discussing the constitution? . . . That's not the issue, economic problems are the issue." [30]

In 1971 the provincial government of Quebec rejected a federally sponsored charter for a new Canadian constitution, which would have replaced the British North America Act. Quebec's premier, Robert Bourassa, said that the charter was unacceptable because of its "uncertainties," especially the question of whether Canadian provinces would retain their traditional authority over health and welfare matters. Other French-Canadian spokesmen went further, explaining that the new charter was intolerable because it would make Quebec "a province like the other provinces without regard for its particular problems and pressing priorities." [31]

Canada's development troubles cannot be laid only at the door of ethnicity; indeed the independence and parochialism of most of the ten provinces have dampened the mutual disliking of the French and English. Canadians in the west, a great proportion of whom are recent immigrants of ancestries other than French and English, simply do not care much about the English-French communal issue.[32] However, sectional preoccupations have combined with Quebec separatism to hamstring a central regime burdened with growing service and planning obligations.

When a nation has managed to achieve jurisdictional centralization and political unity, its leaders are extremely reluctant to give them up. The British endured centuries of violence and civil war along the way to establishing a constitu-

29 *New York Times,* February 12, 1969.

30 *New York Times,* December 11, 1969.

31 *New York Times,* June 24, 1971.

32 Some non-English, non-French Canadians have started to demand governmental protection for their own ethnic heritages. Prime minister Trudeau has had to promise Canada's Germans, Ukrainians, Scandinavians, Chinese, and Indians that his regime's goal is not biculturalism but "multi-culturalism," *New York Times,* October 10, 1971.

tional monarchy and a bicameral parliament that bring all power under one authority in London. They are not likely to whimsically throw off that accomplishment. Under a unitary system the British were able to withstand attempted foreign invasions. They also industrialized faster than most other nations, spread their culture and rule around the globe, and enjoyed generations of stability while other countries were embroiled in revolution. Today it is all too easy to imagine Britain as an eternally stable, law-abiding polity, free from costly internal strife. This is the Britain pictured by most peoples in former British colonies, which, ever since the eighteenth century, have sought to emulate it politically. American political scientists like Woodrow Wilson, along with nation-builders in Canada, India, and Nigeria, have looked longingly at Britain's two-party system, its merger of executive and legislature, its entrenched political legitimacy symbolized by an unwritten constitution, its loyal civil service, its civilized public debate. Wilson and fellow anglophiles, however, shrugged their shoulders and recognized that their own countries could never match Britain's social homogeneity, insularity, and developmental head start. Lacking these, other nations would have to cope with conflict and fragmented power.

What this simplistic portrayal of Britain's political accomplishment overlooks is the amount of blood shed to create the current system. For centuries the monarch was little more than one of several rival lords. Tensions between parliament and the king stimulated conspiracies and public uncertainty until the nineteenth century. Ireland, Scotland, and Wales were brought under London's rule by coercion. British political development was neither smooth nor peaceful.

Presently there is wide-ranging debate in Britain over whether the hard-won unitary system is still relevant. Many official reports and authoritative commentators propose a "devolution of power." [33] Two principal conditions prompt

[33] A thorough analysis of proposals for devolution of power has been done by a member of Parliament, J. P. Mackintosh, in *The Devolution of Power: Local Democracy, Regionalism and Nationalism* (Baltimore: Penguin Books, 1968). See also Great Britain's *Report of the Royal Commission on Local Government in England, 1966–69* (London: HMSO, 1970)

the current reexamination of the utility of the British unitary system. First is a general feeling — intensified by serious problems blocking economic growth — that an industrialized mass society in the post–World War II era needs complex decision-making structures. Policy questions are too numerous and technical to be handled effectively by the House of Commons and cabinet and civil service generalists. Because of the enormous complexity of public affairs, authority must be parceled out and new, specialized agencies created. Second is the emergence of Scottish and Welsh nationalism and a new flare-up of Northern Ireland's ancient communal hatreds.

Foreigners commonly use the terms "English" and "British" interchangeably, but the British themselves rarely do. The English comprise an ethnic group — the dominant ethnic group. Their language. laws, and history shape British political culture. The British are a heterogeneous group, and their chief common identity is political. The United Kingdom consists of Britain (England, Scotland, Wales) and Northern Ireland. The 1536 Act of Union combined Wales and England. The Treaty Union of 1707 merged Scotland and England. The settlement of 1922 severed the six countries of Northern Ireland and brought them under London. Now it appears that these arrangements are not necessarily permanent. As the pressures that affect development have changed, political linkages have been sorely tried. All sectors of Britain are feeling the strains of underdevelopment, and there is a growing awareness of the unevenness of the development that has taken place. Relations between the English on the one hand and the Irish, Scottish, and Welsh on the other are subverted; the non-English groups believe they have been neglected by London.

Until London stepped in and took direct control in March 1972, Northern Ireland had its own parliament at Stormont equipped with considerable authority. The Ireland Act of 1949, which elaborated on the relationship between Ulster

---

Anthony Lewis, former *New York Times* reporter for the Supreme Court now covering Britain, has recommended that Britain adopt a written constitution for the sake of guaranteeing liberties in a complex and increasingly heterogeneous society. Anthony Lewis, "A Case for a Written Constitution," *Spectator* 220, no. 7289 (August 3, 1968): 290–91.

and Britain, provided that Northern Ireland could not be severed from the United Kingdom by a unilateral act of the British parliament. The Act thus represented a limited experiment in federalism.[34] The Catholic minority complained that this English-sanctioned autonomy enabled Ulster's Anglo-Protestants to rule in a highly discriminatory fashion. Until the 1969 riots broke out in Londonderry and Belfast, revealing Stormont's weakness, the central government in London was loath to intervene in Northern Ireland. The collapse of public order, however, compelled London to send British troops to supplement the largely Protestant police force and to investigate Catholics' claims of being short-changed in jobs, housing, and electoral districting.[35] Then, as Catholics and Protestants became increasingly polarized and the Unionist party (Protestant) regime at Stormont demonstrated an inability to maintain peace, London found itself deeply mired in Ulster politics, a situation it had tried to avoid throughout the twentieth century.

Initially, British troops were welcomed as neutral buffers between the two warring ethnic groups. By 1971, the troops had become targets for firebombs and sniper bullets, and Britain was being labeled "imperialist" by Northern Irish Catholic militants. Bernadette Devlin, Catholic civil rights leader, Socialist, and member of Parliament from Londonderry, stated her belief that the focus on unification with Eire (the Irish Republic) and attacks on British troops were under-

[34] There is some question about whether the theory of parliamentary supremacy could be used to override this provision and thus permit unilateral action by Westminster. Charles Aikin, "The Structure of Power in Federal Nations," in John D. Montgomery and Arthur Smithies, eds., *Public Policy* (Cambridge, Mass.: Harvard University Press, 1965), 14:330.

[35] London's recommendations were contained in the report of an official commission of inquiry into the police of Northern Ireland. The Hunt Report (after Lord Hunt, chairman), recommended that the Special-B Force, a part-time police force of eighty-four hundred men, feared by Catholics, be disbanded and that more Catholics be recruited into the regular police. *New York Times,* October 16, 1969. One month earlier, the Cameron Commission (Lord Cameron, Scottish High Court judge, chairman), investigating the causes of the 1969 riots, published its findings, sustaining many of the Catholics' complaints of job and housing discrimination. The report was excerpted in *New York Times,* September 12, 1969.

standable but did little to further the North's development: "The energies of the people are too important to be wasted on the British army, which can only bring suffering and personal tragedy. But," she said, "let me make one thing clear. Although I feel that rioting is useless as a political tactic, I sympathize with those who go on the streets in defiance of the apparatus of British imperialism." Miss Devlin's target was the Unionist regime at Stormont, which divided natural economic allies — Catholic and Protestant workers — from each other:

> It is safer for the Unionist government to allow the under-privileged and underemployed people of the Shankill, the Falls, or Bogside [poor Catholic and Protestant sections] to express their resentments and frustrations against the soldiers in the streets, and against one another, rather than have it directed in a coherent way against their real oppressors.[36]

Northern Ireland's sacrosanct autonomy had created a civil rights problem. London's hands-off policy implicitly sanctioned Protestant dominance and thus helped to create conditions that finally led to interethnic violence. Then came belated intervention by armed troops, which threatened to precipitate full-scale civil war in Ireland. As young British soldiers were injured and killed in Ulster and as television gave Britons a ringside seat for the seemingly endless violence, popular sentiment for disengagement grew. Even the Ulster Protestants, who had traditionally looked to London for protection, began to see that most Britons felt no strong bonds of identity with

[36] Bernadette Devlin, "This Time I Am Here as Bernadette Devlin, Socialist," *Village Voice*, February 18, 1971, p. 16. A study by two British political scientists concluded that the intervention of the British peace-keeping force in Northern Ireland left the Catholic minority isolated and "put an end to all immediate hopes of reform." R. S. P. Wiener, one of the researchers, explained: "The presence of the British Army served a number of symbolic functions. . . . It seemed to legitimize the Protestant backlash; the Catholics, unable to protest any longer, had to watch the election of Ian Paisley (the anti-Catholic leader) and the establishment of a powerful Protestant bargaining position. The Catholics, therefore, found themselves in a worse position than when they had started and a situation had been created where protest was automatically regarded as extremism." Report of a forthcoming book by R. S. P. Wiener and John Bayley, *Ulster: A Case Study in Conflict Theory*, in *New York Times*, August 30, 1970.

Ulster. The realization was perhaps rudest for the most militant Protestant spokesman, Reverend Ian Paisley. In 1970 he was elected both to Stormont and to Westminster. One year later he was making surprising statements about the possibility of Ulster's Protestants eventually unifying with independent Eire. To explain this remarkable turnabout, one observer remarked that Paisley, dismayed at London's indifference to Ulster's fate, began to think of long-range alternatives to the London-Stormont arrangement: "At Westminster, Paisley has observed at close hand the basic ennui that afflicts most British politicians when confronted with Ulster. In this, Westminster is simply reflecting basic electoral perceptions." [37] The experience as an MP at Westminster, according to one of Paisley's associates, "has made him feel more like an Irishman." [38]

Disintegrative forces are so strongly felt in contemporary Britain that some observers have gone so far as to draw parallels with Yugoslavia. A. J. P. Taylor points out that all Yugoslavs have two national identities — one Yugoslav and another Croat, Serb, or whatever. He suggests, "The same is true, I suppose, of the British, who all really think of themselves as Welsh, Scottish, Irish, or English." Taylor sounds like Andrei Amalrik when he makes predictions about Britain's future: "Once it was assumed that these distinctions would fade away. Now it begins to look that the United Kingdom is more likely to dissolve." [39]

[37] Lewis Chester, "The Flexible Fundamentalist," *The Sunday Times* (London), December 12, 1971. Chester referred to a *Times* poll showing most Britons rating the Ulster crisis as less important than unemployment and rising prices.

[38] *Ibid.* There is little evidence that other Ulster Protestants' sense of Irish identity is so strong that they would even consider unification with the overwhelmingly Catholic south.

[39] Taylor, "The Independent Habit," p. 27. Some Britons seem increasingly willing to sever Ulster from the United Kingdom because of London's inability to resolve Catholic-Protestant hostilities. As violence increased in the summer of 1971, a commentator for the left-wing *New Statesman* wrote: "In Ireland, over the centuries, we have tried every possible formula: direct rule, indirect rule, genocide, apartheid, puppet parliaments, real parliaments, martial law, civil law, colonization, land reform, partition. Nothing has worked. The only solution we have not tried is absolute and unconditional withdrawal. . . . It is time the crutch of British 'peacekeeping' was removed and the Irish forced to come of

Evidence that such a dissolution is imminent remains highly ambiguous. Inconsistent popular support for nationalist movements forces one to hedge all predictions. Scottish nationalism had an upswing between 1967 and 1969, followed by a decline. Scots have not been outside the circles of British power, but until recently they have reached those positions through the ranks of the established parties. Five of Britain's twenty-two prime ministers in the twentieth century have been Scots: Arthur Balfour (Conservative), Sir Henry Campbell-Bannerman (Liberal), Ramsay MacDonald (Labour), Harold Macmillan and Sir Alec Douglas-Home (Conservative). In 1969, of the seventy-one MPs in Westminster representing Scotland, forty-four were Labour. twenty-one Conservative, and five Liberal. In addition there was a woman lawyer from Glasgow, the first member of the Scottish National party to be elected in thirty-three years.

Founded in 1927, the Scottish National party (SNP) by 1969 claimed a membership of 125,000 out of a total Scottish population of three million.[40] The high point in the Nationalists' ascendancy was their decisive victory in Scotland's 1968 municipal elections. Nationalists handed the Labour party a humiliating defeat by winning nearly one hundred seats on Scottish town councils. They ran on a platform blaming London for Scotland's high prices, low wages, and great unemployment.[41] But the SNP was undecided about its primary objective. It was on the rise electorally. Yet how much and what kind of autonomy did it want for Scotland? In 1969, at their annual conference, Scottish Nationalists discussed whether their party should simply insist "Put Scotland First" or spell out a program in detail. The conference decided to stay uncommitted

---

age." Paul Johnson, "Ulster: Time to Quit," *New Statesman* (July 23, 1971), p. 102. These sentiments were being expressed in liberal and conservative papers alike when the London Home Office moved to take a more direct role in Ulster's affairs than ever before. See "Ulster: Steady as You Go," *The Economist* (July 31, 1971), pp. 19–20.

40 "Scotland," *Special Report, British Record*, no. 18 (December 30, 1969).

41 *New York Times*, May 9, 1968.

because a precise definition of independence might scare off potential voters. Young radicals in the party were most disappointed; they had hoped for an explicit policy statement. Generally, the SNP chose to stand as a reform party of the left, but even on welfare issues the nationalists split sharply.[42] Then, in 1969–1970, the momentum of Scottish nationalist mobilization was slowed by defeat at the polls. As economic indicators took an upswing, the Labour government during its last months managed to hold on to contested seats in Scotland. The Labour party won an important by-election in Scotland in 1970, overwhelming an SNP candidate by a wide margin. Against Labour's 20,664-vote tally in South Ayrshire, the Conservatives attracted 9,778 votes and the SNP only 7,785.[43] The result was particularly heartening for Labour, which traditionally trails in England and depends on Scottish and Welsh support to make up the difference. Electoral defeat for the SNP reflected the ambiguous nature of Scottish national identity more than it reflected the party's ineffectiveness. In this case it also contributed to Labour's overconfidence about national elections held later the same year, won in an upset by the Conservatives, but the Scottish Nationalists fared poorly then as well.[44]

Scottish nationalism does not rest on a cultural base as well-delineated as that of Croat nationalism or French-Canadian nationalism. As a result, Scots' demands and objectives are vague, and a nationalist party has a hard time drawing up precise platforms. One study of Scottish attitudes concluded that identity is more regional than cultural (language, religion, mores). Regional identity was expressed especially in

[42] "Scottish Nationalists: Left Turn at Oban," *The Economist* (June 7, 1969), pp. 18–20.

[43] *New York Times,* March 21, 1970. This was the first election in Scotland in which eighteen-year-olds voted, but their votes apparently made little difference.

[44] In a series of 1971 by-elections the Scottish Nationalists seemed to revive. They did not win seats but significantly increased their votes over 1970 elections. The SNP's membership, however, still was below its 1968–1969 peak of 125,000. "By-elections: It's Those Nats Again," *The Economist* (September 25, 1971), p. 22.

terms of economics. Scottish nationalism surfaced in British politics in the middle of the 1960's, when the British economy was facing serious problems. The Scottish sense of regional economic deprivation was acerbated by the tightening of purse strings in London. In fact, ever since World War II, the waxing and waning of widespread nationalism "has consistently followed upon the changing state of the British economy." [45] Nevertheless, the differences between Scotland and England are modest, and there is little evidence of political, economic, or educational discrimination. British citizens in the north might describe themselves as "Scottish," but they do not feel themselves to be cultural outsiders or objects of calculated oppression. Hence the ambiguity of Scottish nationalism: although there is a desire for greater control over regional economic affairs — taxation, customs, insurance — there is also a hesitancy about cutting political and cultural ties with England. [46]

If the SNP should win the power of decision, the financial link with London would be the first severed. According to one SNP official, "Every time London sneezes, we catch cold. We're tired of that and we're going to change it." Another party spokesman explained, "Our share is one-tenth of the budget. This means our money pays one-tenth of the cost for the Concorde [supersonic jet] and nuclear weapons and dozens of other items that have no relevance at all for Scotland. What we need," he continued, "is what we're not getting — better education, roads, housing, power stations, new industry." [47] Though still far short of a regional majority, the Nationalists attracted 12 per cent of the total Scottish vote with this message in the 1970 British general election. Their strongest showing was in the western districts, for even Scotland is not of a

45 John E. Schwarz, "The Scottish National Party: Nonviolent Separatism and Theories of Violence," *World Politics* 22, no. 4 (July 1970): 512–16.

46 The Scottish Liberal party submitted its proposal for Scottish home rule to the Crowther Constitutional Commission, which is investigating national reorganization. The Liberal recommendations focused on economic autonomy for Scotland, though stopped short of dissolution of the internal common market. "Scotland: Home Rule All Round," *The Economist* (April 4, 1970), p. 26.

47 *New York Times*, September 11, 1970.

piece developmentally. The west (Glasgow) is lagging economically, while the east (Edinburgh) is gradually narrowing the gap with England.[48]

Like so many other multi-ethnic nations in a rapidly changing world, the United Kingdom has two problems about development. On the one hand, the country as a whole is suffering a development lag. The central government lacks the capacity to apply new technology and organizational skills where they will be most productive and thus is unable to satisfy the rising expectations of its citizens. On the other hand, there are significant internal inequities. Some parts of the country, especially certain regional ethnic groups, are faring much better than others. Current discussions in Britain make the two-dimensional nature of development clear. Politicians and scholars recognize that "devolution of power" is not simply a response to nationalism in Scotland and Wales — let alone in Ireland. It may be a solution to Britain's countrywide political and economic dilemmas. If Britain should break with its past and adopt a written constitution, this would not necessarily mean that political legitimacy is crumbling. Instead such a new instrument would reflect a belief widespread among English, Welsh, Irish, and Scottish citizens that the nation has grown too complex and too pluralistic to rely on implicit arrangements.

As societies become more complex, development pressures more intense, and governments more broadly responsible, political relationships are likely to become more explicit and multi-dimensional. Organization and law replace personal relationships and custom. Americans continue to envy the Brit-

---

[48] *The Economist's* extensive report on the Scottish economy concluded: "From Edinburgh and the eastern shires, it is easy, pleasant and honest to note: that the rate of emigration has fallen; that the number of new jobs which has been created is just about as many as was originally planned in 1965; that earnings are gradually catching up to the English level; that the electronics and other science-based industries are growing rapidly." While in the west, around Glasgow, it is "honest to note: that the Scots are still leaving Scotland; that total unemployment has failed to rise; that job losses have been nearly double the number expected in 1965; that the traditional industries, like coal and shipbuilding, are still declining." "Scotland: A Sense of Change," *The Economist* (February 21, 1970), p. xli.

ish because of their unity and parliamentary democracy, but British reformers are taking a closer look at American federalism with its extended organizational and legalistic complexity. Ethnic mobilization and resultant intergroup conflicts, therefore, may serve as warning signals, compelling national policymakers to seriously reevaluate entire political structures. Scottish, Croat, and Flemish nationalist movements are not simply "special problems." They are harbingers of broad development challenges.

CHAPTER VI

Ethnic Representation in Unitary States

AT FIRST GLANCE the unitary state appears most developed. Its unbroken hierarchy of command and pyramid of representation seem to form the optimal structure for efficient communication and administration. In other words, a polity that can create a unitary system must be highly integrated and thus fairly stable.

Political scientists have learned, however, that structural integration is not always a reflection of societal integration. The contrary can be true as well. For instance, Mexico and Venezuela both have fragmented federal structures; yet both are relatively integrated societies. The discrepancy between form and reality in unitary states conceals the price paid for a seemingly high level of institutional integration. In multi-ethnic societies a unitary system may be feasible only in the presence of exclusion, coercion, or inequality. If a country contains two or more distinct ethnic communities, disintegration or federal fragmentation may be avoided by the ostracism of one of the resident communities. The remaining citizenry can be organized into a unitary system. Sometimes the excluded group is an enthusiastic supporter of this solution; sometimes it is not. Exclusion can take a variety of legal forms, among which the autonomous region is most popular.

Alternatively, a group can be excluded by the redefinition of citizenship requirements. Narrowing citizenship may simply disenfranchise certain groups and lessen their political influence, or it may eliminate the community physically as well as politically, by deportation.

Not all unitary, multi-ethnic states have to resort to such drastic actions; they are too much trouble when one ethnic community so dominates political and social resources that it can be confident that lesser groups will have to assimilate. Autonomy and redefinition of citizenship likewise are uncalled for if most ethnic groups are underdeveloped and consequently ill equipped to impose disintegrative demands on the system.

Like the various federal states, unitary states also can simultaneously adopt two strategies for dealing with different ethnic communities. All ethnic communities do not pose identical developmental problems for a government. Ethnic groups may be divided into five general categories: (1) immigrant groups from noncontiguous countries (Indians in Kenya, Indians in Fiji, Jews in Poland, Koreans in Japan), (2) groups historically residing along a country's borders and having ethnic ties in a contiguous nation (Somalis in Ethiopia, Shans in Burma and Thailand, Germans in the Italian Tyrol, Hungarians in Rumania), (3) aboriginal peoples isolated in a country's interior (Amer-Indians in Guyana, Peru, Bolivia, and Brazil, aborigines in Australia and the jungles of Malaysia), (4) ethnic groups in coastal or fertile lowland regions that are not the original inhabitants but have deep enough historical roots to call themselves "natives" (Laos in Laos, Thais in Thailand, Iraqis in Iraq, Vietnamese in Vietnam), and (5) groups that are no more indigenous than other resident groups but can claim a special identity with the political state because of their alleged contribution to its creation (Eastern European Jews in Israel, Anglo-Saxons in the United States, Great Russians in the Soviet Union, Negroes in Trinidad and Guyana, Americo-Liberians in Liberia).

Each of the five types may have a peculiar political status in a unitary system. The status will depend first on the group's own resources and political mobilization and second on the country's stage of development. Groups whose energies and cooperation are least needed to ensure development at a given time are those most likely to be given a formal autonomous region or ignored. Groups possessing attributes that make their integration imperative either will be lured into assimilation or coerced into submission. There are, in addition, communities — commonly overseas immigrants — whose socioeconomic position makes them highly relevant to national development but whose communal stubbornness and alienness make them seem a threat to the government. They are vulnerable and subject to deportation. For instance, within the last decade Ceylon has repatriated Tamils, Burma has sent home planeloads of Indians, Chinese have been expelled from Indonesia and Vietnamese from Cambodia, and Asians have been forced to leave Kenya. In more extreme cases, a state policy decision has meant internment for thousands of Japanese-Americans and, in the most drastic case, internment and extermination for millions of German Jews.

Modern development requires mobilization but not necessarily the mobilization of every group in society. Groups that government must mobilize are those possessing the skills and resources essential for whatever social and economic change is deemed crucial (for example, groups with the greatest technical expertise, capital for investment, communication control, and administrative experience) and those intimately associated with the nation's identity. Nation-builders would be happier if these groups were identical, but frequently they are not. Moreover, there may be still other groups in the country that possess neither of the two critical characteristics. They do not have to be mobilized except in a minimal way; their political development may be merely a security matter.

An ethnic community's relevance to decision-makers can change. Political autonomy and cultural integrity become hard to protect as the central government seeks to penetrate the community and exert closer control. A community considered a security problem today could be viewed as a manpower resource tomorrow and thus be vulnerable to mobilization pressures. Or security itself may be redefined. Where a military fort on the border once was deemed sufficient, a new

definition of security may require frontier people to be social-
ized into the majority's values. Technology alters security
requirements by shortening distances and speeding communication. For example, since the escalation of the second Indochina war, in the 1960's, the government of South Vietnam has
sharply increased assimilationist pressures against the hill
tribes.

Westerners refer to several Vietnamese tribal groups as Montagnards. Twenty different languages are spoken among South
Vietnam's hill people; the spread of Vietnamese has been
hindered by physical isolation and cultural conservatism. According to some estimates there are more than seven hundred
thousand Montagnards, representing forty distinct ethnic communities. Lowland South Vietnamese commonly refer to Montagnards as *moi,* meaning "savage." There is little structural
unity among Montagnards, and they are culturally, historically, and even physically differentiated from the Vietnamese
majority. Their slash-and-burn agriculture, animist religion,
and tribal society all elicit the scorn of lowlanders, who until
the coming of the French had few contacts with the hill peoples. The French, interested in developing plantations in the
highlands, gave the Montagnards special status and more autonomy than they gave the South Vietnamese. French administrators and Christian missionaries established schools and
hospitals in the hills. Throughout the 1930's Montagnards
revolted against both Vietnamese and French intrusions. Although interethnic contacts increased and plantations were
created during the French colonial period, the Montagnards
generally remained politically disinterested.

As so often happens when colonists depart, the newly independent regime moved quickly to dismantle the divisive
barriers carefully constructed by the European administrators.
The French had seen security in terms of law and order; the
South Vietnamese saw it in terms of mobilization because of
the grass-roots popularity of the war fought by the Viet Minh.
Consequently, after 1954 Saigon incorporated hill regions into
the centralized government. President Ngo Dinh Diem sought
to divest the Montagnards of their communal land and tribal
courts. Assimilation was promoted by moving ethnic Viet-

namese settlers into the hills and regrouping Montagnards into camps where they could be controlled. In the middle of the 1960's army camps were established in the hills by United States Special Forces; later they were taken over by South Vietnamese units. The camps came to resemble nineteenth-century cavalry outposts on the American western plains — desolate and temporary, with barbed-wire surrounding shelters for native refugees whose villages had been destroyed in battle.[1]

When Montagnard resistance hardened, Saigon backed down and modified its disruptive assimilation policies. It had become obvious that resettlement and land transfers, far from fostering allegiance, were driving Montagnards into the arms of the Viet Cong insurgents. Only after anti-Vietnamese revolts (led by the Rhade tribe) in 1964 did the central government enact legislation assuring Montagnards of some autonomy and promising welfare services. Even afterward, Montagnards voiced grievances against lowlanders.[2] They thought they were getting very little from the Vietnamese, although they were taxed and some of their best lands were confiscated and, in the three western provinces, where Montagnards were most numerous, the provincial chiefs were often Vietnamese. It was widely believed that any Vietnamese official expressing too much sympathy toward tribal minorities was reprimanded by his superiors.

Though Montagnard representation in Saigon's national assembly is greater now than it was during Diem's regime, we might wonder whether tribesmen think they wield effective influence over policy-making.[3] Ironically, Saigon's efforts to tighten relations between the Montagnards and Vietnamese authorities may have weakened the military security of the western frontier regions. Not only were the hill peoples explicitly hostile toward the lowlanders because of the adverse

1 *New York Times*, August 10, 1970.
2 Harvey H. Smith et al., *Area Handbook for South Vietnam* (Washington, D.C.: Government Printing Office, 1962), pp. 76–77. See also Robert L. Mole, *The Montagnards: A Study of Nine Tribes* (Rutland, Vt.: Tuttle, 1970).
3 Larry R. Jackson, "The Vietnamese Revolution and the Montagnards," *Asian Survey* 9, no. 5 (May 1969): 326–27.

effects of government policies, but assimilationist policies succeeded mainly in giving Montagnards a greater sense of intertribal unity. What previously had been just a cultural division
between the hill peoples and the majority community had
been politicized.

AUTONOMOUS REGIONS WITHIN UNITARY STATES

In a unitary state the creation of an autonomous region for
a specific ethnic group is a tacit acknowledgment of the
limited capacities of the central government. A central government will expose such a limitation only if it has no choice or
if it believes that limitation is peripheral to the functions on
which it is staking its legitimacy. Unitary states that have be-
haved in accord with the peripheral maxim include the People's Republic of China, North Vietnam, Rumania, Iraq, and,
in a peculiar way, the Union of South Africa. In each case the
ethnic community removed from centralized authority was
considered to be minimally involved in nation-building. The
non-Han peoples along the northern borders of China were
nomadic and remote; they were not linked to the country's
economy. The same was true of the hill tribesmen in the
eastern highlands of North Vietnam; their importance lay in
the strategic territory they occupied, not in their socio-economic roles. But just as nuclear energy and the Sino-Soviet
ideological split made Peking less comfortable with autonomy,
the escalation of the Vietnam War into a second Indochina
war made Hanoi anxious. In both nations the autonomous arrangements remain in force, but under the ever watchful eyes
of the central government.

At about the same time, Iraq's Kurdish peoples (1.9 million
in a population of 5 million) drove their government into a
concession. The Kurds occupied sensitive border areas but
were barely integrated into Iraq's society. Although they share
Islam with Iraqis, racial and linguistic characteristics separate
them from the Arabs. After years of inconclusive warfare,
Baghdad finally acknowledged its inability to subdue the
Kurds. A new constitution drawn up in 1970 was "unique in
the Middle East" because of the administrative autonomy it
permitted. Nonetheless, the central government reserved the

power to make policy on oil, the Kurds' most valuable asset.[4]

What is granted can be withdrawn. If ethnic group autonomy is delegated from above rather than defined and defended from below, it is only as durable as the central regime's view of its political needs. The Hungarian minority in Rumania discovered this. Several distinct cultural groups coexist in Rumania, though the country is more homogeneous now than it was prior to World War II. Ethnic Rumanians comprise almost 86 per cent of the population. The largest minorities are Hungarians, 9.4 per cent, and Germans, 2.3 per cent; other nationalities such as Serbs, Ukrainians, and Bulgarians amount to less than 3 per cent of the population.[5] The more Rumanian development has relied on nationalism, the greater a threat the small Hungarian population has seemed. Soviet economic and military domination of Eastern Europe is the political fact of life that makes Rumanian cultivation of nationalism so essential and difficult.

The Rumanian constitution of 1952 provided for a Hungarian autonomous region. At that time it appeared that the best way to deal with this unassimilated community was to separate it from the mainstream of national political life. The 1956 uprising in neighboring Hungary reversed this decision. Policy-makers in Bucharest feared that Transylvania, where more than a million Hungarians lived, might become an opposition stronghold. So in the late 1950's central policy shifted from autonomy to assimilation. The Hungarian Bolyai University was merged with the Rumanian Babes University; Rumanian was gradually introduced as the sole language of education, law, and public services. The vast difference between

---

4 "Iraq: Two Nations in One State," *The Economist* (March 21, 1970), p. 25. Almost a year after the signing of the new constitution, the Kurdish chief, general Mustafa al-Barzani, voiced his skepticism about the arrangement: "To lead a people in peace is more difficult than to lead it in war; it is easier to fight than to achieve development." He was complaining about Baghdad's failure to fulfill its pledge to assist the Kurds with economic aid. Literacy among rural Kurds is less than 10 per cent. Tuberculosis, trachoma, typhoid, and malaria are more widespread among Kurds than among Iraqi Arabs. *New York Times,* December 31, 1970.

5 Paul Lendvai, *Eagles in Cobwebs: Nationalism and Communism in the Balkans* (New York: Anchor Books, 1969), pp. 420–21. Seymour Kurtz, ed., *New York Times Encyclopedic Almanac, 1970,* p. 858.

Rumanian and Hungarian languages is a major ethnic barrier. In 1960 the autonomous region was renamed "Mures-Hungarian Autonomous Region," and the proportion of Hungarians was reduced from 78 per cent to 62 per cent of the population. Finally, in 1967, the autonomous region was completely abolished and replaced by three counties. Though the move was accompanied by guarantees of cultural freedom and nondiscrimination, the influx of Rumanians to Transylvania and a general policy of "Rumania first" meant displacement of ethnic Hungarians as the governing class.[6] So long as Rumania's development relies on nationalist consolidation to offset Soviet hegemony and so long as Hungary's political evolution takes a more liberal path than Rumania's, Rumanian party leaders will regard the existence of a geographically compact Hungarian minority as dysfunctional.

Autonomy makes most sense for an ethnic group that is peripheral to development. The central government does not require its manpower, its emotional attachment, or its resources. All that is needed is assurance of nonaggression, permission to develop a communication and transportation infrastructure, and minimal cooperation in activities such as tax collection, internal security, and census-taking. If this arrangement works smoothly, perhaps mutual trust eventually may build up to a point at which the excluded ethnic community accepts greater integration and interdependence. But this can come about slowly and only if development pressures do not change and make that group or its territory vital to overall planning.

APARTHEID: A PSEUDO-SOLUTION

There is a dilemma when a ruling group is unable or unwilling to permit integration of an ethnic community that is critically involved in the development process. The apartheid ("separateness") policy of the Republic of South Africa illustrates what can happen when a government confronts this

---

[6] Lendvai, *Eagles in Cobwebs*, pp. 421–23. Rumanians are now approximately 65 per cent of Transylvania's population. In 1910 they amounted to only 53 per cent.

dilemma *in extremis*. Nearby Rhodesia has moved toward a similar policy because of its own inability to make integrative choices, though its white minority regime has been forced to modify that scheme somewhat in its desire to reestablish friendly relations with Britain.[7] South Africa is further along in economic modernization than Rhodesia, and the dilemma is this: while South Africa is becoming a major industrial nation, it is attempting forcibly to separate the nation into autonomous social sectors. Industrialization and the urban expansion that goes with it mean greater interdependence than ever before. Yet apartheid blindly ignores this axiom and prescribes separation.

South African segregation is essentially and explicitly racist: there is no way for a person to assimilate into the dominant ethnic sector except biologically. Language, mores, religion, and historical identity are indeed factors separating South Africa's numerous groups, but each cuts across racial lines and is not the criterion used by the Nationalist party and its supporters to classify citizens. Whites, Indians. Chinese, Japanese, and persons of multi-racial parentage are meticulously separated into different legal categories, each with its own political status and limitations on mobility. Striking evidence of the racial (as opposed to the ethnic) basis for distinction is the fact that English-speaking and Afrikaans-speaking whites (the lat-

[7] Just before the Rhodesian-British "Salisbury Agreement," the Rhodesian regime had put forward a bill that provided for segregation of the European (white) community from 23,000 Asians and persons of mixed races by allowing for the eviction of persons of one race who "infiltrate" the area of another. The foundation of the racial segregation plan is the Land Tenure Act, which allocated *equal* territories for the 5 million Africans and 230,000 whites in Rhodesia. *New York Times,* November 27, 1970.

Whether this land bill will stand in the future is just one of many questions raised by the 1971 agreement worked out between Rhodesia's Ian Smith and British foreign secretary Sir Alec Douglas-Home. Theoretically, discrimination against Africans is to cease. The most controversial part of the agreement concerns voting criteria. Will the concessions granted by Smith's government ensure African majority rule in a decade or, as most observers contend, a century? One of the most thorough attempts to work out the time it will take for Africans to gain enough qualified voters to achieve an electoral majority is by Dr. Claire Palley, a British political scientist. See Claire Palley, "The Blacks' Best Hope — A Majority in 2035," *The Sunday Times* (London), November 28, 1971.

ter being of Dutch and French Huguenot descent) are legally indistinguishable, despite their cultural differences. Nor are distinctions made between the various African tribal groups (Zulu, Basuto, Xhosa, and Venda).

On the other hand, microscopic concern with biological origins courts absurdity and confusion.[8] Japanese and Chinese citizens have different legal status. According to government spokesmen, the eight thousand Chinese are considered a separate racial group with a "separate identity" and may use white facilities only if whites do not object. The Chinese are too few for the government to provide "separate amenities" for them. They are "colored" in the eyes of the law and thus cannot own property except in their own areas. They are likewise prohibited from cohabitation with persons of other races. South African Japanese are classified as "honorary whites," but no Japanese are citizens. They are businessmen and professionals on temporary permits. As "honorary citizens," Japanese have absolute rights to use white facilities. The Chinese hope that they will be reclassified as "honorary whites." [9]

Apartheid is the South African government's plan to create eight separate "homelands" for 16 million Africans, who will be resettled and, theoretically, allowed to run their own affairs free from white interference. At a distance the scheme looks rather like what the Kurds fought for in Iraq or what Montagnards are demanding in South Vietnam. But the dark side of African autonomy is exclusion. For an ethnic group that depends on the advanced sector of society for its own employment and livelihood, for an ethnic group whose well-being is directly affected by central decision-making, separation from the mainstream is a form of oppression, not communal liberation.

South Africa's blacks are already integrated into the nation's economy; their situation is not analogous to that of Brazil's Indians or China's nomads. Four million blacks are

---

[8] According to the 1960 census, whites (40 per cent English, 60 per cent Afrikaner) made up 19.3 per cent of the population, mixed-blood colored, 9.4 per cent, Asians 3.0 per cent and "Bantu" (Africans) 68.3 per cent. Leonard M. Thompson, *Politics in the Republic of South Africa* (Boston: Little, Brown, 1966), p. 30.

[9] *New York Times,* July 23, 1970.

employed in the white industries. Even with bureaucratic restrictions, 80,000 new black workers enter the expanding white economy every year.[10] Integration has also taken the form of black migration to the cities and to areas where white enterprises provide jobs. The 1970 census showed that in a black population of 16 million, 8 million blacks are registered in white areas — twice the number of whites. When the government launched "separate development" in 1951, only 5 million blacks were in white areas.[11] It is questionable whether the desolate territories designated "homelands" can support even the 4.5 million people there now.

As a solution to South Africa's development dilemma — that is, its need to pursue industrialization and a market economy together with its inability to adjust the political system to the racial ethnic integration that such economic change requires — apartheid has fatal flaws and in the long run is doomed. Ironically, it contains the seeds of its own destruction. Apartheid antagonizes businessmen and foreign countries on whom South Africa relies for customers and investors. It foments hostility between whites and nonwhites. It fragments the white population along ethnic lines of English and Afrikaner and politically divides the Afrikaners among themselves. It has the potential to hasten the political mobilization of the African majority.

So far, foreign investment in South Africa has hardly been damaged by international protest. In 1969 the *Wall Street Journal* reported, "The book value of 275 American companies' investments in South Africa is now estimated at over $750 million. . . . That's nearly double the book value of only a half a dozen years ago." [12] On the other hand, the need to build trading relations with black governments surrounding South Africa has been a source of friction between the ruling Nationalist party of prime minister Vorster and radical Afrikaner segregationists. In addition, the labor market is compelling industrialists to reappraise the rationality of apartheid.

---

10 *Washington Post,* June 26, 1970.
11 *New York Times,* October 20, 1970.
12 *Wall Street Journal,* December 11, 1969.

Especially wasteful is the law restricting black workers to the most menial jobs. Modernization means mobility; mobility leads to a breakdown of ascriptively based social stratifications. This in turn fosters new competitive relations in a previously compartmentalized society. New lines of competition call for political processes and institutions able to balance interests without dampening mobility.[13]

Industrial managers are not particularly concerned with the lack of political means to cope with increasing mobility; they watch their cost indexes and see waste. The chairman of Johannesburg Consolidated Investment, one of the country's biggest mining firms, told his white shareholders that the national Job Reservations Law, dividing the work force along racial lines, needs revision: "By this law, which is based partly on the ideology of separate development and partly on the desire to protect the white employee from competition by the nonwhite employee, we impose a deliberate restraint upon the growth of our economy." [14] On top of the loss of efficiency and inevitable inflation resulting from artificially high wage scales is South Africa's labor shortage. It, too, is the product of successful modernization. The South African Bank's bulletin for June 1970 noted an ominous slowdown in economic growth. It blamed the lag on the shortage of skilled and semi-skilled workers.[15] Other South African observers have gone a step further and have blamed racial job restrictions for insufficient manpower. One of the country's white economics professors has predicted that the national economy would come to a

[13] Pierre L. Van den Berghe's comparison of racial social evolutions in Brazil, Mexico, the United States, and South Africa underscores the inevitability of this competition-producing mobility as economies advance. See his *Race and Racism: A Comparative Perspective* (New York: Wiley, 1967).

In South Africa blacks now constitute about 68 per cent of the population but receive only 19 per cent of the national income, whereas whites, with approximately 19 per cent of the population, get 73 per cent of the cash income. *New York Times*, August 4, 1970.

[14] B. A. B. Watson, quoted in the *New York Times*, November 19, 1969. A thorough analysis of the dilemmas modernization poses for advocates of apartheid is contained in Heribert Adam, *Modernizing Racial Discrimination: South Africa's Political Dynamics* (Berkeley: University of California Press, 1971).

[15] *New York Times*, August 4, 1970.

standstill if total apartheid were achieved.[16] These warnings from businessmen do not reflect a necessarily libertarian ideology, though they might in some cases; rather, they suggest how imperative modernization and commitment are to material production and continuous growth. A British journalist has remarked that "South Africa today is probably the only country where the big-business community is visibly to the left of the government, and big finance is less conservative still." [17] In early 1971, the Afrikaner Nationalist regime gave in to business pressures and relaxed apartheid restrictions in certain construction projects. Amid protests from white labor unions, the government permitted Africans to work as bricklayers and plasterers on "white" projects.[18]

If complete separation is to work, at least the dominant white population should be tightly cohesive. But ethnicity and ideology, as well as different economic roles, divide South African whites. Conflicts between the 40 per cent of whites who are English speaking and the 60 per cent who are Afrikaans speaking go back to the colonial period and the Boer War. Genuine conflicts of interest persist between the two communities even in the face of a potentially hostile black majority. Some issues are ethnic — use of the two national languages in the government and schools, the inequality of occupational and educational status, with the English tending to hold most of the higher positions. Religion also divides the two white communities. Afrikaners are almost exclusively Protestants of the Dutch Reform Church; Calvinism and the church have become pillars of apartheid ideology. The English are religiously divided among Protestants, Catholics, and Jews. Anglican clergymen have taken public stands against the government's racial policy. The English-language press in South Africa has criticized apartheid, though it has

[16] *Ibid.*

[17] Norman Macrae (editor of *The Economist* of London), "Foreign Report: What Will Destroy Apartheid?" *Harpers* (March 1970), p. 40. Leftists in the United States and elsewhere are less sanguine about the egalitarian influence of business in South Africa. See, for example, Daniel Schechter, "Polaroid Apartheid: Pull Tab, Wait 60 Seconds," *Ramparts* 9, no. 8 (March 1971): 47–50.

[18] *New York Times*, February 9, 1971.

not challenged the basic premise of white superiority. As the official ideology is pushed to extremes, differences between whites are likely to become more apparent. On the other hand, mobilization by angry blacks might generate a fear among whites that could overcome their internal ethnic differences.[19]

Politics and commerce highlight the ethnic split between English and Afrikaner. While the English have held sway in business, the traditionally rural Afrikaners have controlled political power since shortly after World War II. Not only in parliament and the cabinet, but in the civil service and military, Afrikaners occupy most decision-making positions.[20] The vote is restricted to whites, and Afrikaners thus can exploit their 3-to-2 numerical superiority and their geographical concentration. Extension of the franchise across the color line would have improved English electoral prospects. Nevertheless, the English agreed to the principle of exclusive white power, though it meant they would remain a political minority within a white elite.[21] The English are weakened further by their social heterogeneity and the impotence of their own party spokesmen. The Nationalist party, the governing party since 1948, is virtually an Afrikaner ethnic party. Although it receives the support of some English-speaking voters because of appeals to white unity, its leadership, organization, and outlook are overwhelmingly Afrikaner: "In one sense the Nationalist party is more than a party. It deems itself to be the legitimate political home for an Afrikaner, irrespective of wealth, occupation or class. The Afrikaner who does not support the Nationalist party is not a true Afrikaner, but a traitor." [22]

---

19 A study of racial attitudes among white South African students concluded that Afrikaner students were more in favor of discrimination against blacks in housing, employment, and voting than were their English counterparts. On the other hand, English as well as Afrikaner students share the traditional stereotype of the black African as "lazy, primitive, happy-go-lucky." See Thomas F. Pettigrew, "Personality and Sociocultural Factors in Intergroup Attitudes: A Cross-national Comparison," *Journal of Conflict Resolution* 2, no. 1 (1958): 29–42.

20 Thompson, *Politics in the Republic of South Africa*, p. 111.

21 H. J. Simons and R. E. Simons, *Class and Colour in South Africa, 1850–1950* (Baltimore: Penguin Books, 1969), p. 613.

22 Thompson, *Politics in the Republic of South Africa*, p. 152.

Nonetheless, the ideological fuzziness of apartheid is apparent in its confusing racial categories, its vague definition of separate development, and its puzzlement over the requisites for continued economic prosperity. Currently there is growing debate over whether apartheid in the sense of segregation within the same region should be replaced entirely by "separate development," transporting all blacks to tribal reservations far from the cosmopolitan center. These questions are starting to fragment the Afrikaner community internally, and the Nationalist organization is finding it difficult to contain the intracommunal controversy. On the eve of the 1970 general election an ultra-segregationist wing split off and formed the Hertigte Nasionale party (Reconstituted National party). Labeled by the Nationalists "traitors to the Afrikaner cause," the renegades ran on a platform of maximum territorial separation of races through creation of independent Bantustans (native areas) and Afrikaner supremacy. They accused the Nationalists of betraying their own ethnic community.[23] Finally they opposed the government's trade relations with neighboring black nations. Nationalist party leaders dubbed the opposition *verkramptes,* the cramped ones. But unquestionably right-wing Afrikaners made it difficult for the regime to reassert its ethnic leadership without alienating the rest of the white voters. The party's indecision during the election led it to restrict job openings for blacks even more. Africans were forbidden to become telephone operators, typists, cashiers, or receptionists except in their homelands. Then, in the face of business protest, the policy was hedged and modified. Although Afrikaners are losing their small-farm rural complexion, the English still comprise the largest part of the country's business leadership. One way for the Nationalist party to offset the Hertigte splinter party was to make a more concerted appeal for English backing. But policies such as the labor restrictions were likely to have the opposite effect, reaffirming English-speaking support of the small United party.[24]

[23] *New York Times,* November 2, 1969.
[24] "South Africa: Election Attitudes," *The Economist* (April 18, 1970), p. 38.

Election returns shed light on the problems of governing a racially exclusive state by a virtually ethnic party. The moderate and white English United party gained eight seats in parliament, while the strongly liberal Progressive party, which had only one seat, managed to increase its per cent of the vote. The Hertigte party lost all its contests.[25] As the imperatives of social and economic modernization make mobility and interdependence inescapable, the Nationalist regime's dilemma is thrown into sharp relief. The English community's political impotence has encouraged it to avoid facing the dilemma. While the Afrikaners were rooted in the *platteland,* rural outback, isolated culturally and physically from the dynamics of modern development, they too could overlook the fundamental ideological inconsistency of apartheid. But as South African society grows more urban and industrial, even the banning of television will not keep the contradiction out of sight. Thus the urbanization of the Afrikaner may be as significant to South African development — that is, to the confrontation and resolution of the conflict between modernization and racial separateness — as the urbanization of the blacks.

South Africa's nonwhite population embraces a multitude of ethnic groups. Asians, who as shopkeepers and clerks have close dealings with blacks, frequently are the target of blacks' animosity because they cannot take out their frustration on the whites. The blacks are only now evolving into a single ethnic community. For centuries they have been divided among several tribal groups. The white government has sought to preserve ethnic barriers among the African population with policies such as conducting black schools in the tribal mother tongue and defining homelands linguistically and tribally.[26] Despite these restraints, tribal distinctions have been fading steadily as a growing proportion of blacks enter the urban-industrial world. Apartheid, in addition to separating blacks from whites, was intended to separate blacks from blacks. Detribalization, the demise of intertribal rivalries, and the emergence of a broader African ethnic community threaten white supremacy. If Xhosa and Zulu join in a com-

25 *New York Times,* October 30, 1970.
26 Van den Berghe, *Race and Racism,* p. 106.

munity that transcends tribal identity, the white community will be more vulnerable than it was in the past. Black leaders such as those in the African National Congress know this and are skeptical of tribally segregated Bantustans. In his preface to a study of the 1960 African revolt in the Transkei, Ronald Segal interprets the Nationalist regime's retribalization program:

> The racial dominion of Afrikanerdom — as Dr. Verwoerd (then Prime Minister) himself has proclaimed — hopes to weaken that (African) nationalism through division. . . . If the Xhosa and Zulu can be made to struggle against each other for what passes with so many modern peoples as national dignity, what energy or resolve will be left for the struggle against white rule? [27]

Segal contends that retribalization programs are up against the effects of diamond and coal mining and South Africa's expanding industrialization:

> In kitchen and labour barracks, Xhosa and Zulu became together "kaffirs," then Natives, recently Bantu, always African. . . . Apartheid, therefore, if it is to accomplish its purpose, was faced with the problem not of stopping any further detribalization, but of actually engaging in a new and massive campaign — unique in Africa and indeed the world today — of retribalization.[28]

The politically important division could turn out to be that between urbanized blacks and rural blacks. However, class is unlikely to fragment blacks so long as all suffer under the same racist discrimination. Black workers allowed to live within the white metropolitan areas are classic examples of what Ted Gurr describes as "relative deprivation." [29] Another scholar observes, "The more money a rich urban African makes, the more he comes up against the limitations of what he can do with it." [30] He is forever insecure because he can be

---

[27] Ronald Segal, "Preface," in Govani Mbeki, *South Africa: The Peasants Revolt* (Baltimore: Penguin Books, 1964), pp. 7–8.

[28] Ibid.

[29] Robert Ted Gurr, *Why Men Rebel* (Princeton: Princeton University Press, 1970).

[30] Anthony Sampson, *London Observer*, reprinted in *Washington Post*, May 3, 1970.

"resettled" at any moment. He can see with his own eyes the better life accessible to whites doing comparable work. He is not so poor as to be a passive fatalist. He is a potential revolutionary.

It is estimated that if the economy of South Africa continues to grow at its present rate, the average nonwhite will reach the average black American's 1970 standard of living in 1990.[31] The South African black is seriously hampered by a lack of organization and barriers to gaining political skills. Moreover, the white government is equipped with superior force and a coercive administrative apparatus.

Given these conditions, rural blacks may have more chance than urban blacks to develop politically and gain leverage to alter the South African system. This may seem unlikely because whites are creating rural Bantustans and forcing blacks to move there. However, the homeland territories eventually could have a political function quite different from that intended by their creators.

Less than one-fourth of South Africa's blacks currently live in Bantustans, most of which exist only on paper. The reserves comprise a mere 13 per cent of the country's land — poor land, at that. (Valuable land is occupied mostly by whites.) There is some evidence that black leaders in these territories are eager to exploit them for the sake of black political development, but their utility as a base for unified black mobilization is reduced further by their geographic fragmentation and their linguistic definition. Finally, they are dependent on the central government for their budgets, and African administrators serve at the pleasure of the whites in Pretoria.

The most fully realized of the eight Bantu "nations-in-waiting" is in the coastal province of the Transkei. Only about fourteen thousand whites live in enclaves there, and this low figure is a big reason why the Transkei is the experimental model for separate development. Blacks in the Transkei are Xhosa tribesmen. When the province's chief executive, Matanzima, gave outspoken support for the policy of separate development, he was written off as a puppet of

31 Macrae, "Foreign Report," p. 42.

Pretoria. Matanzima is a paramount chief of the Xhosa tribe, as well as leader of the Transkei's ruling political party. Black parties are legitimate only within the Bantustan. Matanzima claims that protesting discrimination is a waste of time and that blacks should concentrate on developing the territories allotted to them. Whites refuse to surrender control of the Transkei police, defense, transportation, communications, and foreign affairs. Ironically, this means that there is probably more official and social contact between whites and blacks in Transkei than elsewhere in South Africa. Just as important, Matanzima's admittedly nominal power at least gives a black official acess to policy circles, which blacks have not had before.[32]

Whether Bantustans become vehicles for African political development and system transformation will depend not only on the government's devotion to the concept of separate development but on the Africans' own perception of their usefulness. Zululand's administrative and tribal chief has emerged as one of the most enthusiastic advocates of exploiting the homelands for the benefit of Africans. His formal powers as head of the Zulu Territorial Authority are infinitesimal, but his political potential as leader of the Zulu and perhaps all blacks is enormous. Since his inauguration he has been in demand as a spokesman for African interests. Unlike the Transkei, Zululand contains a sizable white community, which possesses the little valuable land existing in the generally poor area. There are no seaports and few roads. With little economic activity, it is unlikely that the Zulu homeland could support South Africa's 3.5 million Zulu. The chief, Gatsha Buthelezi, has told the government that no more Zulu can be resettled in the territory unless whites relinquish their land holdings. He has demanded that Zulu schools be conducted in English — "the language of bread" — and that industry be promoted to provide jobs for returning tribesmen. The Zulu chief, like his Xhosa counterpart, owes his post to white sufferance, but he has used it to press the government

---

[32] This description is based on a firsthand report by Jim Hoagland, "Black South African Leader Charts Tribe Land's Independence," *Washington Post,* July 5, 1970.

for change. He argues that its own apartheid policy requires far-reaching assistance to blacks.[33]

If urbanization is mobilizing and politicizing blacks by bringing them face to face with discrimination and bases for comparison, the isolated Bantustans may stimulate new ethnic confidence and solidarity. Either, or a combination of both, could intensify the white government's development dilemma to the point that a choice finally will have to be made between unadulterated modernization and isolated traditionalism.

There are at least two ways to describe what is happening in South Africa today. We can view it as the development crisis of a whole political system struggling with pluralist tensions, or it can be portrayed in terms of the development trends of separate ethnic groups on a collision course. Political choices in South Africa are not just those facing a nation but those before individual communities. Nor is it simply a matter of the Afrikaner regime stubbornly resisting change. The current crisis is due in large part to the fact that change has come to the Afrikaner community: it has achieved political development over the past half-century. Rather than standing still, Afrikaners have grown in communal self-confidence and political effectiveness to the point of overcoming the humiliation of their defeat in the Boer War at the hands of the British. Proud nationalism has replaced the old embarrassment of the rough Afrikaner farmer. Ethnic pride is the cornerstone of the Afrikaner-led Nationalist party. South Africa's trouble lies in the fact that other ethnic groups also have been maturing politically. Black Africans communicate across tribal lines and begin to think of themselves as a political community. Through new outspoken chiefs, homeland parties, and national associations Africans are overcoming their debilitating sense of inferiority and their passivity. South Africa's future will be born out of the convergence of these two developments.

---

[33] Reports on Zululand and South African black advances are included in a series of articles by Marvine Howe, "Zulu Chief Urges Self-Rule in South Africa," *New York Times*, July 13, 1970, and "Blacks in South Africa Developing a New Awareness," *New York Times*, July 12, 1970.

ISRAEL: THE "INVISIBLE" ETHNIC MAJORITY

South Africa seems to be an aberration, far out of step with worldwide development. Actually it is not unique, or at least the variables that combine to shape South African politics are not unique. The ruling group's strategy for coping with those conditions is singular, not the conditions themselves. Few other countries have found it necessary to grasp at so extreme a formula because their attitude toward modernization has been less ambiguous, the disparity between their ethnic groups has been narrower, and the resources available to the government have been more flexible. When a regime has all these things working in its favor, a unitary system may be created without any structural concessions to ethnic pluralism. Ceylon, Guyana, Trinidad, Cuba, and Israel all contain two or more significant ethnic communities and yet have unmodified unitary systems. All are physically small, with competitive parties, and a relatively high degree of political mobilization. Ceylon's and Guyana's political systems are the most ethnically defined, Israel's and Cuba's the least. Yet ethnicity remains a salient factor in each country. Ceylonese and Guyanan parties are organized along communal lines; ethnic issues such as language, ascriptive recruitment, and religion are central in electoral contests. In both Guyana and Ceylon governments have had to put down interethnic violence. Unitary structures and ethnic communalism can and do coexist.

By contrast, Israel's ethnic distinctions are politically implicit rather than explicit. They are acknowledged by the country's political figures but are not strong enough to organize parties around or to define electoral issues. This relationship between ethnic affiliation and Israeli politics could change; currently there are movements in opposite directions. Among the Eastern and Western European immigrants political distinctions are fading, whereas between Israel's Oriental Jews and European-American Jews the differences are gaining political importance. Although they appear diametrically opposed in terms of ethnic relations, these two trends are headed in the *same* direction developmentally.

Each testifies to Israel's expanding citizen involvement in national affairs.

In the United States and Soviet Union the word "Jew" denotes an ethnic category, but in Israel the term is an umbrella for a variety of nationality groups. An immigrant's original motherland, rather than his religion, defines his ethnicity. It identifies him linguistically and cuturally. In the distribution of political power, national origin divides insiders from outsiders. The inner circle of Israeli decision-makers has been monopolized by immigrants from Eastern Europe. Most of them entered what was then Palestine between 1903 and 1914. They were imbued with a faith in labor and Zionist-socialist ideology; they were suspicious of westernized Jews from England, Germany, and the United States.[34] This group built the labor, the welfare, and eventually the political insitutions that led to the founding of the new Israeli state in 1948. Until recently, most pary leaders and cabinet ministers had their roots in Eastern Europe. But their influence derived as much from membership in the so-called Second Aliyah, the pre-1914 emigration wave, as from ethnic characteristics.

Today the Second Aliyah has passed from a "near monopoly on power in Israel to a disproportionately large share in power."[35] Between 1949 and 1961, for instance, the non-European membership in the ruling Mapai party delegation rose from 10 to 30 per cent. By 1963, Mapai's eleven cabinet ministers included six men born in the twentieth century, two native Israelis, one Iraqi immigrant, and four persons who entered Israel after 1930. Time is perhaps the greatest subverter of East European hegemony; death and old age are eliminating these early immigrants from positions of leadership. In addition, Israel's economic and social advancement has meant that pioneering, egalitarianism, and collectivism are less relevant; change has devalued Eastern European agrarian idealism and labor socialism. Finally, as the state takes on more responsibilities and as the citizenry is swollen

---

[34] Rafel Rosenzweig and Georges Tamarin, "Israel's Power Elite," *Transaction* 7, nos. 9–10, (August 1970): 27.

[35] Leonard J. Fein, *Politics in Israel* (Boston: Little, Brown, 1967), p. 152.

with new immigrants, the Second Aliyah has been compelled to open more political posts to outsiders.

As in Australia and Canada, immigration has underwritten Israel's growth. But the price of the immigration policy has been diluted homogeneity and a more fragile consensus. Aside from the small Arab-Muslim population, the least assimilated group in contemporary Israel is Jews from African and Asian countries. By 1964 Jews born in Asia and Africa comprised 28.7 per cent of the total population, those born in Europe and America 31.9 per cent, and Israel-born persons 39.4 per cent (43.2 per cent of these were children of Afro-Asian fathers).[36] In the first half of 1969 more than one-third of the fifteen thousand new immigrants came from Africa and Asia.[37] Yet at present the Oriental Jews are on the periphery of the political system. The blurring of ethnic lines and the equalization of influx among European Jews have not gone far enough to assimilate the most culturally distinctive and socially underdeveloped of the country's citizens. Oriental Jews were ignored by the early settlers; later elites held them in contempt. They are still underrepresented in the Knesset, the cabinet, and administrative offices, as well as in the parties and powerful labor associations. To date they have not resorted to a party of their own but have pursued assimilation through the established political framework. When Oriental Jews become more sure of themselves as Israeli citizens and acquire the skills of literacy and organization, this passivity could be traded in for determined communal politics.

The Oriental Jews' feeling of exclusion could provide a basis for the practice of communal politics in the future. Their exclusion derives from cultural peculiarities perceived by other Israelis. In national elections most Oriental Jews vote for one of the major political parties. Conscious of the new voting strength of the Afro-Asian immigrants, the parties have nominated a larger number of Oriental candidates. However, already candidates have been put up in municipal elections to represent "Oriental" interests.[38] A vocal minority among

36 Ibid., p. 38.
37 *New York Times*, November 2, 1969.
38 Fein, *Politics in Israel*, pp. 159–60.

the Oriental Jews has asserted that it will not be satisfied with anything less than the political supremacy justified by its proportion of the population.

These militants, mainly young Israelis from North Africa, organized a group modeled after the American Black Panthers and took to the streets to demand an end to discrimination against Oriental Jews. They were joined by young European Jewish sympathizers.[39] The Israeli Black Panthers, like their American counterparts, argued that ethnic and racial discrimination was not just one group's problem: it "is rooted in the very nature of Zionism and the Israeli state." Their supporters went on to interpret the 1971 demonstrations as a furtherance of class struggle and the fight against imperialism in the Middle East.[40]

Surrounded by unfriendly neighbors, Israel cannot afford such communal divisiveness. Whether communalism will be translated into domestic political conflict depends on how closely the Oriental Jews' own development runs parallel to widening acceptance by older immigrants.

[39] See Amós Elon, "The Black Panthers of Israel," *New York Times Magazine* (September 12, 1971), pp. 33, 150–55.

[40] The Middle East Research and Information Project, "Cultural Chauvinism in Israel," reprinted in *The Great Speckled Bird* (Atlanta, Ga.), July 12, 1971, p. 15.

CHAPTER VII

Political Development
of Ethnic Groups

IN A MULTI-ETHNIC NATION problems of political development
are defined largely by the kinds and rates of political development inside individual groups. Development for a single ethnic group refers to capacity to channel social mobilization and
to satisfy or deflect external demands. Ethnic groups, like nations, must be able to adapt institutions, recruit new sorts of
leaders, propose new goals, and fashion new strategies to meet
changing conditions inside and outside the community.

However, the trials of development for an ethnic group are
not identical to those of a nation. First, the ethnic group is
defined by its *cultural* attributes to a greater extent than is a
nation. Ethnic groups are collections of people who feel tied
to each other by certain cultural bonds. Consequently, an
ethnic group's political appeals and goals give primacy to cultural matters such as language, religion, and social mores.
When the political interests of members lose this cultural
dimension, members become more class oriented, though organizations may still make appeals to an individual's attachment to the ethnic community. A second difference between
ethnic and national development is the relative importance
of assimilation. Nation-states are anxious to protect their sovereignty. Their leaders debate the wisdom of alliances and

supranational cooperative projects, but rarely is a national regime compelled to decide whether to dissolve into a larger polity. Since the decline of feudal fiefdoms and city-states, nations almost by definition have adopted as their first commandment, "Thou shalt preserve thy integrity." This is not so with ethnic groups, which constantly are caught up in debates over whether they should exist at all. Does the best hope for the community's members lie in assimilation, sloughing off peculiar cultural traits and associations for the sake of joining the larger mainstream? If this is the consensus, political development entails gaining entry into national parties, the civil service, the army, and the legislature. It means creating organizations and tactics to press for an end to discrimination and ascriptive criteria in public life. On the other hand, some communities conclude that the benefits of assimilation are not worth loss of identity, compromised values, and weakened interpersonal bonds. In this case, political development calls for mobilizing around explicitly communal symbols and needs. It means reviving communal institutions that have been permitted to decline. It requires a new self-consciousness about exactly what ethnic distinctiveness entails. Once a nation-state manages to win independence, the argument over separateness, and assimilation ends; political development involves exploiting independence to meet the needs and expectations of the citizens. For an ethnic group the argument never ends; it continues to shape the resources and priorities of communal development.

"GETTING IT TOGETHER"

For an ethnic group to be effective in politics it has to raise the communal consciousness of its individual members and tighten collective bonds. In several recent local elections in the United States, black Americans demonstrated a new solidarity at the voting booth. Some opponents implied that this age-old American tactic of electoral campaigning is peculiarly black. They referred to it as bloc voting, pronouncing "bloc" so that it sounds distinctly like "black." In fact, all sorts of communities operating within electoral systems have sought unity at the polls to increase their political leverage. Many communities never achieve political consensus because they are too fragmented socio-economically or cannot agree about the wisdom or propriety of communal consolidation. Few ethnic groups face a simple choice between assimilation and communalism. Typically, a group must determine whether communalism is to be a short-term strategy or an ultimate goal. Furthermore, a group's perception of the options and their payoffs evolves as development conditions change in the larger society and within the community itself.

By "getting it together" American blacks mean both arousing individual ethnic awareness and creating bonds of trust and cooperation between members previously alienated from one another. Leaders trying to get their group together may be frustrated by what seems an unbreakable vicious circle. Men have been taught to disparage their ethnic heritage, to think of themselves negatively. Plagued by lack of self-confidence and positive identity, they shy away from commitments to their fellow men; yet only collective identity and joint action can pull men out of their passivity and convince them that they have worth as individuals. Black psychology tries to cope with the personal side of the dilemma; black history and community action groups are directed at the collective dimension. According to the black psychologist Charles W. Thomas:

> The black-psychology movement begins on a different assumption than white psychological counseling of blacks. Our work is to help all Afro-Americans appreciate the necessity of becoming black and using their blackness as a mental-health model. The black ethic, black history, the black communion — all our teaching efforts support the patient in his effort to gain self-esteem, to define himself in terms of his potential and to master his environment by changing it.[1]

The prominent lines of cleavage within ethnic groups are class, generation, tribe, and degree of assimilation into the larger ethnic culture or modern way of life. A group's problems in forging unity will vary according to the divisions that fragment it most. For example, the Malaysian Chinese — and

[1] Charles W. Thomas, "Different Strokes for Different Folks," *Psychology Today* 4, no. 4 (September 1970): 52.

overseas Chinese throughout Southeast Asia — are split by dialect, income, Westernization, and education. On the other hand, it is chiefly class that internally divides Catholics in Northern Ireland. American Indian leaders since the eighteenth-century have struggled against tribalism, and today there are the additional cleavages of reservation versus nonreservation, rural versus urban, differences in education and Anglicanization, plus growing generational conflicts.

An irony of development is its tendency to acerbate differences inside ethnic groups. As a nation expands opportunities for participation in its economy and politics, disparities in power, wealth, mobility, and cosmopolitanism may intensify within a community. In an earlier and more restrictive period internal differences were overshadowed by common experiences of discrimination or exclusion. Accelerated development permits at least some members of a community to break out of the imposed confines. These few develop new skills, invest capital in modern enterprises, send their children to the national university, cultivate political liaisons with representatives of other groups. A little development may be as dangerous as a little knowledge. It bestows its benefits on only a minority, while most people of the community remain spectators.

At the outset the danger in incomplete development may be hard to see. More obvious and warmly applauded by anxious nation-builders are the first signs of interethnic communication and cooperation between the persons in each community who are able to enter the widened marketplace, university, or legislature. Interethnic contacts thus take place among the most worldly or modernized members of the various ethnic groups. Initially, the elite coloration of the contact is not worrisome. National policy-makers (and colonial patrons, if they are still on the scene) are grateful for any signs of increased integration. As long as social and political mobilization does not spread to all sectors of the population, this kind of top-level integration is functional. Within each ethnic group there is respect for, and dependence on, those few men who can deal with external power structures. The majority's deference stems from its own continuing reliance on subsistence agriculture or marginal commerce. Both limit the resources that most community members can devote to schooling, political activity, and travel.

Narrowly based integration among elites crumbles when change penetrates more deeply into all groups. In other words, development does not breed more development. The first phase, which initiates cooperation among at least the cosmopolitans of several ethnic groups, is not succeeded automatically by a second phase generating cooperation among majorities of all groups. In the United States, Trinidad, and Malaysia, for instance, the diffusion of mobilizing forces actually has undermined the integration that already existed. Communal elites lose credibility in the eyes of their own ethnic constituents. They are labeled sellouts, communal traitors, Uncle Toms, Uncle Tomahawks. At the same time, the relatively uncosmopolitan and lower-class persons in each ethnic group grow more restless, more politicized, and often more communally chauvinistic. As they reject their own elites they simultaneously become more hostile toward members of other ethnic groups. Communal violence in Belfast, Los Angeles, and Kuala Lumpur is not just an interethnic phenomenon; the explanation lies *within* the individual communities themselves.

Just how wide the gaps are between cosmopolitan elites and their ethnic constituents and thus how difficult it is to prevent communal divisiveness depends on the cleavages within the community. An outsider is likely to view an ethnic group as if it were homogeneous. When trying to explain the resistance of an ethnic group to assimilation or to political absorption, we stress the shared qualities that set all members of the ethnic group apart from the rest of the society. Ethnicity, however, can and usually does embrace diversity within its commonality. Intragroup diversity leads to different rates of development and politicization.

In extreme cases a community exists mainly in the eye of the beholder but has little meaning for the alleged members. In these instances, only conflict with outsiders may stimulate communal consciousness. Black slaves who arrived in the American colonies represented not a single ethnic strain but a variety of African tribal cultures. Slavery, Reconstruction, and civil rights battles forged black Americans into a recognizable ethnic group, and much the same comment applies to Africans in South Africa. The so-called Montagnards of South Vietnam are more a collection of tribes with their own languages, family structures, and belief systems than they are a single ethnic community, though a sense of unity seems to be growing among them. Tribal division in the past aborted several uprisings against hegemony of the lowland Vietnamese. The Rhade tribesmen led but had minimal support from other Montagnards. American Indians are in a development phase somewhere in between those of the Montagnards and black Americans. They are on their way to "getting it together" but remain tribally distinctive.

THE PLURALISM OF THE AMERICAN INDIAN

The American continent contained a plural society long before Winthrop and Penn arrived to establish their separate colonies. Before the European invasion there was not one Indian society but a plethora of tribal ethnic communities, some of which were in communication. The first effort to build a nation out of this diversity was creation of the League of Iroquois in the sixteenth century. A confederation of five (later six) nations — Mohawk, Oneida, Onondaga, Cayuga, and Seneca (the Tuscarora joined in about 1722) — the league predated both the Swiss and American federal systems. In 1754 Benjamin Franklin used the Iroquois League as a model for his own unsuccessful Albany Plan for a union of the American colonies. There were other experiments with inter-tribal confederations: the Creek Confederacy appeared in the 1600's; the Pueblos in the Southwest united under the leadership of Pope in 1680; Joseph Brant (Thayendaegea) and Tecumseh, two of America's greatest Indian statesmen, forged alliances among various tribes during and after the American Revolution.[2]

Despite nationalist efforts, American Indians remained tribally divided and isolated from one another. The current In-

[2] Shirley Hill Witt, "Nationalistic Trends Among American Indians," in Stuart Levine and Nancy O. Lurie, eds., *The American Indian Today* (Baltimore: Penguin Books, 1970), p. 95. For a study of Tecumseh's nationalist leadership in the early 1800's, see Alvin M. Josephy, Jr., *The Patriot Chiefs* (New York: Viking Press, 1969), pp. 129–74.

dian renaissance, however, has not been at the expense of tribal identity. Communal political development of the past decade suggests that the causal relationship between ethnic identity and intra-ethnic subdivision is complex. There is not a simple dichotomy between identification as an Indian and tribal attachment. Instead, pride in tribal membership and awareness of common cause among Indians of all tribes have increased together. The Allotment Act of 1887, giving Indians rights to private property, was intended to transform them into solid yeoman farmers.[3] The Act precipitated detribalization accompanied by demoralization and alienation. The Indian leader Black Elk eloquently expressed the sense of communal loss:

> I did not know how much was ended. When I look back now from this high hill of my old age, I can still see the butchered women and children. . . . And I can see that something else died there in the bloody mud, and was buried in the blizzard. A people's dream died there. . . . *The nation's hoop is broken and scattered. There is no center any more, and the sacred tree is dead.*[4]

Individual self-confidence declined as tribes were broken up. This seems peculiar to whites who imagine tribal life to be stifling or oppressive. But in the minds of leaders of the present Indian revival, tribal association and individual self-respect are not opposites; they reinforce one another. The tribe protects and nourishes the individual with its brotherhood and encouragement of participation: "The Indian has a free spirit. . . . And his tribe is his source for that. Like home base."[5]

Thus the reaffirmation of the tribe socially and politically

[3] One of the ironies of Indian development in the hands of whites is the case of the Comanches of Texas, who had a long history of settled agricultural economy. When land-hungry whites drove them out of Texas, they moved north and became buffalo hunters. Later, when whites demanded northern lands as well, they lectured the Comanches on the virtues of becoming like the white man and settling down to agriculture. See Dee Brown, *Bury My Heart at Wounded Knee: An Indian History of the American West* (New York: Holt, Rinehart and Winston, 1971), p. 246.

[4] Ibid., p. 446. Emphasis added.

[5] Vine Deloria, Jr., quoted in Stan Steiner, *The New Indians* (New York: Delta Books, 1968), p. 140.

is important for American Indian development, for two reasons. It strengthens individual Indians' self-respect and capacity to act. In addition, it provides an identifiable base for organization and defines concrete issues — for example, land and water rights — around which Indians can mobilize. Retribalization became government policy during Franklin Roosevelt's New Deal. Previous administrations had tried to acculturate the Indians. The programs of the Bureau of Indian Affairs (BIA) during the 1930's, however, were grounded on the assumption that Indian communities could be economically viable. In 1934 Congress passed the Howard-Wheeler Act (also known as the Indian Reorganization Act), which altered relationships between Indians by authorizing the establishment of tribal governments. Both the Act and BIA policies breathed new life into tribes; they also fostered intertribal contacts.[6] Then World War II sent many Indian men off the reservations to serve in the military and work in wartime industries, as World War I had done in a smaller way. This new mobility put Indians in touch with one another across tribal lines, and intertribal conferences sponsored by the BIA added structure to these contacts. Not until 1944 was the National Congress of American Indians, the first all-Indian national organization, founded. In a sense the new body took up where Tecumseh had left off, using tribal communities as a base for broad Indian resistance to white America's encroachments. Whereas Tecumseh had sought a military alliance against frontiersmen expanding westward and the federal army, the National Congress of American Indians, composed of tribes and individuals, set as its task the dissemination of Indian viewpoints in Washington. The raiding party was replaced by the lobbyist.[7]

The combination of urban migrations, persistent white com-

---

[6] Witt, "Nationalistic Trends Among American Indians," pp. 102–03.

[7] An analysis of the triangular relationships of BIA officials, congressional committee members, and white lobbyists is contained in J. Leiper Freeman, *The Political Process,* rev. ed. (New York: Random House, 1966). The new Indian pressure groups are attempting to break up this triangular relationship, which has long put oil and mining interests, for instance, ahead of the interests of Indians.

mercial encroachments on Indian rights, and the influence of the blacks' civil rights movement generated tribal as well as intertribal activism. Indian political mobilization in turn forced federal authorities to halt their vacillations over the future of tribal reservations. In a landmark message to Congress, the Nixon administration in 1970 declared that the federal government was abandoning its efforts to terminate reservations, the keys to tribal self-rule. Prefacing his proposed legislation, Nixon said:

> Because termination is morally and legally unacceptable, because it produces bad practical results, and because the mere threat of termination tends to discourage greater self-sufficiency among Indian groups, I am asking the Congress to pass a new concurrent resolution which would expressly renounce, repudiate and repeal the termination policy as expressed in House Concurrent Resolution 108 of the 83rd Congress.[8]

Nixon declared that his legislation would "explicitly affirm the integrity and right to continued existence of all Indian tribes and Alaskan native governments." Referring to Indians' charges that for a century the white government had tried to break treaties unilaterally, the president concluded, "The historic relationship between the federal government and Indian communities cannot be abridged without the consent of the Indians." Shortly thereafter the BIA shifted its policies to reduce its historic paternalism and allow greater Indian self-government.

Some older Indian tribal leaders feared the change would expose them to challenges by young militants. Some militants were new recruits within the BIA. In the months following Nixon's announcement, these young Indian officials discovered that red power required bureaucratic leverage — and endurance — as well as public mobilization. A reporter for the *Washington Post* found that after an enthusiastic, optimistic start, Nixon's innovations on behalf of Indian self-rule became bogged down in a quagmire of resistance not only from congressional committees but from BIA career bureaucrats

8 President Richard M. Nixon, "Message to Congress on Indian Affairs," excerpted in *New York Times,* July 9, 1970.

and other agencies in the Department of the Interior: "Many of the [Indian] activists recruited from outside now share a sense of impending doom, the feeling that the opportunity for dramatic change has been lost to the oldliners, who know more about the rules of bureaucratic gamesmanship and the uses of political clout." [9]

Outside of the BIA, interests and forms of political action vary widely among the revitalized tribes. Puyallup Indians of Washington won a court case against the state department of fisheries for violation of tribal fishing rights.[10] Santo Domingo Pueblo Indians of New Mexico took steps to break the political monopoly of the local Spanish-speaking community. They concentrated their political efforts on getting Pueblo Indians to turn out to vote for Indian candidates for the local school board.[11] In Oklahoma the Original Cherokee Community Organization (OCCO) mobilized Indians on behalf of power for the rural, poor Cherokee full bloods and against the tribal regime of W. W. Keeler, a federal appointee, one-sixteenth Cherokee, chairman of the board of Phillips Petroleum and ally of Oklahoma white elites.[12]

The most celebrated example of Indian militancy was the seizure of Alcatraz, the insular former penal colony in the middle of San Francisco Bay. Militants invited Indians of all tribes and regions to participate, though their strongest support came from urban Indians living in San Francisco, Oakland, and Berkeley. Indian occupiers were distressed by their own infighting but were encouraged by the variety of tribes represented on the island. "Alcatraz has got us back together

[9] William Greider in *Washington Post*, August 1, 1971. Revealing accounts of BIA paternalism and inability to protect Indian interests are found in Edgar S. Cahn, ed., *Our Brother's Keeper: The Indian in White America* (New York: New Community Press, 1969); Vine Deloria, Jr., *Custer Died for Your Sins* (New York: Macmillan, 1969). Collusion between tribal officials and the BIA is described by former Sioux chief Robert Burnette in *The Tortured Americans* (Englewood Cliffs, N.J.: Prentice-Hall, 1971).

[10] *New York Times*, January 31, 1971. An account of the origins of this controversy is in American Field Service Committee, *Uncommon Controversy: Fishing Rights of the Muckleshoot, Puyallup, and Nisqually Indians* (Seattle: University of Washington Press, 1970).

[11] *New York Times*, December 1, 1969.

[12] Peter Collier, "The Theft of a Nation: Apologies to the Cherokees," *Ramparts* 9, no. 3 (September 1970): 35–45.

again, although it's a frail thread," remarked one Indian leader. "And if we lose this, it will take us another 150 years to get it together again." [13] The slogan of the Alcatraz militants expressed their hope for an end to the tribal parochialism that for generations has undermined Indians' political leverage: "Alcatraz is not an island."

The American Indian experience qualifies the easy assumption that intracommunal pluralism retards political development. American Indian tribes have different needs and claims, but rarely do they directly compete with one another. Internal subdivisions can be functional if they provide bases for individual participation, sustain ethnic identities in the face of alienating change, and do not foster unavoidable conflicts of interest among community members. On the other hand, intra-ethnic divisions are politically dysfunctional when they make communal leaders mutually suspicious, stimulate conflicting interests, and acerbate inequalities within the ethnic community. The most common dysfunctionalisms are intracommunal class antagonism and gross disparities in modernization. Though commonly lumped together, they are analytically separable. It is possible for one sector of a community to be urbanized and integrated into industrial and commercial life while still remaining low on the ladder of intra-ethnic stratification.

COMMUNAL UNDERDEVELOPMENT AND CLASS CONFLICT

Two ethnic groups suffering from political underdevelopment as a result of debilitating intracommunal friction are the Protestants of Northern Ireland and the Malays of Malaysia. Ulster Protestants and Malaysian Malays both confront domestic other ethnic communities similarly divided. *Ethnic conflict can be irreconcilable and thus most harmful to na-*

---

[13] Susan Lydon, "Where Indians Used to Play," *Earth Times*, no. 3 (June 1970), p. 28. After a nineteen-month occupation, in June 1971 the Indians were ousted from Alcatraz by the coast guard. They then seized an abandoned Nike missile site across San Francisco Bay in El Cerrito, only to be removed three days later. John Trudell, a leader of the small band, announced, "They've always dealt with us with a show of force. We don't want to get hurt, but we're not afraid of that. We'll be back. America hasn't heard the last of the Indians." *New York Times*, June 20, 1971.

tion-building when each of the chief contestants is politically underdeveloped. Fraught with internal dissent and suspicion, each community is incapable of presenting leaders who can negotiate and institutions that can accurately represent the community's views. In this situation communal differences deteriorate into violence that no regime can effectively control. The common picture of two ethnic groups, each politically developed, escalating conflict to the point of civil war may be less accurate than the picture of two ethnic groups, each politically immature, moving uncontrollably toward destructive confrontation.

Underdevelopment may be masked by communal unity cemented by artificial causes. Alternatively, underdevelopment can show up when leadership initially is based less on positive constituent support than on majority apathy or impotence. The development gap is exposed as leaders fail to broaden their support while the majority grows politically conscious. Ethnic immaturity also takes the form of a communal associational structure that reflects past levels of constituent interest and is too inflexible to adapt to increased mobilization. If it makes a group more capable of acting responsibly and coherently, "getting it together" — in the sense of creating vehicles of cooperation to match current levels of social mobilization — can foster communal development and national integration as well. The two are not necessarily incompatible. Both Malaysian Malays and Northern Ireland's Protestants comprise dominant communities, albeit not overwhelming in numerical superiority. On the Malayan peninsula Malays confront a Chinese community of approximately 35 per cent of the total population, plus an Indian community amounting to 11 per cent. For their part, the Ulster Protestants must come to terms with a Catholic Irish community that comprises 34 per cent of the population of the six counties that became part of Great Britain in 1921. Not only do Malays and Northern Ireland's Protestants have the advantage of numerical superiority, they command political power as well. Their respective numbers and power notwithstanding, however, each ethnic group falls dramatically short of political development. The glaring evidence of their underdevelopment is not their inability to dominate rival ethnic communities but their common vulnerability to internal factionalism, which undermines communal leaders' capacity to govern.

The street fighting that broke out in Londonderry and spread to Belfast in 1969 did more than reflect the unresolved Catholic-Protestant hostility that had jeopardized Northern Ireland's stability for five decades. The riots also revealed schisms within the Protestant community itself, and these were exploited by extreme Protestant chauvinists. The fiery spokesman for anti-Catholicism was Ian Paisley, an evangelical minister. Many journalistic reports laid the blame for violence at his feet. But in terms of political development, Paisley was more a product than a cause of the Protestant community's outbreak. Beneath his evangelical anti-popery lay the Protestant aristocracy's centuries-old reliance on sectarian fears to maintain dominance in their own ethnic community. The Unionist party, the Protestant and ruling party in Northern Ireland, has been led by this upper class, which traces its descendants back to the English and Scottish colonists who settled and subdued Ireland in the seventeenth century. Unionist policies protected English Toryism and the interests of a privileged class. Catholic citizens have suffered most from the social and economic stagnation resulting from Unionist rule, but lower classes within the Protestant community have not fared much better.[14] If the elite Protestant leadership was more secure, it would be less afraid of the consequences of political integration. Although Ireland was divided to give Protestants a comfortable voting majority in the North, this insurance was not enough to inspire Unionists with the confidence to integrate Catholics into the new polity. The Protestant elite remained unsure of its own ethnic backing. In the words of one Irish historian:

> The new unionist government proceeded to do the opposite: protesting their apprehension of Catholic, nationalist and republican threats, they showed by their actions and policies

[14] In mid-1969 Ulster's overall unemployment rate was 7.5 per cent, compared with 2.2 per cent in Britain. The most severe economic conditions were in the largely Catholic areas to the south and west. Unemployment was 20 per cent in Kilkeel on the southern border and 13 per cent in Londonderry (two-thirds Catholic) in the west. "Putting Catholicism on the Map," *The Economist* (August 23, 1969), p. 21.

over the years that their real fear was of a union of the Protestant and the Catholic working classes. A nineteenth-century-
style ruling caste, supported (at times uneasily and relevantly)
by an aggressive Protestant middle class, established, and maintained for half a century, power in Northern Ireland by a
classic application of the principle of *divide et impera*.[15]

Why, then, did the Protestant community not split along
class lines and thus dilute the ethnic cleavages threatening
Northern Ireland's security? There have indeed been numerous attempts to combine Catholic poor and Protestant poor
into a single class movement. The fate of these movements has
been similar to the fate of populist efforts to merge poor white
farmers and poor black farmers into a single political movement in the American South. In each case the upper class of
the dominant ethnic group intervened with warnings of cultural peril. Sectarianism and racism, each raised to the level
of ethnic loyalty by association with language and culture,
have managed to hold an ethnic community together. In the
long run, solidarity could not be built with flimsy material.

The Irish civil rights movement and Ian Paisley's emotional
following reflect different sides of the same coin — the Protestant elite's failure to develop programs and institutions relevant to transformations within the Protestant community,
especially urbanization and industrialization of all classes.
The weakness of the Unionist regime is due not simply to
fragile ties with the Protestant proletariat; it is due also to
factionalism within the elite itself. A Danish social scientist,
Anders Boserup, questions whether Unionist politics is as
thoroughly controlled by the traditional landed class as its
domination of top party post suggests. In 1966 agriculture
contributed only 9.4 per cent of Ulster's GNP, and the landed
class is now intertwined with the newer industrial managerial
class. Furthermore, Boserup observes, "Unionist economic
policies, which provide large subsidies to new industries while
traditional ones are given insufficient assistance to keep them
alive, hardly suggest a predominance of the traditional inter-

[15] Liam de Paos, *Divided Ulster* (Baltimore: Penguin Books, 1970), pp.
103–04.

ests." [16] Brian Faulkner, Ulster prime minister and the first member of the business wing of the elite to take over the Union party leadership, in 1971 introduced reforms to encourage Catholic participation in policy-making. But ethnic polarization had gone too far, and violence worsened rather than abated.

The civil rights movement began among middle-class, modernizing students at Queens University. Its founders intended it to be noncommunal, to join enlightened Catholics and Protestants in demanding that the Unionist party end its anti-democratic mode of government. Civil rights marches in Londonderry eventually resulted in violent clashes.[17] The Unionist party and its leaders had portrayed the group as a Catholic group and had thus shrouded civil rights demands in a veil of communalism. While it was true that the Catholics were the most legally deprived sector of the population, the civil rights spokesmen were arguing for the modernization of Ulster's whole political system and charged the Catholic Church, the most powerful institution within the Catholic community, with aiding and abetting the retardation of modernization.

Liberals and Socialists tried with incomplete success to avoid becoming merely communal advocates. As civil disorder broke down, though, their ranks split ideologically and ethnically.[18] But Unionists' disunity was equally acute. Ian Pais-

[16] Anders Boserup, "The Politics of Protracted Conflict," *Trans-action* 7, no. 5 (March 1970): 22. Other perceptive analyses of the escalating conflict in Northern Ireland are Roger Scott, "Ulster in Perspective: The Relevance of Non-European Experience," *Australian Outlook* 23, no. 3 (December 1969): 246–57; Paul F. Power, "Conflict and Pluralism: The Case of Northern Ireland" (Paper presented at the annual meeting of the International Studies Association, San Juan, Puerto Rico, March 17–20, 1971).

[17] A personal account of the beginnings of the civil rights movement is in Bernadette Devlin, *The Price of My Soul* (New York: Vintage Books, 1969).

[18] Within the Catholic community, factions formed around socialism, liberal reformism, and Irish Catholic chauvinism. Interestingly, similar divisions appeared among American Irish Catholics as they were appealed to for financial aid. Some responded to the civil rights issue; most responded to the ethnic discrimination issue. See Sara Davidson, "Bernadette Devlin: An Irish Revolutionary in America," *Harpers* (January 1970), pp. 78–87.

ley's support grew, especially among Protestant workers. His appeals were communal, but they contained strong doses of anti-elitism as well. In 1969 Paisley ran against the Unionist prime minister in his own district and managed to accumulate an impressive tally. In the following election he was victorious, and his ascendency to Stormont, Ulster's parliament, signaled a further Unionist fragmentation.

The Catholic's own progress in formulating and articulating political interests was no more the root cause of the street fighting and virtual occupation by the British army than was the rhetoric of Ian Paisley. The Catholic minority's political transition stems in part from the opening of university places for Catholic young people such as Bernadette Devlin, subsequently an MP at Westminster. Introduction of welfare services from London, not subject to Stormont's control, made it less likely that Catholics would emigrate, despite unemployment, as they had in the past. As welfare recipients, Catholics were more conscious of the benefits that could be had if they were permitted full opportunity to participate in the modern economy. Unemployment among Catholics had long been far above Britain's and Ulster's average because of inferior education, job discrimination, and the lack of economic expansion in the six counties. The opposition Nationalist party, led by the small Catholic middle class and the conservative Catholic Church, did little to exploit the new conditions to build a Catholic political force.[19] Consequently, both institutions were unprepared to channel the mobilization sparked by the civil rights movement. The chief beneficiary of this unpreparedness was the outlawed militant Irish Republican Army. Support for its guerrilla tactics against British troops was small initially but grew as Catholics became convinced that no one else would give them physical protection. The Catholic community, in other words, was saddled with political underdevelopment restricting its ability to deal with internal disorder and external threat.

Both Malaysia's Malays and Ulster's Protestants had the

---

[19] Conor Cruise O'Brien, "Holy War," *New York Review of Books* (November 6, 1969), p. 9.

advantages of numbers, patronage of the colonial power, a sense of communal cohesion, a political party able to dictate national policy. But class divisions within the two ethnic groups have had differing effects on communal development. Whereas Ulster Protestants have been politically retarded by their elite's reliance on sectarian xenophobia, the Malays' political problems result from their leaders' conviction that cosmopolitan pragmatism in the capital would prevent ethnic restlessness in the hinterland.

The Malay English-speaking elite led the country through a Communist insurgency and out of British colonialism. Men like former prime minister Tunku Abdul Rahman and his successor, Tun Abdul Razak, were sensitive to the resentment that many Malays felt toward the urbanized and educated Chinese and Indians. Continually they reminded non-Malay politicians that this was a latent force not to be roused foolishly by claims for Chinese as an official language and other demands offensive to Malay pride. This caveat was one of the strongest elements holding the tricommunal Alliance party together after its creation in 1952. Though nominally a partnership of equals, the Alliance was heavily weighted toward the Malay party, the United Malay National Organization (UMNO). The other partners were the Malayan Chinese Association (MCA) and the Malayan Indian Congress (MIC). The MIC and especially the MCA were politically trapped: they dared not leave the Alliance and thus the government, but their communal constituents depended on effective defense of Chinese and Indian interests.[20] The UMNO, simi-

---

[20] As the political paralysis became apparent to their ethnic constituents, the MCA and MIC lost support. Both fared poorly in the 1969 elections. For a perceptive discussion of divisions within the Malaysian Chinese community, particularly conflicts over the best way to reconcile Malaysian citizenship with Chinese communalism, see Wang Gung-wu, "Chinese Politics in Malaya," *China Quarterly*, no. 43 (July–September 1970), pp. 1–30. The Chinese community was in a shambles after the MCA's electoral defeats of 1969 and the communal riots that followed. Six months later the community convened a meeting of Chinese spokesmen from all points on the communal spectrum. Out of this emerged a liaison committee composed of several MCA men and younger professionals as well. The hope was that internal divisiveness could be patched over and new communal leaders groomed so that the Chinese could withstand the mobili-

larly, used predictions of Malay backlash to check Chinese and Indian activism but pursued policies that did little to diminish Malay anxieties or cope with increasing politicization of Malay nonelites.

There were two principal reasons for the failure of the Malay elite to adapt and thus forestall progressive underdevelopment between the time of Malaya's independence in 1957 and the traumatic commual riots of 1969. First was the leaders' own commitment to Malaysian modernization. Acquiescence to Malay cultural interests would have sidetracked efforts toward this primary goal. Education, the cornerstone of modernization, would have had to be switched from three languages to one, Malay. Malayization would have been costly and might have cut Malaysia off from its useful contacts with British and Australian universities.[21] Deference would have had to be shown to Islam, a salient part of Malay ethnic identity. Although UMNO leaders did invest money in new mosques, they perceived the modern society as essentially secular. The UMNO and the Alliance as a whole chastised the Pan-Malay Islamic party (PMIP) for its wasteful indulgence in religious symbolism.

The unwillingness of the Malay elite to come to terms with Malay chauvinism also stemmed from a genuine fear that to do so could end only in a breakup of the delicately balanced plural society. Tunku Abdul Rahman, Tun Razak, and their colleagues needed Chinese and Indian votes to ensure continued Alliance rule and Chinese and Indian economic resources to underwrite national modernization. More fundamentally, Chinese and Indian support was a requisite for the Alliance's legitimacy. Non-Malays were more or less stuck in Malaysia. With immigration and citizenship restrictions narrowing all over the world, Chinese and Indian Malaysians could not depart, even if they wanted to, leaving the federa-

zation of the newly self-conscious Malays. See James Morgan, "Malaysia: Confessional Victory," *Far Eastern Economic Review* 71, no. 8 (February 20, 1971): 11.

21 Analysis of the politics of Malaysian education is contained in Cynthia H. Enloe, *Multi-Ethnic Politics: The Case of Malaysia* (Berkeley: Center for South and Southeast Asia Studies, 1970).

tion to the devices of the Malay community. The federal regime had to find a formula for preserving at least minimal harmony among the three groups. The Alliance's strategy called for symbolic and cultural concessions, plus special Malay preference in the civil service and land development schemes for rural Malays.[22] For the non-Malays there were guarantees of laissez-faire economics and some voice in national policy-making through the Alliance's tripartite structure.

Though fraught with problems, the Alliance's formula worked for about twenty years. The crisis came when gradual changes within the Malay community finally outstripped cultural tokenism and centralized UMNO control. In a sense, Malay communal political status slipped from developed to underdeveloped in the course of two decades. Leadership by English-speaking, modern, educated Malays was adequate as long as most Malays were relatively apolitical, rural, and content with cultural symbolism. But as Malays began migrating to cities on the west coast to take up jobs and educational opportunities, they had more contacts with Chinese and Indians who seemed to be reaping disproportionate advantage from the nation's economic advances. Overall, the ratio of non-Malay to Malay incomes was approximately 7 to 4.[23] But to change this ratio would compel the UMNO to betray its pledge to the MCA and MIC. The Malays had political dominance,

[22] Rural development programs have faltered especially when they tried to go beyond well-digging and road-building to changing rural Malay values. Gayl D. Ness, *Bureaucracy and Rural Development in Malaysia* (Berkeley: University of California Press, 1967).

[23] James Morgan, "Malaysia: How Big the Imbalance?" *Far Eastern Economic Review* 69, no. 39 (September 26, 1970): 22. The most celebrated Malay chastisement of the Malay elite's insensitivity to economic inequality is former UMNO parliamentarian Mahatir bin Mohamad's book *The Malay Dilemma* (Singapore: Asia Pacific Press, 1970). Mahatir concludes that "the dilemma of the Malays is that not only is there little effort made to right the economic wrong from which they suffer, but it is also wrong to even mention that economic wrongs exist at all. The whole idea seems to be that the less they talk about it the more the country will benefit from the economic stability built on Chinese economic domination. . . . The Malay dilemma is whether they should stop trying to help themselves in order that they should be proud to be the poor citizens of a prosperous country or whether they should try to get at some of the riches that this country boasts of, even if it blurs the economic picture of Malaysia a little" (pp. 60–61).

while Chinese and Indians enjoyed economic freedom. Meanwhile, radio, television, and the Malay-language press mobilized Malays outside the urban centers. Construction of schools in rural villages encouraged Malays to consider university education and to puzzle over the University of Malaya's English medium of instruction and high percentage of Chinese and Indian students.

Events of May 1969 remain clouded, but it is generally believed that riots in the wake of the general election were touched off by discontented Malay youths in Kuala Lumpur (who may, in turn, have been angered by Chinese youths' post-election celebrations). Newcomers to the city, often underemployed, living in Malay reserves within the city limits, often unable to speak English or Chinese (the principal commercial languages), cognizant of the benefits of modernization beyond their reach — these were the newly mobilized persons the UMNO had not absorbed. The 1969 election returns showed support for the Alliance (UMNO-MCA-MIC) declining not only among Chinese and Indian voters but among Malay voters as well.[24] Yet the only organized communal alternatives were a minute radical Malay party, Parti Rakyaat, and the tradition-bound PMIP. Chinese and Indian communities had dozens of associations; Malay groups tended to be UMNO spinoffs. Political underdevelopment characterized not just the UMNO but the Malay community as a whole.

---

[24] I was in Malaysia during the 1969 elections and subsequent communal riots, but there remain differences among first-hand observers over just what occurred and what caused the riots.

It is estimated that "while the Alliance's share of the total West Malaysia vote declined by 10.1 per cent, its share of the Malay vote declined by 13 per cent and its share of the non-Malay vote by 7.9 per cent." K. J. Ratnam and R. S. Milne, "The 1969 Parliamentary Election in West Malaysia," *Pacific Affairs* 43, no. 2 (Summer 1970): 220.

Early returns from the 1970 Malaysian census reinforced evidence from the 1969 elections and riots. The state of Selangor, where Kuala Lumpur is located, was left most politically unsettled by the elections; the riots were most violent in Kuala Lumpur. The 1970 census shows Selangor to be a rapidly growing state, outstripping all others in population. Moreover, Selangor's growth, according to government statisticians, stems in large part from the influx of unemployed youths from rural areas. See James Morgan, "Malaysia: Richly Censed," *Far Eastern Economic Review* 72, no. 19 (May 8, 1971): 7.

Experiences of Ulster Protestants and Malaysian Malays testify to the dynamism of development. Political development is measured by demands upon the group's policy-making and policy-articulating processes. Those demands change as the group's relations with other communities are altered. They also change as conditions *within* the ethnic group evolve. Secondly, these two cases serve as warnings against the facile assumption that hegemony provides immunity from the trials of development. Dominant ethnic groups, as well as less-powerful communities, must be prepared for the emergence of new needs and new relationships. The political crises of Northern Ireland and Malaysia stemmed in part from the failures of dominant ethnic communities to respond to forces increasingly factionalizing them. In each instance the result was communal violence and leaders' loss of credibility.

ETHNIC GROUPS IN TRANSITIONAL SOCIETIES

"Getting it together" requires constant attention; once achieved, the goal is not secure. Among the principal variables determining the difficulty of creating group cohesion is discontinuity in the larger society. If a country is in transit from one major development phase to another, values will be ambiguous. Social issues, distinct from so-called bread and butter issues, are likely to be the focus of political contests. These sorts of issues are especially relevant to ethnic identity and thus will stimulate citizens' awareness of their ethnicity. As social issues are replaced by questions of material welfare, ethnic identification may be harder to arouse because citizens are likely to think of themselves either as mobile individuals or as members of a socio-economic class. During transitional periods, ethnicity is most easily appealed to for collective action.

Another variable that helps explain fluctuations of ethnic identification and communal solidarity is breadth of opportunity. If one ethnic group is systematically excluded from avenues of mobility, its members will come together out of a sense of common deprivation. However, their exclusion makes it difficult for them to exploit their cohesiveness politically. They lack the resources for communication and access to the government that effective political action requires. In this situation communal solidarity may have no outlet except rebellion, with little likelihood that rebellion will produce system change. American Negro slaves, American Indians, and Southeast Asian hill tribes all have revolted to little avail.

A narrow opening of the door of opportunity also presents dangers for ethnic groups. It permits a few group members to learn sophisticated skills and to gain security and prestige. These few can then take on the responsibilities of leaders and liaisons, bargaining on behalf of their less-fortunate brethren and instructing them in the ways of the larger society. However, the mobile minority comprises a new elite. Intracommunal inequality intensifies; class antagonisms emerge. In the end, the ethnic group is politically handicapped by its own disintegration.

A classic illustration of the dangers posed for ethnic groups of minimal opportunity is the relationship between field slaves and house slaves in the antebellum American South. Malcolm X made a strong case against the house slave. He curried the white master's favor; he did his best to mimic white life styles; he was detached from the misery of the field slaves. Malcolm believed that black middle-class leaders of the twentieth century were analagous to house slaves. They were dependent more on white approval than on the support of their black constituents; they sought assimilation into affluent white society so single-mindedly that they had sloughed off black styles and values. The analogy was forceful and was employed by numerous lower-class black leaders after Malcolm was assassinated.[25]

Historically, relationships between house slave and field slave may have been considerably more ambivalent. Eugene D. Genovese, a student of American slavery, cites data indicating that house slaves were not uniformly passive and deferential. Some took leading roles in slave rebellions. Diaries of white slaveholders are filled with puzzled entries after the flight of a

25 Malcolm X: "I'm a field Negro. If I can't live in the house as a human being, I'm praying for a wind to come along [when the house is ablaze]. If the master won't treat me right and he's sick, I'll call the doctor to go in the other direction." Malcolm X, *Malcolm X on Afro-American History* (New York: Pathfinder Press, 1970), p. 64.

"loyal" house slave. Only on large plantations did house slaves live separately from the rest of the blacks. On a typical, small plantation they lived in the regular slave quarters and married field slaves. Lines separating the two types of slave were rarely sharp. The house slave remained ambivalent not only in his relationships with fellow blacks but toward the whites he served as well.[26]

If possibilities for mobility appear to be wide, ethnic group solidarity is especially hard to maintain. The broader the opportunities, the more likely persons are to think of themselves as individuals judged on their own merits; ethnic affiliation is viewed as irrelevant or burdensome. A popular strategy used by nation-builders to stave off communalism is to broaden the ladder of mobility so that men will concentrate on their personal careers and think of their fellow citizens as competing individuals rather than as ethnic representatives. Universal education, civil service exams, expanding economies — all encourage men to relegate their ethnic identities to lower importance.

However, widened opportunity frequently turns out to be nothing more than a chimera. When men who think of themselves as individualists discover how limited and discriminatory the system is in practice, ethnic ties regain their salience. This has happened among the West Indians in Britain. Pakistani and Sikh immigrants came to Britain without high expectations, but newcomers from the West Indies were anticipating equal opportunity and improved standards of living. This outlook diminished their reliance on communal associations; most West Indians expected to succeed because of their personal qualities. Collective bonds were further weakened by the diversity of their backgrounds. West Indians did not have a sense of national identity. They shared a common language and Caribbean culture, but individuals from St. Kitts, Jamaica, and Trinidad were distinct in each other's eyes. In search of individual advancement, West Indians branched outside their own community. Government studies showed that

[26] Eugene D. Genovese, "American Slaves and Their History," *New York Review of Books* (December 3, 1971), pp. 38–39.

they were more likely than Asian immigrants to live in apartments managed by British landlords and that they had more contacts with white Britons. Consequently, West Indians also had more experiences with discrimination.[27] Because their expectations were higher and their experiences more negative, West Indians were the first among Britain's immigrants to turn to militant political action. Recognition of their common condition came later than to Asian immigrants, but when it did crystallize, it elicited aggressive political participation.[28]

[27] W. W. Daniel, *Racial Discrimination in England* (Baltimore: Penguin Books, 1968), pp. 36–41, 45; see also E. J. B. Rose and Associates, *Colour and Citizenship: A Report on British Race Relations* (London: Oxford University Press, 1969), pp. 419–33.
Another study found that most West contacts with white Britons were in fact confined to the workplace. Very little white-black contact occurred through voluntary association. In a sampling of West Indians, for instance, a mere 2 per cent of the men and virtually none of the women belonged to a political party. R. B. Davison, *Black British: Immigrants to England* (London: Oxford University Press, 1966), pp. 127–31.

[28] West Indian immigrants to the United States also are noted for their belief in the Puritan work ethic, education, and individual responsibility. Shirley Chisholm, Stokely Carmichael, and Malcolm X are among the most prominent black Americans of West Indian origin. The Bedford-Stuyvesant section of Brooklyn has the largest concentration of voluntary black immigrant West Indians. One West Indian New Yorker asserts that because West Indians never experienced the sanity-robbing harshness of post-slavery oppression they feel out of place among their fellow blacks in the United States: "Black Americans move, insistently, to understand their ravished psyches, to give specific meaning to the black experience. West Indians seem to tether, to recoil from the harsh search for identity, to wash themselves in abstruse talk of multi-racism. . . . This does not mean that West Indians have been inactive. . . . But the mass of West Indians in New York are hostile to any movement that trumpets blackness." Consequently, when black power advocates in Trinidad sparked an army mutiny in 1970, New York West Indians were shocked: "It was as if, no matter where one turned and how fast one ran, one could not escape the threatening panorama of blackness." Orde Coombes, "West Indians in New York: Moving Beyond the Limbo Pole," *New York Magazine* (July 13, 1970), p. 32. See also Richard Blackett, "Some of the Problems Confronting West Indians in the Black American Struggle," *Black Lines* 1, no. 4 (Summer 1971): 47–52.
The year 1968 is often cited as the turning point in Britain's black politics. Stokely Carmichael, himself a West Indian and black power advocate, visited Britain in the summer of 1967. His talks with black groups throughout the country and the publication of his book (co-authored with Charles Hamilton) *Black Power: The Politics of Liberation in America* (New York: Random House, 1968), acted as catalysts to the incipient British black power movement. A microcosm of the development is the biography of one

A third factor affecting the unity of ethnic groups is the number and relative authority of communal institutions and associations. Where influence is wielded by one institution, the likelihood of internal disintegration is reduced. The church played a commanding social and moral role for southern European immigrants in the United States; the trade union functions in a similar fashion for the Punjabi community in Britain.[29] By contrast, Jewish communities in Britain and the United States and overseas Chinese in Thailand and Malaysia are crisscrossed by multitudes of associational bonds. Proliferation of institutions sharpens members' political talents, but it can paralyze the community's dealings with external authorities.

As an ethnic group is politicized it generates additional associations. This is one of the risks, as well as one of the burdens, of political mobilization. When the Punjabis in Britain, for example, lost confidence in the efficacy of their Indian Workers' Associations, they began to break away and launch new organizations, thus fragmenting the traditionally united Punjabi community but injecting new vitality into political life for the rank and file.[30] As French Canadians and Northern Ireland's Catholics have demonstrated, communal cohesiveness per se is no guarantee of political influence or economic security. If cohesiveness is rooted in isolation or authoritarian domination by a tradition-bound institution, then political development may have to be achieved at the cost of internal friction and division.

Lastly, an ethnic group's ability to take joint action for the sake of the collective good depends on there being a consensus concerning ultimate goals. Is the group intent upon its own disappearance, its absorption into a larger society? Or do members want to preserve their cultural distinctiveness and

---

young British black and his discovery of the British Black Panthers in the late 1960's. See "The Birth of a Black Panther," in Derek Humphrey and Gus John, *Because They're Black* (Baltimore: Penguin Books, 1971), pp. 134–47.

[29] Dewitt John, *Indian Workers' Associations in Britain* (London: Oxford University Press, 1969), p. 119.

[30] Ibid., p. 158.

associational ties but press for a redistribution of the country's benefits? There will be those who want nothing less than political autonomy and cultural integrity for the group. Ethnic groups rarely reach a firm agreement on ends prior to exerting political pressure. Typically, persons with common cultural ties create a community as they debate these essential questions, for they force individuals to define their own loyalties and the outer limits of their communal affections. For ethnic groups as well as for nation-states, conflict engaged in seriously and sincerely can be the germ of integration. Consequently, the fundamental disputes present within the contemporary American black community do not necessarily portend its disintegration; they may signal political and ethnic self-consciousness.[31]

In a single week in September 1970, three black conferences met separately in Philadelphia, New Orleans, and Atlanta. The participants were separated more by ideology than by miles. The Congress of Racial Equality (CORE) met in New Orleans to map out new strategies to compel federal and state governments to end racial discrimination. In Atlanta, the African People's Congress defined black identity in supranational terms, calling for unity of black peoples all over the world under the banner of pan-Africanism. Blackness could shelter a diversity of political styles and programs. Radical poet-playwright Imamu Baraka (LeRoi Jones) declared, "I would rather make a political alliance with Whitney Young [leader of the moderate Urban League who died in March 1971] than with Abbie Hoffman [the white Yippie leader]

[31] A study of black youths in Detroit after the riots of 1967 concluded that riots grew out of feelings of blocked opportunity in youths who were certain of their own worth. A sense of confidence, not powerlessness, provided the force behind black militancy. "New Sense of Self-Efficacy Characterizes Black Militants' Recent Riot, Analysis Shows," a summary of findings of John Forward and Jay Williams, in Institute for Social Research, *Newsletter* (Summer 1970), pp. 5–7. Similarly, a study of the aftermath of the 1965 Watts riot found that the concept of black power had support among Watts blacks before the riot. But the riot had the effect of increasing politicization, racial partisanship, and blacks' control of their own community. David O. Sears, "Black Attitudes Toward the Political System in the Aftermath of the Watts Insurrection," *Midwest Journal of Political Science* 13, no. 4 (November 1969): 543–44.

because Whitney Young controls masses of black people's minds." [32] Baraka was indirectly chastising Black Panthers, who were meeting in Philadelphia. The Panthers rejected pan-Africanism; they linked the cause of American blacks to that of oppressed peoples and political radicals of all cultures and races.[33]

The two black ideologies clashed directly two months later when the Panthers convened the second session of their constitutional convention in Washington. Students at Howard University, alma mater of Stokely Carmichael, chief advocate of pan-Africanism, refused to permit the Panthers to use the Howard Auditorium. Howard's rental fee also exceeded the Panthers' funds. The Panthers' troubles at their Washington convention in 1970 were followed by an open split between the party's two best-known leaders, Huey Newton and Eldridge Cleaver. Factions clustering around the two disagreed over both organized discipline and political strategies. Essentially, the Newton wing wanted to concentrate on organizing within the black community and on fighting court battles where they were crucial to those organizing activities. Cleaver and his supporters were more intent on building alliances with white underground groups and were willing to sanction violence. The Newton-Cleaver split became public after Newton expelled two New York Panthers for jumping bail only to have Cleaver welcome them to political exile in Algiers.

Communal political development is not measured by the degree of internal conformity. Rather it is judged by the extent to which intragroup conflict stimulates political awareness and participation.[34] Controversy can clarify alternatives

---

[32] *New York Times,* September 5, 1970.

[33] *New York Times,* November 28 and 30, 1970.

[34] A recent attitudinal study of blacks in Detroit found an unusually high level of ideological subtlety and consistency among persons of high and low education. Joel D. Aberback and Jack L. Walker, "The Meanings of Black Power," *American Political Science Review* 64, no. 2 (June 1970): 380–82. See also by the same authors *Race in the City* (Boston: Little, Brown), forthcoming.

For analyses of the Panthers' intramural tensions see Phil Tracy, "The Cleaver-Newton Split: Civil War Within the Revolution?" *Village Voice,* March 11, 1971; Earl Caldwell, "The Panthers: Dead or Regrouping," *New York Times,* March 1, 1971; Ross K. Baker, "Panther Rift Rocks

and their ramifications for communal well-being. According to these criteria, ideological splits are likely to be more functional than class cleavages for developing ethnic groups.

Whole Radical Left," *Washington Post*, March 21, 1971; Richard Moore, "A Black Panther Speaks," *New York Times*, May 12, 1971. Moore, one of the Black Panthers who jumped bail in the New York bombing case (the jury later found all thirteen accused Panthers not guilty) wrote from Algiers: "Newton's harping on survival programs is not in the interest of the people. Just as the refrom programs instituted in the Philippines by ex-Huk leaders were geared to remove the mass base of the revolutionary Huks, Huey's programs are geared to remove revolutionary mass action that could jeopardize his new-found material freedom and position [for example, Newton's penthouse apartment in Oakland, California]."

CHAPTER VIII

Political Development
and Communal Power

POLITICAL DEVELOPMENT is incomplete if it halts with the stimulation of ethnic awareness and group pride. Such new consciousness has to be channeled to influence the rest of society or the part of society impinging on the group's well-being. Politics is the sphere of social life where public issues and goals are defined and authoritative policies to deal with areas of public concern are formulated. An ethnic community increases its control over its own welfare to the extent that it shapes the perception of issues and the assignment and management of priorities. Some ethnic groups are only marginally affected by most public decisions. They need far less power to be developed than does an ethnic group whose affairs are constantly affected by public policy. Still, it can be extremely difficult for even a marginal community to obtain the leverage it needs.

Political development is measured not only by the extent of power but by its relevance. For instance, Tibetans in southwestern China have some influence over local policies related to religion and cultural affairs, but their impact on China's foreign policy toward India is almost nil. Foreign policy decisions ultimately determine the external pressures Peking exerts on Tibet, so that without power at least to modify China's outlook on foreign affairs, the Tibetans are grossly underdeveloped.

Furthermore, the quality of power requisite for development does not remain static. At one time, for instance, military skill and effective weaponry may have been the most critical needs for the protection of an ethnic group's integrity, whereas a generation hence access to mass media may be crucial. Not only resources but targets change. In the past the ministry of war made the decisions most pertinent to the lives of group members; now perhaps the ministry of mines or ministry of education is paramount. The relative effectiveness of political influence depends on the nature, limits, and flexibility of a group's resources, the depth of government penetration into a group's affairs, and, finally, the accessibility and vulnerability of the penetrating authorities.

Strategies and tactics employed by any group are limited by the group's resource potential. Some ethnic communities must cultivate influence under severe constraints. The influence exerted by groups that are numerically weak and have little claim to legitimacy is especially limited. Small, newly immigrated communities suffer from such constraints. So do small groups that live in geographically remote areas and have been peripheral to national history. In such instances, power has to be exercised with minimal waste, and it must be directly on target. As advertising men say, the "rifle method," not the "shotgun method," is needed. If the target of influence is inaccessible, then a group with a minimal power potential may be forced to accede to majority policies at times, maintain a low profile, and hope that pressure will lift as the society passes on to other problems. If a low profile does not give adequate protection, the group may seek marriages of convenience with outsiders or emigration to another country. This strategy of ethnic politics has frequently been mistaken for undignified passivity. But, though it may be that in some cases, in other situations minimal compliance, low visibility, patience, and survival demand considerable communal cohesion, respected leadership, and individual self-confidence.

The final test of any group's development is whether the group broke up and disappeared into the mainstream as its members generally desired or, if members sought preservation of communal distinctiveness, whether bonds and values survived intact.

THE PALE OF LEGITIMACY

Ethnic groups possessing minimal potential leverage include the Asian community in Kenya, the Chinese in South Vietnam, the Jews in Russia, Japanese Americans during World War II, and Meo tribesmen in Laos. The first four of these communities are fortunate because they are closely in touch with the developed sector of the society. Their members live near urban centers, engage in modern commerce, receive information about forthcoming political decisions and their implications. However, these four groups and others like them are viewed by the majority of citizens as somehow alien, even though the country as a whole is pluralistic. They seem to lie just beyond the pale of legitimacy and are politically crippled by mutual distrust and unacceptance.[1] These groups possess education, cohesiveness, some wealth, urban skills, information. But for them to employ these politically exploitable resources too actively would prove dysfunctional. It would escalate tensions between the group and the majority of citizens, prompting the majority to urge the government to place additional limitations on the group's maneuverability. When a country is in the midst of war or is mobilized by nationalism, communal assertiveness is all the more dangerous.

Meo tribesmen of Laos traditionally live in remote hill villages, practice an animistic religion, and grow opium. During decades of warfare they have tried to protect their communal integrity. Since 1940, Laos has passed from French to Japanese control, back to the French, then to the Lao; currently it is torn by a civil war dividing Laotians and attracting foreign intervention. Wars, in their displacement of people and destruction of landscapes, change not only distributions of power but environments: "In recent years [the Meos'] en-

---

[1] "Beyond the pale" has its origins in ethnic xenophobia. "Pale" refers to medieval dominions of the English in Ireland. To be "beyond the pale" was to be outside the boundaries of acceptability or belonging.

tire environment has been drastically altered — the hills have become the scene of almost continuous warfare, most of the Meo have been relocated into refugee camps, and their traditional economic patterns can no longer be followed." [2] And yet, despite stress and dislocation, Meos remain communally distinct. Intermarriage of Meo and non-Meo is rare, and there are conscious efforts to preserve ethnic boundaries. The strategy for accomplishing this has been a topic of controversy among Meos. Increasingly, however, tribesmen of several persuasions have looked for protection outside the mainstream of Laotian politics.

Meos are a small minority (5 to 10 per cent) in one of the world's least stable political systems. Ancient Lao royal rivalries were patched up but never fully resolved by French colonizers. After independence in 1954 old conflicts pitting Lao elite families against one another resurfaced, though they were intertwined with nationalist and ideological disputes.[3] Upheavals in Vietnam and later in Cambodia hastened Laotian national disintegration. Laos is a patchwork of ethnic enclaves, yet during all the political maneuvering the principal actors were ethnically Lao. For centuries the Lao had controlled the rice-cultivated lowlands and thus had dominated Laos' cultural, political, and economic affairs. Non-Lao peoples were tribal, geographically isolated from one another and from the Lao, peripheral to nation-building, and scorned by lowlanders. Of all the hill tribes the Meo was the most united and assertive; today it is the only tribe formally represented in the national assembly. The Kha (meaning "slave" in Lao) and Tai tribes are even more at the mercy of policies dictated in Vientiane, Hanoi, Saigon, Moscow, Washington, and Peking.

The Meos are politically divided and can be found fighting on both sides of the Laotian civil war. One faction is led by Touby Lyfond; it backed the French in the first Indochina

[2] G. Linwood Barney, "The Meo of Xieng Khouang Province, Laos," in Peter Kunstadter, ed., *Southeast Asian Tribes, Minorities and Nations*, vol. 1 (Princeton: Princeton University Press, 1967), p. 289.

[3] For accounts of Laotian involvement in the first Indochina war and in cold war struggles thereafter, see Arthur J. Dommen, *Conflict in Laos: The Politics of Neutralization* (New York: Praeger, 1964); Bernard B. Fall, *Anatomy of a Crisis: The Laotian Crisis of 1960–61* (New York: Doubleday, 1969).

war and has amicable relations with the neutralist regime in Vientiane. It would be more nearly accurate to say that Meos in general are not represented in the national assembly, but Touby's Meos are. A French-trained Meo military officer named Vang Pao lately has challenged Touby's authority and has led pro-government Meos into a client relationship with the United States. On the other side are Meos following one-time district chief Faydang. They are allied with the Pathet Lao and its foreign sponsors, the North Vietnamese. Faydang and Touby (like Lao political rivals) are related, but their split is so deep that it is local wisdom to say that "whatever Touby's people do, Faydang's people will do the opposite." [4]

The Pathet Lao has elevated Faydang to the party official-dom and has made concessions to Meo communalism. We know much less about anti-government Meos than about pro-government, pro-American Meos. The autonomous, CIA-supported, Armée Clandestine is commanded by Vang Pao and composed largely of Meo tribesmen.[5] Most of its operations have been in the north central area around the Plain of Jars, the Meos' traditional home region.

The Meo have been involved in other wars to protect their interests. In 1896 Meos in Xieng Khouang province rebelled against the French, and in 1919 they slaughtered Lao officials whom the French used as intermediaries for tax collection and labor recruitment.[6] Vang Pao and his army, though supplied with arms and equipment never before available to isolated hill peoples, are risking more of their community's integrity than were their rebellious ancestors, for they are increasingly dependent on the Americans for food, ammunition, and mobility. The fact that Meos are traditional enemies of all the ethnic groups living around them adds to their dependence

---

[4] Barney, "The Meo of Xieng Khouang Province, Laos," pp. 274–75, 280–81.

[5] Members of other tribal groups have been recruited as the supply of adult male Meos has dwindled. *New York Times,* March 16, 1971.

[6] As a result of the uprisings, the French created special Meo districts in the Plain of Jars region. The rival Meo leaders, Touby and Faydang, came from the two clans that controlled this district. Alfred W. McCoy, "French Colonialism in Laos, 1893–1945," in Nina S. Adams and Alfred W. McCoy, eds., *Laos: War and Revolution* (New York: Harper & Row, Colophon Books, 1970), pp. 79–81, 97.

on American patronage. Yet Meos have scant influence on long-range American Indochinese policy and thus have little to say about the length and focus of the war or the terms for peace. However, especially after Congress limited the president's military authority outside Vietnam, Vang Pao's Armée Clandestine became valuable to the United States government. The Meo commander's own objective appears to be an autonomous Meo kingdom spreading through most of northern Laos. Vang Pao has used his CIA-supplied aid to cement alliances with other Meo clans in the area and entrench his own leadership.[7]

The cost of the Touby–Vang Pao strategy for communal preservation has been high. Meos are fighting Meos in the civil war. Both sides are dependent on allies who dictate overall policy with only token deference to Meo wishes. Proud Meo tribesmen have become homeless refugees reliant on outsiders for subsistence. Tribal people in government as well as in Pathet Lao areas have been forced to flee to government refugee camps to escape American bombing and battlefield operations. Sam Thong, thirty miles southwest of the Plain of Jars, was constructed in the early 1960's with American aid. Its twin city, Long Cheng, headquarters of the Armée Clandestine, is twelve miles away. In the early 1960's twenty thousand or thirty thousand tribal people, principally Meo, lived in the Sam Thong–Long Cheng area. By 1970 approximately a quarter of a million Meo and other tribal peoples had become residents of the two Quonset hut towns. An additional fifty thousand to one hundred thousand refugees were relocated to the west and northeast.[8] Civil war was urbanizing a once isolated, village-oriented ethnic group. The effects of such radical alterations on Meo communal integrity are as yet unclear.[9]

[7] Fred Braufman, "Presidential War in Laos, 1964–1970," ibid., p. 252.

[8] Ibid., p. 251. Sam Thong later came under attack and was evacuated.

[9] The urbanization of Indochina (South Vietnam now is estimated to be at least 40 per cent urban) as a result of the war is a topic of heated controversy. An excellent summary of statistics and their political overtones is in Laurence A. G. Moss and Zmarak M. Shaliz, "War and Urbanization in Indochina," in Jonathan S. Grant et. al., eds., *Cambodia: The Widening War in Indochina* (New York: Washington Square Press, 1971), for Laos see pp. 195–97. The policy piece that set off so much controversy

Refugee villages in Laos reportedly are overcrowded, congested, and unsanitary, with mortality rates as high as 250 per cent above normal in some cases.[10] By early 1971 even Vang Pao's celebrated military force was heavily strained. Enlistment of Meo tribesmen to the army was at an all-time low, and the average age of new recruits was reportedly fifteen years. The Meo population numbers between one hundred fifty thousand and three hundred thousand. In the last decade approximately ten thousand have been killed in battle. Added to this is the high death rate due to the traumas of constant migration.[11]

The Meo tradition is one of independence and a well-developed internal social structure. Meos have sided with whatever external force seemed likely to maintain an equilibrium. But the second Indochina war is different from any conflict Meos have fought in. Its dislocation and destruction are so far-reaching that involvement could subvert rather than sustain Meo ethnicity.

Perhaps the resource Meo leaders most lacked was information. If they had had a larger picture of the Indochina conflict, they might not have accepted arms from the United States as early as the late 1950's. The following testimony from 1970 hearings before Senator Edward Kennedy's subcommittee on refugees underscores the communal loss due to inadequate information. Ronald Rickenbach, testifying before the subcommittee, had been an AID refugee relief officer in Laos:

> Mr. Rickenbach: Ten years ago when [the Meos] were first armed they had a choice. I don't think there was the animosity then that exists today. I believe that leaving them

is Samuel P. Huntington, "The Bases of Accommodation," *Foreign Affairs* 64, no. 4 (July 1968), pp. 642–56.

[10] U.S. General Accounting Office reports on AID refugee program, reported in *New York Times,* February 7, 1971. See also "Refugee and Civilian War Casualty Problems in Laos and Cambodia" (Hearing before the subcommittee to investigate problems connected with refugees and escapees, Senate Judiciary Committee, 1970).

[11] Henry Kamm included these figures in an extensive firsthand report on the Meos in the Laotian war in *New York Times,* March 16, 1971. See also R. P. W. Norton, "Laos: The Rocky Road to Peace," *Far Eastern Economic Review* 71, no. 4 (January 23, 1971): 44.

independent would have made them better off under some
type of subservient role with the North Vietnamese than
what has ensued as a result of this ten-year war. . . .

Senator Fong: The Meo people are intelligent people, aren't
they?

Mr. Rickenbach: Well, sir, I think they are very intelligent
within their own realm, yes, sir. I don't think they had the
knowledge or sophistication to pass judgment on our [United
States] Southeast Asian policies.

Senator Fong: Do you think they have been duped into picking
up arms to fight their enemy?

Mr. Rickenbach: To put it in very simple terms, the ethnic
Vietnamese were their enemy; there was no duping involved.
If you give a Meo a gun, he'll go and hunt a Vietnamese for
you, but we knew what was going on in Southeast Asia and
I contend that the Meo did not know the ramifications of
what they were doing. I think if they had to do it over
again, the Meo wouldn't pick up a gun.

Senator Fong: Even though it was against the North Vietnamese?

Mr. Rickenbach: Yes, sir. I contend that they would somehow
come to a settlement. If they could have foreseen what this
was all about, they wouldn't have done it.[12]

Other weak ethnic groups are compelled to rely on their
own ingenuity and adaptability when foreign sponsors are unable or unwilling to provide protection. Kenya's Asians illustrate political underdevelopment due not only to the group's
own weakness and ambivalence but to its long dependence on
a foreign intermediary. Throughout east Africa, Asians comprise not more than 1.5 or 2 per cent of national populations.
They depended on British colonial rule to sustain law and order, though they could not influence British decisions made in
London. Kenyan African nationalists believed that commercial control by non-Africans was intolerable in an independent nation, and the colonial administration served as a
bulwark against the ouster of Asian as well as British businessmen.

Initially after Britain granted Kenya its independence,

12 "Refugee and Civilian War Casualty Problems," p. 37.

Asians were only mildly restricted through commercial licensing. Within several years, however, they were being deported. A British passport became a valuable possession to an Asian in the 1960's, but the British polity by that time was embroiled in an ethnic controversy of its own, and Asian immigrants were unwelcome in Britain as well as in Kenya. When a young Kenyan girl was caught in a plane traveling between Kenya and Britain, unable to get off at either airport, the Asians' plight was made dramatically clear. Kenya's Asian community was unprepared to deal with this crisis.

During the colonial period Asians played little part in Kenya's politics. The actions they took were taken as individuals. The Asian community was equipped with communal associations, but it did not feel the need to create expressly political organizations. British laws militated against political activism, but this condition frustrated Africans more than the politically reticent Asians, who generally stood aloof from Kenya's nationalist movement; indeed, they feared its vitality. Unlike their relatives in India, they were immediately concerned more with commercial opportunity than with national integrity. Kenya's Indian leaders did issue public declarations favoring Kenyan self-government, but in private most Asians were uneasy about independence. Ambivalence about colonialism was a brake on their involvement in Kenya's politics, which was the politics of nationalism.[13]

Indicative of their persistent ambivalence was the Asians' decision to remain in Kenya after independence but to opt for British, not Kenyan, passports. They believed that ties with Britain provided the best insurance. Of the hundred sixty thousand Asians residing in Kenya, approximately one hundred twenty thousand took British passports. Not surprisingly, their allegiance was the first questioned by African nationalists, and they became the prime targets of the government's Africanization economic campaign.[14]

Political development for Kenya's Asian community in-

---

[13] Yash Tandon, "A Political Survey," in Kharam P. Ghai, *Portrait of a Minority: Asians in East Africa* (London: Oxford University Press, 1965), pp. 76–77.

[14] *New York Times*, January 19, 1969.

volves coming to grips with two paramount circumstances: African nationalism, which presses for economic autonomy to undergird political sovereignty; and withdrawal of the British buffer and the inhospitable situation in Britain that makes emigration from Kenya not too feasible. Underdevelopment was the result of the failure of Asian leaders to acknowledge these circumstances and to alert the community to their political ramifications.[15]

Sometimes the harshness of reality makes the limited options so starkly visible that an ethnic group is compelled to cope with them. Kenya's Asians continued to trust in the protection of a foreign benefactor until it was too late. Japanese Americans were not retarded in their political development by any such delusion. They were caught in a state of declared war between the United States and their would-be patron, Japan. Pearl Harbor stripped away wishful thinking more cruelly than did Britain's departure from Kenya. American pride in its historic "melting pot" aside, one hundred twelve thousand persons of Japanese descent — American citizens as well as noncitizens — were uprooted from their Pacific Coast homes and resettled.

In 1942, without pretense of due process, Japanese Americans were transported to ten relocation camps in the interior, and most were confined for the duration of the war. The popular view has been that the pragmatic, docile Japanese (docile when they were not fighting in China or the Philippines) recognized the necessity of accommodation and worked to assimilate into the American mainstream in order to re-

15 Overseas Chinese in Southeast Asia frequently have been retarded by similar delusions of foreign protection. Since 1956 the People's Republic of China has been reluctant to come to the aid of overseas Chinese communities. See Stephen Fitzgerald, "China and the Overseas Chinese: Perceptions and Policies," *China Quarterly*, no. 44 (October–December 1970), pp. 36–37. Peking's reticence notwithstanding, the small (2 per cent) but commercially potent Chinese community in Indonesia became the victim of violence following the coup and countercoup of 1965. Peking was charged with complicity in the abortive Communist coup. The culturally exclusive domestic Chinese minority served as a surrogate for Peking for the enraged Indonesian anti-Communists. See Lie Tek-Tjeng, "The Chinese Problem in Indonesia Following the September 30 Movement," *International Spectator* 24, no. 12, 1151.

establish the majority's trust. Recently, however, a study of Japanese behavior in the relocation camps has concluded that behavior interpreted by the guardians as pragmatic assimilation was in fact dictated by Japanese ethnic tradition. The discrimination that justified Japanese detention actually reinforced a sense of ethnic identity. Interviews with former detainees revealed tactics for survival drawn directly from their own ethnic culture, not from wholesale adoption of American values. The basic Japanese values that stood them in such good stead were accommodation and cooperation:

> The respondents spoke of resolving conflict through cooperation, invoking the higher synthesis of yin and yang, rather than savage partisan duels to the social death. Demands only heighten social recoil, intensify "contentiousness" and smother progress toward a higher synthesis. . . . The American response to delinquency is primitive — to jail the youngster, since guilt must be assigned. The Japanese response is for parents to cooperate with the police, forming an umbrella above the child during his rehabilitation.[16]

The political strategies of communities in which resources are scarce must be subtle and flexible, and because their position is so precarious, their members must be particularly sensitive to society's complex relationships and the ramifications of public policies. Occasionally an ethnic group, like the Japanese Americans, is so adroit that the less-perceptive majority mistakes accommodation for assimilation:

> The majority society read its own priorities into the ethnic tenacity of the Japanese and saw no reason to debate the diverse background and motives that inspired them. *Indeed, it is far more flattering to concede that the Japanese had been Americans all along than to entertain the suspicion that ethnicity is admirable in its unredeemed state.*[17]

[16] Ronald O. Haak, "Coopting the Oppressors: The Case of the Japanese-Americans," *Trans-action* 7, no. 12 (October 1970): 31.

[17] Ibid. Emphasis added. Japanese Americans live under several different ethnic conditions in the United States. In Hawaii, where they are a sizable minority and close to strategic military bases, they were not detained. Today they comprise 34.3 per cent of Hawaii's nonmilitary population, and their political strategy is increasingly assertive. They are a majority in

THE POSITION OF MIDDLE POWER

A second broad class of ethnic groups has substantial, though restricted, political power potential. These groups usually have the dual advantages of contact with society's developed sectors and its ruling bodies, plus communal resources adaptable to political ends. Some of these ethnic communities are not very large, but they can concentrate their numbers in local elections or focus energies on decentralized institutions. If they have broken out of a pariah status, they can base communal activism on nationally sanctioned rights. Groups relatively integrated into the larger polity broaden their support by allying not with foreign powers but with other domestic ethnic groups. Their political leverage remains limited, however. There is little chance for ethnic groups in this second category to become the principal architects of national policy or even to exert long-range influence without the support of other domestic forces. Such communities are most effective when they pinpoint one or two policy areas and institutions as most critical to their welfare and concentrate their resources on them. However, conditions are rarely arranged so conveniently for the ethnic activist, particularly as group members become integrated into the larger society. The number of relevant policies mushrooms and a group then must direct its attention toward a multitude of political arenas simultaneously. Resources are spread thin; priorities are hard to determine; intracommunal conflict escalates. As this frustrating expansion occurs, groups are attracted by the separatism that goes with autonomy. Only thus can the ethnic community gain control over widely diverse policies affecting it. The alternative under these conditions is individualism and the loosening of communal bonds except for purely social occasions, each member being encouraged to find his own

---

the state legislature and have been the strongest element in Hawaii's Democratic party since governor John A. Burns, a Caucasian, helped them organize in 1954. Despite the markedly different political-social setting, Japanese Americans in Hawaii are motivated by many of the ethnic values prominent in the World War II camps: working for the group, pride, faith in education. *New York Times*, October 24, 1970.

formula for coping with the newly complex relationships and demands resulting from integration.

Canada's French community represents a group in this middle-power position. It has reached a level of integration and modernization where separatism has special appeal. Until World War II, French Canadians were relatively insulated from the onslaught of modernization. This was due partly to their concentration in a single province, Quebec, and partly to their general unwillingness to surrender familial, religious, and moral values antithetical to modernization.[18] There is still a popular saying that French-Canadian boys aspire to be priests or ice hockey players because "That's where the status is." The Liberal party could always count Quebec as a safe province, with little competition from the Conservatives. Voters turned out in higher percentages for provincial elections than for federal elections — quite the opposite from the United States voting pattern. This was a firm indication that French Canadians' interest lay in politics closer to home.[19]

Economics has been the major force drawing French Canadians out of their provincialism and into political mobilization. In contrast to their behavior two or three decades ago, French Canadians presently are exploiting a political potential they had always possessed but left dormant. Business and industry moved into Quebec with English-speaking Canadians and Americans. One young French professor of marketing recalls that his friends were shocked when he announced that he would major in business. "It was the cult of the liberal professions," he explained.[20] Most Frenchmen were outside the world of modern economics or only tangentially integrated into it, lacking means to control it. In the 1960's the combination of English and American economic expansion and rising unemployment among Quebeckers stimulated politicized in-

[18] Traditional and transitional French Canada are described in Horace Miner, *St. Denis: A French-Canadian Parish* (Chicago: University of Chicago Press, Phoenix Books, 1963); Everett C. Hughes, *French Canada in Transition* (Chicago: University of Chicago Press, Phoenix Books, 1963).

[19] Howard A. Scarrow, "Patterns of Voter Turnout in Canada," *Midwest Journal of Political Science* 5, no. 4 (November 1961): 361.

[20] *New York Times,* January 25, 1971.

terest in the province's economy and its ethnic ramifications. The last census showed Quebeckers of English descent to be best off economically, holding 77 per cent of jobs in the province paying $15,000 a year or more. At the same time in Quebec 8.9 per cent of the labor force was unemployed, nearly 3 per cent more than the average for Canada as a whole.[21]

Newly mobilized political activists among the French-speaking population pressed both federal and provincial régimes. Ascendancy to the prime ministership by a French Canadian, Pierre Trudeau, did not assure French influence but did increase sensitivity to French interests at the very time they were channeling ethnic concern into politics. In Quebec the Liberal party preserved its rule, but not without contest. The Parti Québeçois, running on a platform of separatism, managed to secure 24 per cent of the vote in the 1970 provincial election. The Liberal regime was also challenged by the Quebec Liberation Front (FLQ), an extralegal organization intent upon separation and an ideological revolution.

Political development for French Canadians is dynamic as it is for all groups and nations. In their case, transitional strains are generated by conflicting strategies of prime minister Trudeau, the Quebec Liberal party, the Parti Québeçois, and the FLQ. All agree that the central problem is the unequal distribution of economic rewards and influence or, more precisely, exclusion of French Canadians from the modern sector of the economy. This has class overtones, of course. The separatist program of Parti Québeçois culled its strongest support from low- and middle-class French-Canadian workers.[22] However, a principal barrier to French participation in business and technological affairs is ethnic: finance, trade, and manufacturing are conducted overwhelmingly in English. Even when a French Canadian does get a job, his chances for advancement and salary increases are limited. At the core of the French community's internal conflict is the question of how much needs to be altered so that French Canadians can enjoy respect, equality, and mobility. Should the entire eco-

21 *New York Times,* November 14, 1970.
22 *Wall Street Journal,* October 27, 1970.

nomic structure be transformed? Is capitalism itself to blame for the community's disaffection? Radicals of the FLQ and the more moderate Parti Québeçois reply to these questions in the affirmative. They demand separatism, meaning sufficient autonomy for the French to restructure their entire economic system and their economic relations with the United States. They believe communal well-being depends on such a vast range of factors that it cannot possibly be secured by piece-meal tinkering within the Canadian polity. Liberal adminis-trations in both Ottawa and Montreal deny that such major surgery is necessary. Instead they focus on narrower problems: language, education, and job recruitment.

Among French Canada's potent political resources is French identification with the nation's founding. General Wolfe's de-feat of the French on the Plains of Abraham in 1759 made con-solidation of the colony under British rule possible, but French Canadians' right to maintain their own culture was a cornerstone of the British North American Act of 1867. Theo-retical bilingualism and provincial autonomy are two endur-ing consequences of that recognition. Their unique legal and historical status permits French immigrants to make claims on the federal government that other immigrant groups cannot. This, plus Quebec's long-standing support of the Liberal party, motivated prime ministers Pearson and Trudeau to seek a solution to the language problem. A four-year study of bilingualism and biculturalism commissioned by Lester Pear-son produced a report in 1967 urging English Canadians to recognize French as one of two official languages. The royal commission concluded that although almost one-third of Cana-dians spoke French, the country was far from bilingual in its political and economic relations. To achieve bilingualism in fact as well as in theory the commission recommended that more bilingual schools be established in English-speaking prov-inces and that bilingualism be the norm in local governments serving French-speaking citizens.[23] Two years later, with bi-partisan support, the federal parliament passed the Official Languages Act. It provided that in areas where more than 40

[23] *New York Times*, December 7, 1967.

per cent of the populace spoke a "minority tongue" all civil servants must know both English and French. The objective was twofold: to make government more accessible to French Canadians and to recruit a greater number of French speakers into the civil service.[24]

Quebec's provincial regime is pressed even harder to relieve French frustrations. Resources convertible to political leverage are all the more potent at the provincial level. Quebec Liberals rely on French votes; the regime's legitimacy derives from confidence. On the other hand, economic growth and the province's financial viability require outside capital. For the nonseparatist Liberal administration of Quebec, then, the problem is one of widening French participation in the economy without scaring off English-speaking investors. Since the death of traditionalist premier Duplessis in 1959, the accent has been on industrialization and education. As French Canadians grew more politicized and militant, however, the ethnic implications of both policies gained in importance. Industrialization and education alone were unacceptable unless they permitted conservation of ethnic, especially linguistic, heritage. McGill University's dean of law capsulized the French-Canadian dilemma: "How to be both utterly modern and utterly French speaking in an utterly North American setting." [25]

The strategy adopted by Quebec Liberals for resolving this

24 "The plan calls for doubling the number of bilingual civil servants to 50,000 (out of a total of 250,000) by 1975. Among the 350 highest-level officials, most of whom work in Ottawa, the requirement is for 60% to know both languages by 1975, compared with the current 30%. Since most of the relatively few French Canadians currently in civil service already speak English, the biggest problem is teaching French to those of English origin." *Wall Street Journal*, October 20, 1969.

25 *New York Times*, September 28, 1969. Since 1969, McGill, an English-speaking university, has come under heavy attack, especially after it dropped French studies.

An attitude study of French-Canadian professional men — lawyers, engineers, business executives — showed that Quebec nationalism is not a rejection of modernism. Most of these highly educated, urban men believed that their French identity could — indeed *must* — be preserved while the fruits of science, technology, and organization were pursued. See Erwin C. Hargrove, "Nationality, Values, and Change," *Comparative Politics* 2, no. 3 (April 1970): 473–99.

dilemma was to make French the "language of work" in Quebec. The provincial government had to persuade English and American businessmen to do this, though its leverage on business was weaker than in areas such as education of the civil service. Premier Robert Bourassa, a Harvard-trained economist elected in 1970, hoped that the language-of-work issue would direct French-Canadian militancy away from national constitutional change, where success was improbable, to economic change, where progress was within reach. Premier Bourassa intervened personally in the first language dispute of its kind, between General Motors and the United Auto Workers at an assembly plant outside Montreal. The company eventually agreed to cover the cost of simultaneous translation at bargaining sessions but rejected demands that French be made the language of work for the twenty-four hundred assembly-line workers. Although most workers were French Canadians, 20 per cent of their foremen spoke little French and most technical terms were in English.[26]

The Liberal administration holds the advantage of ethnic affiliation with the French community, support for its policy in Ottawa, and an electoral mandate, plus English fears of French separatist ascendancy. On the negative side, however, Liberals face the likelihood that political mobilization and rising expectations will outstrip the government's ability to transform the economy. The more politicized ethnic pride becomes, the more stubbornly do French Canadians refuse to surrender ethnic identity for the sake of material welfare. A student supporter of the FLQ called business students "traitors" because they "wind up working for the Americans here or in Ontario or in America." Another student went further: "I refuse to learn English . . . even if it means I can't get as good a job."[27]

A test of the Bourassa regime is its ability to impress En-

[26] *New York Times,* October 4, 1970.

[27] *Washington Post,* November 1, 1970. The most outspoken, autobiographical account of an FLQ member is Pierre Vallières, *White Niggers of America* (New York: Monthly Review Press, 1971). In its description of childhood, political radicalization, and growing ethnic pride, Vallières' autobiography is comparable to Bernadette Devlin's and Malcolm X's.

glish elites with the seriousness of this emergent ethnic pride. "Quebec may be part of North America, but culturally it is different," the premier warned English-speaking businessmen. "If you force Quebeckers to work in English, you will risk a social explosion. If you enable them to work in French, you will avoid unrest and revolution. You will also raise morale and increase production." [28] Bourassa was issuing a caveat to English Canadians.

The other side of the coin is a development challenge for the French-Canadian political establishment. Its success at overcoming political underdevelopment caused by rising expectations depends on the Liberal regime's persuading English Canadians to develop. This is a typical problem confronting an ethnic group at the second level of political potential. The group is too limited politically to shape national affairs on its own. Consequently, its development is measured by how far and how fast its leaders move the dominant communities to expand opportunities for economic mobility and political participation.

Many ethnic groups in the middle range of political potential possess the assets of the French Canadians: significant numbers, affiliation with a major national party, control of a federal subunit with substantial powers of its own, historical identification with the nation's origins. Even with more modest resources, an ethnic group can develop to the point where it plays an important role in decisions affecting its communal interests. Transfer of services from the private to public sector, together with decentralized authority and officials elected by local constituencies, all inflate otherwise modest resources. Among intracommunal conditions that extend political potential are group self-consciousness and solidarity and organizational structures relevant to local issues. In addition, targets must be precisely defined yet touch fundamental concerns of the community, and tactics should be appropriate to the ethnic culture though sanctioned by the larger society. American Puerto Ricans illustrate what can be done under these circumstances.

28 *New York Times,* September 13, 1970.

There are only 1.8 million Puerto Ricans in the United States. Many are handicapped by inability to communicate in English. They are the most recent of the country's immigrants, coming from a largely agrarian society to the most densely urban section of the United States. Their high unemployment rate is only the most visible indication of Puerto Ricans' disadvantaged position. A report by the Bureau of Labor Statistics on four ghetto areas showed Puerto Rican unemployment at 9.6 per cent, against 6.8 per cent for blacks and 4.5 per cent for whites.[29]

Nevertheless, Puerto Ricans have resources they have begun to exploit for the sake of greater control over their own environment. First, there is growing nationalism in Puerto Rico itself, testified to by the strength of the statehood and independence movements and militant resistance of the United States military draft during the Vietnam War.[30] A second resource is the maturing generation of Puerto Ricans born in the United States and familiar with its ways. One million of the 1.8 million ethnic group members are concentrated in one city, New York. There is also the stimulation of the black civil rights movement. In a modern, participant system such as the American, experiences are quickly transmitted from one group to another. Each group need not start from home base. Model Cities and War on Poverty programs in the 1960's placed more authority into local communities, and services in New York came necessarily into the public domain. Finally, the cultural attributes of the Puerto Rican community encourage political organization: the bonds of Catholicism, closely knit family units bridging the generation gap, a common language.

For a long time Puerto Ricans in New York were subject to decisions made by politicians and administrators and scarcely affected by Puerto Rican influence. Of several groups that have sought to mobilize Puerto Ricans' resources for political development, a former street gang, the Young Lords,

---

[29] *New York Times,* January 10, 11971.

[30] Arthur Liebman, "The Puerto Rican Independence Movement," in John R. Howard, ed., *Awakening Minorities* (Chicago: Aldine, 1970), pp. 151–66.

has been most successful.[31] The Young Lords began in Chicago and was a neighborhood gang until its leader was sent to jail and politicized. In jail he redefined his gang's enemies: the Latin Kings, Paragons, and Black Eagles were replaced by Chicago's Urban Renewal Agency, the local alderman, and the United States government.[32] Chicago and New York branches of the Young Lords have remained autonomous. Though in agreement on many issues, they believe that any move toward national organization would undermine their greatest asset, the groups' intimate links with local urban neighborhoods. Localized political action dictated the sorts of issues the Young Lords concentrated upon — urban renewal projects, free breakfast for neighborhood children, medical care. These issues not only directly affected neighborhood life but impinged upon the family, still the crucial unit for Puerto Ricans. The Young Lords hired architects to draw up alternative urban renewal plans; they organized squatters to sit in vacant apartment houses; they occupied a church until its laymen permitted its use for a day-care program; they "kidnaped" a mobile X-ray unit to assure more tuberculosis testing for Puerto Ricans; they conducted door-to-door canvasses to test Puerto Rican children for paint-induced lead poisoning.[33]

31 Herman Badillo was the first Puerto Rican elected to Congress, in 1970. Representing a multi-ethnic constituency in the Bronx, Badillo protested the decision of the House's Democratic leadership to place him on the Agriculture Committee. He succeeded in getting his assignment switched to the urban-oriented Education and Labor Committee. *New York Times*, February 4, 1971. In the same election four Puerto Ricans won seats in the New York state legislature. All four represented districts in New York City's South Bronx. Their legislative proposals for the 1971 session reflected problems of the Bronx and Puerto Ricans: migrant labor, narcotics, and housing. *New York Times*, December 6, 1970.

32 Interview with Jose "Cha Cha" Jimenez in Frank Browning, "From Rumble to Revolution: The Young Lords," *Ramparts* 9, no. 4 (October 1970): 20.

33 For descriptions of these activities see Ibid., pp. 19–25; "Squatters in New York," *Village Voice*, June 25, 1970, p. 9; *New York Times*, June 18, 1970; Jose Thlesias, "Right on with the Young Lords," *New York Times Magazine*, June 7, 1970, pp. 32, 84–94.

In another arena, the New York hospital workers union, the Young Lords' programs seemed too general and impractical to attract support. Local 1199 of the Drug and Hospital Workers Union is composed largely of blacks and Puerto Ricans and is considered one of the American labor movement's most devotedly progressive unions. Nonetheless, "the vision of the Lords seemed too general [to the rank and file] and, therefore,

Each activity has served to bring Puerto Ricans of all ages and political persuasions together. The Young Lords have severe critics within their own ethnic community, but focus upon grass-roots interests and local institutions has tempered some of the initial opposition, especially among adults. The controversy that gave the widest coverage to the plight of New York Puerto Ricans involved the Young Lords and Lincoln Hospital. Once again the militants chose an institution whose services were critical for all members of the community, publically authorized, locally based, concrete, yet symbolic. The Young Lords' original charge was that hospital physicians were guilty of willful neglect in the treatment of a pregnant Puerto Rican woman, who needlessly died. The gang demanded administrative changes within Lincoln Hospital to make it responsive to community needs.

What separated this issue from others pursued by the Young Lords was that health care was becoming a political issue for *all* sectors of American society. Hospitals, medical schools, doctors, and public health administrators were under fire not only from neglected ethnic communities but from assimilated middle-class suburbanites as well. The questions that the Young Lords raised were ethnically salient, but they also had supra-ethnic significance.[34] An ethnic group does not have to suppress its cultural distinctiveness to augment its political influence. In fact, there are instances in which its ethnic consciousness

---

irrelevant. The Lords were talking what seemed like rhetoric. The members needed the machinery, the system, the pre-established processes through which gains, however small, could be realized. The Lords were thrown out [of the pre-negotiation mass meeting]." This same observer, however, concludes her study of Local 1199 with the conviction that the union's preoccupation with short-term gains and its refusal to come to grips with the fundamental inequities of the entire American health system eventually will make it unable to serve the interests of its black and Puerto Rican rank and file. Elinor Langer, "The Hospital Workers: 'The Best Contract Anywhere'?" *New York Review of Books* (June 3, 1971), pp. 30–37.

[34] The Lincoln Hospital case is described in Ellen Frankfort, "Accounting to the People: Lincoln Hospital Crisis," *Village Voice*, October 1, 1970, pp. 24, 44–45; Puerto Ricans' health service problems in the Bronx, are discussed in the context of the *national* health crisis in Barbara and John Ehrenreich, *The American Health Empire* (New York: Vintage Books, 1971); see especially chapter 18, "Health Workers in Revolt: Lincoln Brigade II," pp. 253–67.

alerts it to general developmental challenges before other citizens are aware of them. A small ethnic group that is integrated far enough into the larger society to rely upon its institutions and services can further its own interests most effectively when they reinforce needs of the general society. The case of the Puerto Ricans in New York City and their dissatisfaction with public health facilities suggests that transitional ethnic groups can locate problems of modernism more readily than can the most modern sectors of society.

THE ETHNIC POWER TO GOVERN

A third class of ethnic groups embraces those with the potential to shape not only public policy relevant to their communal affairs but policy for all parts of a nation. Ethnic groups can govern as well as be governed, and the simple fact that an ethnic group formulates policy does not obliterate its ethnicity. These most potentially influential communities sometimes are overlooked by students of ethnic politics because they are not "minorities."

Malays in Malaysia, Protestants in Ulster, and Afrikaners in South Africa are all distinctly communal in their political behavior despite their command of governmental machinery.

The experience of these dominant groups indicates that political superiority is not synonymous with political development. Sinhalese of Ceylon, Negroes of Trinidad, and Anglo-Saxons in the United States are other dominant ethnic groups currently crippled by underdevelopment. In some instances underdevelopment means that the ethnic elite has failed to provide channels of meaningful participation for newly mobilized members of its own community. In other countries the ruling community has been unable to convince weaker ethnic groups of the legitimacy of unequal distribution of influence, or it has not created structures that reallocate power. In still other cases incomplete assimilation of weak groups into the dominant culture testifies to underdevelopment. Underdevelopment, like development, can appear in a variety of guises. Ethnic groups fortunate enough to possess resources for dictating national policy have several options when they try to harmonize relations with less-powerful communities. Which of those options they select will be determined by the dominant group's own culture and goals. The choice also will reflect the strategic attributes that contributed to its hegemony in the first place. Finally, options are narrowed by the resources and goals of the nation's other ethnic groups.

Usually a dominant group does not have a clear-cut choice and has to find some agreeable combination of alternatives. Nor does it operate in a static society, in which status distinctions between ethnic communities are fixed. Domestic and external environments evolve in ways that upset old equilibriums and invalidate standard assumptions about group roles. Of course, a major source of change is intracommunal development of the sort described earlier. Ruling communities must adjust to the rising political awareness and expectations of the ethnic groups they traditionally dictated to or ignored. In modernizing nations adjustment normally means widened avenues of political participation and reforms that distribute society's rewards more equitably. We commonly presume that such innovations tend to weaken the hegemony of the dominant ethnic group and eventually diminish the political relevance of ethnicity altogether. In the long run national modernization and the political sophistication of ethnic groups produce a secular and pluralistic polity. It will be a pluralism of roles, interests, and functional associations; gone will be the primordial cleavages of communalism. In other words, if a ruling ethnic community wants to enjoy the fruits of modernism, it should resign itself to surrendering its communal superiority. It can take comfort, instead, that its privileged members as individuals have a head start in cultivating skills relevant for life in an industrial, urban, managerial society.

There are, however, ethnic groups that attempt to modernize the nations they rule without giving up communal hegemony. Where ethnic minorities exist with significant power potential of their own, ruling communities count on two conditions. First, they assume a gradual transition during which complex changes can be programed and coordinated in a way that avoids harsh dislocations that would undermine established authority. Second, they count on weaker ethnic groups' remaining relatively isolated from modern innovations, except where deliberately introduced to them by the policy-makers. This marriage of controlled gradualism and selective isolation is the foundation of development programs in South Africa and Rhodesia. It is also the basis of the America-Liberians' effort to maintain their century-old political monopoly while simultaneously modernizing Liberia.

American Negro settlers migrated to the west coast of Africa in 1822 to escape slavery, and in 1847 Liberia declared its sovereignty as a nation-state. The settlers shared with the indigenous African tribes a common racial identity. But race was less important than culture in defining America-Liberians' sense of belonging. The culture they brought with them was that of the American South of the 1820's, with a special emphasis on family to offset the fragmentation of slave society. Like their fellow Americans of that era, the settlers were contemptuous of the "uncivilized" African tribes. As they followed their own manifest destiny into the interior, they imposed communal authority — moral and coercive — over the indigenous Africans. Behind a facade of democratic procedures intended to stave off British and French colonial encroachments, America-Liberians enjoyed a virtual monopoly of political power. In the hinterland beyond Monrovia, the capital, African tribes occasionally rebelled, but they were too isolated from the resources of government and from one another to launch an effective attack against the settlers.

Liberia's experiment in programed modernization began after the election of president William V. S. Tubman in 1943. Tubman, a descendant of one of the founding families who compromised the America-Liberian upper class, took office with the support of poorer America-Liberians and tribal peoples. Without surrendering the community's claim to being the "civilized" sector of society, Tubman set about to stimulate economic growth and to integrate tribal peoples into the Liberian nation. The arrival of the Firestone Rubber Company in the 1920's, the wartime demands of the 1940's, and the later discovery of iron ore all contributed to the breakdown of caste barriers between the indigenous Africans and the America-Liberians.[35] Tubman's regime had to tackle the

---

35 Robert H. Jackson, "Social Structure and Political Change in Ethiopia and Liberia," *Comparative Political Studies* 3, no. 1 (April 1970): 53.

problem of sustaining economic development without disturbing intercommunal relations. His solution was to permit tribal persons to enter the outer circle of social and political privilege, while he kept a tight rein on top-level policy machinery. Tubman hoped that a slight acceleration of social mobilization would prevent violent, uncontrollable mobilization. "Economic development, instead of undermining Americo-Liberian control of the Republic, might finance more modern and efficient means of control." [36] Not only would foreign investment be used to build roads connecting interior tribes with Monrovia, but for safety's sake increased revenues would help modernize the police and army and enrich the Americo-Liberian elite. Government revenues multiplied more than eightfold between 1950 and 1960.[37]

Political parties are vehicles for exclusion as well as for integration, and nowhere is this more obvious than in multi-ethnic societies with communally defined party organizations. Liberia's single-party system revolves around the Americo-Liberian True Whig party. President Tubman's unification policy of expanding tribal involvement made the single-party system indispensable. Party patronage was used to channel newly mobile citizens and coopt potential opponents. Revenues from foreign investment allowed the True Whig party to employ more cadres and expand the political job market to meet emergent demands. Whereas in the past the Americo-Liberians had perpetuated the communal status quo by colonial administrative control, under Tubman's guidance they could buy support.[38] Upwardly mobile tribal individuals risked ouster from privileged status if they insisted upon flaunting their tribal origins. The passport for entrance into middle ranges of political influence was acculturation into Americo-Liberian society.[39]

Deliberate gradualism calls for considerable political acumen

[36] J. Gus Liebnow, *Liberia: The Evolution of Privilege* (Ithaca: Cornell University Press, 1969), p. 71.
[37] Jackson, "Social Structure and Political Change in Ethiopia and Liberia," p. 54.
[38] Ibid.
[39] Liebnow, *Liberia: The Evolution of Privilege*, p. 214.

and sensitivity, mechanisms that can both control and be sensitive to social change. The possible flaw in the Americo-Liberian strategy lay in its overwhelming reliance on one man, William V. S. Tubman. The government's outreach to the tribes was made through Tubman's highly personal contacts. His personal authority became a principal pillar of Americo-Liberian domination; then, in July 1971, he died at the age of seventy-five. Now, as more persons outside the Americo-Liberian community are educated, migrate to Monrovia, and take posts in bureaucracy and business, the dominant ethnic group may lose its claim to legitimacy — that is, its corner on "civilization." The problematic character of the Americo-Liberian formula for continued political superiority was underscored every time a Liberian asked, "After Tubman, what?" We do not yet have the answer.

CONCLUSION: RECURRING PATTERNS
OF DEVELOPMENT

Political development stripped of its uniquely modern characteristic is the capacity to make and administer public policies that reconcile needs and goals. Groups as well as entire systems develop — or fail to develop. For one ethnic community within a nation-state, creating the resources and strategies appropriate to contemporary demands is a complex process having two fundamental dimensions: intracommunal integration and mobilization, and exercise of influence on external environments. The process is not likely to be exactly the same for any two ethnic groups, even within a single nation at the same point in its history. Nevertheless, certain significant patterns recur in a host of cases.

First, intragroup cohesiveness varies according to how strongly members believe that individual mobility in the larger society is possible without the frustrations of ascriptive recruitment. Another factor determining group cohesiveness is the extent of social and economic inequality inside the community and whether that gap undermines the authority of ethnic leaders. In numerous instances intra-ethnic distrust has led to an escalation of interethnic tensions; people in the lowest strata of two mutually hostile communities lose faith in their established leaders and become newly convinced that they are being cheated in any elite-to-elite negotiations.

Still, not all internal differentiations obstruct an ethnic group's move toward concerted action. If, as in the case of the American Indian, the subdivisions can serve as interlocutors of the alienated individual and the larger community, and if, in addition, those subunits can crystallize ethnic issues that are otherwise abstract, then they may promote communal mobilization.

With regard to the utilization of group resources to shape public policy, once again there is hardly a "typical" ethnic group. Broadly speaking, three classes of ethnic groups are measured by their potential political influence. The first category includes groups that, even if fully developed, could do little more than assure their own security. They search for the most effective means of deflecting pressures originating from a polity they cannot hope to govern. A second category embraces ethnic groups most commonly studied by political scientists — groups that in theory are capable of influencing government actions impinging on their communal welfare but are unable to direct more than one or two spheres of policymaking. Within this second category, obviously, there is a broad spectrum of political potentials. Ethnic groups experiencing the hardest time finding means to match needs are those integrated into modern societies. They discover that scores of governmental activities, not just one or two, seem critical for the group's betterment. Yet communal numbers and monetary resources stretch only so far. The temptation under these circumstances is either to modify the group's ethnic goals for the sake of building alliances with other groups or to opt for total separation.

Finally, a third class of ethnic communities includes those equipped with historical roots, numbers, and formal authority sufficient to shape decisions affecting the whole nation. If the group's ethnic identity is closely bound to the nation's identity, it may not even appear to be an ethnic group. It will simply be the norm, the mainstream into which all minorities are submerged. Only when minorities (or oppressed majorities) self-consciously assert the worth of their own cultures is the ethnicity of "invisible" ethnic communities exposed. Ukranian nationalism reveals the ethnic chauvinism of the Great Russians; Turkish nomads' resistance to the Red army reveals the ethnicity of the Han Chinese; the black power salute challenges and exposes the ethnicity of Anglo-Saxon Americans.

Our analysis would be grossly distorted if it left the impression that ethnic groups make or break their own development. In practice, of course, the materials a community has to work with, along with the obstacles it has to overcome, are created largely by extracommunal forces, often quite deliberately in order to curb the development of ethnic groups. For instance, the efforts of Soviet Jews to mobilize their community are made extremely difficult by Moscow's restrictions on cultural and religious communications. Similarly, the perpetuation of the historical fragmentation of the American Indians is due in large measure to congressional and bureaucratic decisions aimed at weakening tribal identities and making Uncle Tomahawks out of Indian leaders. The economic impotence of many ethnic groups results not just from failure to succeed in the worlds of commerce and industry but from systematic exclusion from jobs and education and governmental inability to sustain general economic growth. In periods of recession ascriptive criteria are particularly prevalent because jobs are few and "you can't hire everyone." American blacks perhaps know best the meaning of "last to be hired, first to be fired."

Frequently, well-meaning attempts to focus attention directly on an ethnic community — instead of seeing it only through the concerns of the larger society — perpetuate this distortion, for they suggest that a community has autonomy, that it is the architect of its own destiny. The consequence is what some critics have called "blaming the victim" — that is, explaining the poverty of Pakistan's Bengalis or America's blacks in terms of Bengali or black characteristics, when in fact their deprivations are the product of the whole system's underdevelopment.[40]

In most cases — though the precise mix will depend on

40 William Ryan, *Blaming the Victim* (New York: Pantheon, 1970).

levels of integration — ethnic groups have greater potentials for altering their political status than most observers realize. Politicians and scholars alike often are surprised (and embarrassed) by the unpredicted strategic agility and impact of newly mobilized ethnic communities. On the other hand, no ethnic group, even a remote hill tribe, is truly its own master. It must cope with crises it did not precipitate, pursue mobility in economies whose institutions it did not create, lobby for bills in legislatures it did not design. Political scientists are more guilty than other social scientists of focusing on the nation-state as if it were a natural "given" and thus seeing ethnic groups only in the context of "problems" they pose for nation-builders. In their effort to rectify this disciplinary imbalance, political scientists should beware of going to the opposite extreme, treating ethnic groups as if they were fully responsible for their own political developments.

With this caveat in mind, we might take a new look at national development. In multi-ethnic states where several communities are undergoing political mobilization, national development may be conceived as the sum of communal developments plus the central government's capacity to cope with those separate developments and their accumulated consequences.

CHAPTER IX

Revolution and Ethnic Conflict

REVOLUTIONS ARE RARE. The modern period, stretching from the birth of industrialism to the present, commonly has been labeled a revolutionary era. But, in fact, genuine revolutions have been the exception, not the rule. Their rarity is due to the difficulty of matching the right social conditions with men who perceive their potential and possess means for exploiting them in the name of change. In societies fragmented along ethnic lines revolutions are more difficult still.

A revolution is a particular form of socio-political change. Evolutionary development, programed reform, coup d'état, and rebellion are also forms of change, but they are distinct from revolution. The mobilization and overthrow phases of a revolution are compressed into a short time period, usually less than a decade, perhaps only a year. This partly explains the shock and emotion that accompany a revolution. Moreover, revolutionary change is radical; it goes to the roots of society, shaking its fundamental outlook on relations among men, its criteria for legitimacy, and the distribution of power.

The medium of revolution is violence. A society reaches a point that makes revolution likely usually because pressures for necessary reform have been so bottled up that normal — legitimate — modes of accommodation have lost their credibility and efficacy. In their stead, large sections of the citizenry use extralegal — illegitimate — methods.

Incumbent regimes and those with a stake in the status quo cannot tolerate such illegitimate action and still retain power and authority; so they resort to coercion. The violence that is integral to revolution reflects the society's acute disjointedness and, specifically, the established system's loss of legitimacy. Revolutionaries are intent upon creating a new basis of legitimate power; counterrevolutionaries attempt to reaffirm the old concepts of legitimacy and thus their own right to govern. In periods of revolution the relationships between values and power are starkly exposed:

> If history teaches anything about the causes of revolution . . .
> it is that a disintegration of political systems precedes revolu-
> tions, that the telling symptom of disintegration is a progressive
> erosion of governmental authority, and that this erosion is
> caused by the government's inability to function properly, from
> which spring the citizens' doubts about its legitimacy.[1]

The only revolutions we have on record are those that have occurred in the transition between premodern ("traditional" is too vague) and modern periods in the career of any given country. Revolutions to date have been modernizing events. The conviction that men can radically alter social conditions — a belief that must be held by revolutionaries — is a peculiarly modern idea. Furthermore, all the revolutions presently "on the books" have propelled their respective countries toward secularism, egalitarianism, a commercial (though not necessarily industrial) economy, exploitation of knowledge, and popular participation in the affairs of state. The extent to which revolutions have actually achieved these aims differs, of course, as do the particular styles and forms they assume. Nevertheless, the direction of revolutions so far has been toward modernization. Whether a country that is already modern, such as Sweden, Japan, France, Britain, and the United States, can experience a full-fledged revolution is a subject of debate among many observers today. At least *by definition,*

[1] Hannah Arendt, "Reflections: Civil Disobedience," *New Yorker* (September 12, 1970), p. 78.

revolution is possible in modern as well as in premodern societies.

One modern element is inherent in revolution: its mass character. Even revolutions with strong individual leaders and effective organizations are characterized by broad support among the general populace. Mass mobilization, in response to widely felt disaffection from the current system and coercive reactions by the incumbent rulers, is a hallmark of revolution. Only with broad popular participation does a revolution touch lives and values throughout the whole society and thus generate radical change. Of course, various parts of the population may play different roles in the revolution, some more central than others. But for the average citizen in the midst of a genuine revolution there is literally no place to hide.

A revolution is a positive as well as a negative phenomenon. If it were intent merely upon toppling the existing system, it would in all probability leave a vacuum to be filled simply by a replica of the old familiar system. Rebellions follow this pattern. When a nineteenth-century European traveler remarked perceptively that China had more rebellions and fewer revolutions than any other nation in history, this was the distinction he was making. Revolutions create something. Political revolts that accomplish nothing more than replacement of rulers from one ethnic group with men of another ethnic group do not produce revolutionary change. Sources of authority, a basis for evaluating government, and beliefs about the limits of citizen obligation and government responsibility remain unaltered if one ethnic group is simply substituted for another in power. The Manchus, foreigners from the north, replaced Han Chinese when the Ch'ing dynasty began in 1644, but China had to wait nearly three centuries before it experienced its first real revolution.

If revolution, then, is a transformation of society's fundamental structure of power and values by violent means and mass participation, the list of actual revolutions turns out to be surprisingly short: United States (1776), France (1789), Mexico (1910), Russia (1917), China (1911 and 1949), Yugoslavia (1945), Bolivia (1952), Vietnam (1954), Algeria (1958), Cuba (1958). This is not like a list of the planets in our solar system or the members of the United Nations. There is plenty of room for debate over what historical event has constituted a revolution. Perhaps the most controversial revolution on the list is the American. Professional historians have filled volumes with arguments over whether the war against Britain brought about a fundamental reordering of American society. As we shall see, certain ethnic minorities should be among the most reluctant to call that colonial conflict a genuine revolution. It would be more nearly accurate to place each of these national upheavals on a continuum according to how closely it approximates theoretical criteria such as brevity, radical social change, and use of violence. The revolutions of China (1949), Russia, and France would certainly be much closer to the pure form than those of Bolivia, Mexico, and the United States.

If the list were extended to include abortive revolutions — conflicts generated by widespread discontent and radical goals that failed to bring mass, violent upheaval to fruition — then other countries could be added. Malaya, the Philippines, Burma, Laos, and Indonesia experienced unsuccessful revolutions in 1948; some of them dragged on for a decade, and others are still simmering. Bolivia witnessed efforts of Cuban and native guerrillas to mobilize a revolutionary movement in the 1960's. The Hungarians' unsuccessful attempt to oust the communist party regime in 1956 had a revolutionary dimension, as did the student-led violence in France in the spring of 1968. The latter failed to topple the Gaullist regime, although it did contribute to the resignation of President de Gaulle a year later.

Another step removed from completed revolution is the existence of would-be revolutionaries in a society, men who consider thorough change through violence the only solution to their country's ills. There is probably no country in the modern world that does not play host to at least a handful of such revolutionaries without a revolution. Some may succeed in precipitating mass conflicts, but many eventually will opt for nonrevolutionary strategies or withdraw from political action altogether. Among this group are men trying to translate ethnic group anger into general revolutionary commitment; theirs is not easy task. This kind of ethnic spokesman is satisfied neither with tokenism and gradual progress within the current system nor with territorial secession without structural change. Usually such a spokesman's greatest obstacle is his ethnic brothers' eagerness to believe that betterment can come without the high price of revolution. Felipe Luciano, local chairman of the Young Lords, lectured Puerto Rican high school students in New York City at their commencement: "The only solution is revolution. Take destiny into your own hands. You are not going to get it by getting people elected to Congress, by a good education or by praying. The only way you are going to get it is by ripping it up." On a day traditionally suffused with hope, Luciano painted a gloomy picture of Puerto Ricans' future in American society as now structured: "Seize the schools, seize the courts, seize the jails where three-quarters of our people are, seize the town before it seizes you. Revolution in this country is not going to wait." [2]

Lists of consummated and abortive revolutions include a vast assortment of ethnic pluralisms. Among the countries that have experienced successful revolutions, France is the exception to this rule; at the time of its revolution, its ethnic composition was relatively homogeneous.[3] Each of the remaining countries contained at least two distinct ethnic groups when revolution broke out. Even so, they differ crucially in the relationship of ethnic pluralism to revolutionary conflict.

In Mexico and Bolivia the polarization that preceded revolution and shaped its course paralleled ethnic racial polarization. In Russia, several large ethnic groups were left outside the mainstream of revolutionary upheaval and were finally incorporated in it only through civil war. In Vietnam and China, ethnic groups inhabiting remote territories were ideologically peripheral but strategically important to the conduct of the revolutions. The American revolution split the dominant English-speaking group and scattered ethnic minorities on both sides in search of protection or acceptance: Indians,

2 Quoted in *New York Times,* June 26, 1970.
3 By 1968, France was more heterogeneous. The abortive spring revolution was ignited in part by students' dismay at the condition of impoverished Algerian workers living in slums near the University at Nanterre.

Scots, and Dutch sided with the Tory loyalists; Anglicized French Huguenots and German Quakers backed the rebels.

Abortive revolutions display relationships just as complex. Malaya's post–World War II Communist-led revolutionary movement never managed to solve the problem of non-Chinese recruitment. At about the same time, the Hukbalahap, or Huk, revolution foundered in the Philippines because of ethnic as well as regional confinement. Though insurgents called for a nationwide upheaval, Huk control remained limited to the Pampango-speaking area of central Luzon. Other Filipino ethnic groups, such as neighboring Tagalogs and Ilokanos, generally shunned the Huks, in part because the historic mutuality of interests of Pampanganos and nearby ethnic communities had thwarted Tagalog-inspired nationalist movements against Spain. At the end of the 1800's the Tagalogs had led the revolt against Spain, and the Pampanganos had stood aside. Tagalog is the national language of the Philippines. The Ilokano to the north are noted for being even more exclusivist than the Tagalogs and thus showed little enthusiasm for a Pampangano-led movement. Although all the ethnic communities of central Luzon faced conditions that augured well for revolution — politicization, high tenancy rates, social upheaval — the Huks' movement was markedly mono-ethnic. This, as much as the well-publicized charisma and sagacity of the late president Ramón Magsaysay, may have been responsible for the government's counterrevolutionary success. Huk leaders seemed less conscious of their ethnic limitations than did the Malayan Communists.[4] Che Guevara was sensitive to the dan-

---

[4] Edward J. Mitchell, "Some Econometrics of the Huk Rebellion," *American Political Science Review* 62, no. 4 (December 1969): 1167–69. A study of Filipino voting patterns found that cultural-linguistic affiliation was a powerful factor determining elector behavior, carrying more explanatory weight than either party affection or socio-economic status. Hirofumi Ando, "A Study of Voting Patterns in the Philippine Presidential and Senatorial Elections, 1945–1965," *Midwest Journal of Political Science* 13, no. 4 (November 1969): 581–86.

The gradual, though resisted, emergence of Tagalog as the Philippines' "national language" is described in Nobleza Asuncion-Lande, "Multilingualism, Politics, and 'Filipinism,'" *Asian Survey* 11, no. 7 (July 1971): 677–92; the author notes the stubborn persistence of linguistic-regional loyalties in the distribution of political patronage as well as in elections.

gers of ethnic parochialism, but in Bolivia he too failed to penetrate the Indian communities and win them over to his revolutionary guerrilla movement.

Ethnic groups are common stumbling blocks for revolutionaries trying to mobilize the broadest possible base in the name of system transformation. Communal barriers can be as much a threat to a radical movement as the government's military force. Either the groups must be penetrated, won over to the cause, and "deethnicized," or the revolution must be directed along a path that makes hostile groups peripheral to victory. At the same time, of course, the grievances of ethnic groups frequently serve as catalysts for what eventually become supraethnic revolutions. A community that has been treated unjustly illuminates profound contradictions within the entire political system — contradictions present but unseen until blatantly exposed in one group's poverty or oppression. Yet, unless that community comprises a majority of the populace, if ethnic grievances do not break out of communal boundaries, the revolution has scant chance for success. Ethnic deprivation may ignite a revolution, but usually it cannot carry the revolution to fruition without external alliances. A community's disaffection has to touch some raw nerve among the general citizenry if it is to escalate beyond rebellion.

There are several reasons why ethnic groups per se rarely become bases of revolution. First, ethnicity is not primarily ideological or political; rather, it is cultural and social. Ethnic groups have enormous potential for political development, but politics remains secondary to other bonds and values shared by members. Second, in times of crisis ethnic communities are harder to expand than are ideological or functional associations. To join a Marxist movement one need only adopt a certain set of goals and abstract premises, whereas to join an ethnic movement one must *belong*, in style, mores, perhaps even language or race. Finally, by being more exclusive and having boundaries more visible, ethnic groups have a difficult time winning the confidence and trust of potential allies. Their objectives seem too parochial and their leadership too alien to excite active participation within the majority. They may provoke sympathy and concern among outsiders, but that generates piecemeal reforms, not the violent overthrow of a political system.

These characteristic obstacles preventing ethnic discontent from being translated into revolution operate so that a large percentage of rebellions and riots are ethnic. In other words, the factors that frustrate ethnic-based revolution increase the likelihood of ethnic riot and rebellion. Riots tend to be only indirectly political; they are brief and usually confined to a small geographical area, typically a city — or several unconnected cities simultaneously. A rebellion, by contrast, is more political, though not highly ideological. It tends to have more organization, range over a wider region, and can last for years. Unlike revolutions, rebellions pursue limited objectives rather than fundamental alternative structures. Rebels fight for specific concessions from the established rulers; revolutionaries fight for a new structure of rule altogether.

Ethnic groups are prone to riot and rebellion. Members of an ethnic group commonly live close together, clustered in one region or concentrated in several separate towns. They experience discrimination and frustration in specific and concrete ways; thus their protests aim at immediate amelioration rather than at abstract transformation. Members of ethnic groups, more than members of most other social groups, have an explicit sense of brother and stranger; this is helpful in mobilizing protest in the absence of entrenched leadership, organization, and formal political platforms.

History is littered with ethnically defined civil wars that outside political sympathizers sought to elevate to revolutions. From the embattled community's vantage point, the critical question is whether alliances and ideological inflation of goals will increase the chances for ethnic self-control and security, or whether it will make the group more than ever a pawn in other people's struggles. Neither ethnic homogeneity nor ethnic pluralism guarantees revolutionary success. Ethnic divisions, however, do pose special obstacles to revolution. In overcoming or bypassing these obstacles, revolutions take on characteristics that ultimately affect their overall impact on society's development. The obstacles and resultant strategies are visible in each of the three phases of revolutionary change:

the accumulation of sufficient causes, the conduct of warfare, and the drive for consolidation after the collapse of the incumbent government.

PHASE 1: ACCUMULATION OF SUFFICIENT CAUSES

Change as thoroughgoing and as violent as revolution necessarily is prompted by severe conditions. Chalmers Johnson has observed, "the very idea of revolution is contingent upon [a] perception of societal failure." [5] Objective conditions and the *perception* of them are both involved. Furthermore, would-be revolutionaries perceive not simply the failure of a policy, political party, or regime in office, but "societal" bankruptcy: the system itself is losing its worth and rightness.

Ethnic grievances alone almost never become sufficient cause for revolution; though they may induce limited violence or reform, by themselves they cannot propel a country into widespread mass violence aimed at system transformation. The discontent of a group that identifies itself ethnically is likely to focus on concrete claims, hard to generalize though more easily politicized than vague claims. Unless the ethnic group can superimpose a more general identity on itself — for example, class identity — the grievances are likely to remain compartmentalized. What ethnic outsiders may do is acerbate weaknesses already undermining authority and effectiveness. If they demand fuller participation in the nation's political process, they may overload already strained institutions. If they insist on greater autonomy or secession, the government could be deprived of territorial and manpower resources needed for development. Neither claim is inherently revolutionary, but each makes system capacity otherwise questionable in the eyes of the majority.

Ethnic conflict between two or more communities also undermines the structure and fabric of a society, but if it goes unresolved the most probable consequence is civil war, not revolution. If ethnic claims are deliberately interwoven into some stage of the revolution, it may — as the Russian case demonstrates — deteriorate finally into civil war. Despite their

[5] Quoted in Henry Bienan, *Violence and Social Change* (Chicago: University of Chicago Press, 1968), p. 67.

analytic separateness, revolution and civil war are difficult to disentangle empirically, especially when ethnic grievances have been a motivation of conflict. Essentially, ethnic problems contribute to the loss of system legitimacy by stretching institutions beyond their capabilities, by compelling governments to resort to coercion to maintain order, and by thwarting official programs instituted to remedy specific dysfunctions.

Some ethnic conditions are part of *long-term* trends that only later subvert systemic bonds of authority and interdependence. For instance, overextension of government jurisdiction to territorial ethnic groups beyond the immediate reach of central control ultimately frustrates a government's efforts to implement coherent, society-wide economic programs, thus revealing to citizens how ineffective the existing system is in coping with fundamental economic change. Or the introduction of new market opportunities may alter relations between ethnic groups so that groups once remote from one another are in close contact, a proximity that generates friction and makes officialdom rely more heavily on coercive force.

Other ethnic conditions will figure among the *short-term,* or catalytic, factors causing revolution. An urban riot between ethnic communities may become a vehicle for politicizing rioters and mobilizing them on a broad scale for the sake of supra-ethnic claims that the established elite cannot hope to satisfy. Or a political system in the throes of a foreign war may be pushed beyond its resources by the eruption of a domestic secessionist movement. The government's loss of citizen confidence during wartime was the final precipitating factor in both czarist Russia and Kuomintang China. Andrei Amalrik foresees the same thing happening in the Soviet Union if it goes to war with the People's Republic of China.[6]

Nevertheless, by itself ethnic group disaffection is insufficient cause for revolution. In fact, at times ethnic fragmentation can serve as a hedge *against* revolution. It may strain the resources of an already fragile system and deprive established authorities of the solid support they need for effective action; however, the same ethnic divisions can so compartmentalize grievances and alienation that the government will confront

---

[6] See Chapter IV, pp. 106–107.

only scattered revolts and narrow demands but not a revolution grounded in mass mobilization.

The double-edged relation of ethnic pluralism to revolutionary causation can produce the worst of all possible worlds: an ineffectual political system and a generally alienated populace combined with incapacity for popular joint action and fundamental change. The result is continuous sporadic violence plus social stagnation. Since 1960, Burma and Laos have endured this unhappy state of affairs, unable to achieve either peace or revolution. Not surprisingly, both countries embrace a myriad of mutually suspicious ethnic groups, as well as one or more insurgent political movements. Until the two countries can incorporate the various ethnic minorities into their political systems, or until the nations break up into separate states, or until the revolutionaries find formulas for cementing a lasting alliance with dissident ethnic groups, Laos and Burma are likely to remain in developmental limbo.[7]

At the other end of the scale are Bolivia, Mexico, and Cuba. What differentiates these three societies from Laos and Burma is the ease with which ethnic frustration could be translated into supra-ethnic protest. The ethnically divided country most likely to transform communal unrest into political revolution is one in which ethnic boundaries are coterminous with socioeconomic class lines, one ethnic group clearly dominates and exploits a numerically large but powerless have-not sector, and

[7] The Burmese ethnic rebellions and Communist insurgencies (there are two, the Communists split into two factions, White Flags and Red Flags) date back to 1948. The civilian regime's apparent inability to subdue the rebels led to general Ne Win's coups in 1960 and 1962. Ousted civilian prime minister U Nu went to Thailand in the late 1960's and there attempted to build an alliance of the Shan, Karen, and other ethnic minority armies and his own anti–Ne Win force. The military government of Ne Win has not succeeded in establishing internal peace. The Red Flag Communists are weaker, and the White Flags have been forced to move away from their Burman base to the Shan states in the north. Nevertheless, in 1970 Burmese development was seriously retarded by the cost of security. In budgetary terms, education and training are only slightly ahead of counterinsurgency expenditures. The rising number of unemployed and underemployed students and bureaucrats in Burma's stagnant economy offers a potential pool of supporters for U Nu's United National Liberation Front. See John Badgley, "The Union of Burma: Age Twenty-Two," *Asian Survey* 11, no. 2 (February 1971): 150–52. For a report on links between Karen rebels and U Nu, see *New York Times*, February 7, 1971.

the oppressed ethnic group is integrated into the country's economic system and has symbolic significance for national identity. Only under these conditions will an ethnic group stand a good chance of spearheading a revolution. Bolivia, Mexico, and Cuba alone of revolutionary nations fill these criteria. However, even under such favorable circumstances the oppressed community may not win major benefits from a revolution fought in its name.

At the time of the revolutions in Bolivia and Mexico (1952 and 1910) their respective Indian populations were cultural and political outsiders but increasingly integrated into the agrarian economy. "Peasant" and "Indian" were labels used interchangeably, especially in Bolivia. In each society they were the least Europeanized or urbanized sector; they represented the exploitation resulting from class stratification and commercialized agriculture. Their *ethnicity* gave their economic oppression its revolutionary salience, for the Indians offered an alternative to colonially linked Spanish culture. Their distinctive presence inspired nationalist rejection of a European social system that depended upon emulation of foreigners and exploitation of man and nature. Non-Indian intellectuals in both Bolivia and Mexico used "Indianism" as a touchstone for revolutionary nationalism. Exploitation, land alienation, and a sense of ethnic foreignness were linked in the cause of the oppressed, non–Spanish-speaking Indian. The intellectual power of Indianism was strongest in revolutionary Mexico. Brilliant muralists such as Diego Rivera raised rediscovery of Indian culture to a revolutionary mythology. "The Indian represented the national, the patently non-foreign. Uncorrupted by imperialist pretensions, he was a symbol of suffering and purity." [8]

Though the legacy and plight of the Indian crystallized revolutionary fervor in Mexico and Bolivia, in neither country were Indians the principal actors or commanders in the revolution. Perhaps for this reason the Indians' immediate circumstances were not radically altered when the revolution ended. They had more land, in some cases, but not much more

[8] Jean Franco, *The Modern Culture of Latin America: Society and the Artist* (Baltimore: Penguin Books, 1970), p. 121.

power. Indianism was an intellectual movement promoted by radical non-Indian artists and writers. Most Indians were illiterate and thus were unable to appreciate, much less judge, the enthusiastic descriptions of their history and values. The Bolivian Indian peasants in their Andean villages were distant spectators during the 1952 revolution, which was concentrated in La Paz, the metropolitan, Spanish-speaking capital. Bolivian Indians persist as a separate cultural group, but their political impact is far less than their numbers require.

In Mexico, rural isolation and miscegenation worked together to reduce distinctly Indian participation in the 1910 revolution. During the eighteenth and nineteenth centuries huge land estates (haciendas) became the bases of Mexican development. But class stratification was not paralleled by strict racial barriers. Some Indians moved to the highlands to escape Spanish control and preserve their ethnic identity, but most Indians were in close contact with their mestizo masters. Prior to the revolution two trends marked Mexican development: Hispanization of indigenous Indians and immigrant Africans, and mestizoization through racial intermarriage. As Spanish culture permeated almost all sections of Mexican life, Indian and African blood ran through the European community. " 'Pure' Indians declined from 98.7 per cent of the total in 1570 to 74.6 per cent in 1646, to 60.0 per cent in 1810, and to 29.2 per cent in 1921 (the year of the last racial census) and to an estimated 20.0 per cent in 1950." [9] At the same time, Spanish speakers multiplied to the point where they comprised 85 per cent of the population in 1900.[10] In fact, though Zapata was the great "Indian" revolutionary chieftain of the Mexican revolution, just one incident in his campaign on behalf of the land-hungry southern peasants can be called genuinely "Indian." According to John Womack, Jr.:

> In Morales's and Arenas's zone [in the southern states of Mexico] the Zapatistas could exert immediate popular influ-

[9] Pierre L. Van den Berghe, *Race and Racism: A Comparative Perspective* (New York: Wiley, 1967), p. 45.
[10] Ibid. By 1960 only 10.4 per cent of Mexico's population spoke indigenous languages and two-thirds of the racially Indian population was bilingual.

ence, and in the one "Indian" episode of the whole Zapatista revolution secretaries composed manifestos in Nahuatl [the local Indian language] for distribution through Tlaxclan and Pueblan villages, to congratulate local chiefs on their defiances of Carranza and to coax them into a renewed allegiance to Zapata.[11]

The revolutionary overthrow of the Porfirio Díaz dictatorship represented the toppling of bourgeois mestizo domination. It was led by an urban intelligentsia (Zapata was an exception) and sustained by grass-roots peasant support. Neither was strictly Indian. But the nationalist and socialist ideology guiding the revolution led to the breakup of feudal haciendas, where so many Indians labored, and to deliberate governmental efforts to step up assimilation of Indians. On the other hand, Mexican respondents to Almond and Verba's *Civic Culture* survey articulated profound disappointment with the long-range results of the revolution. For a majority of Mexicans the revolution is a source of hope but also of political cynicism. Its tenets are the basis of belief, but beliefs remain unfulfilled.[12] The Indianist revival is still part of Mexican national pride, as any visitor to Mexico City and the National University can testify from the Indian-derived public art. Yet few genuine Indians survive. Among the few that do are those in remote regions (such as the highlands of Chiapas) where an "exploitative interdependence between rural Indians and urban *ladinos* (as the local Hispanicized mestizos are still known) still exhibits many characteristics of the colonial period." [13]

[11] John Womack, Jr., *Zapata and the Mexican Revolution* (New York: Vintage Books, 1970), p. 302.
[12] Gabriel A. Almond and Sidney Verba, *The Civic Culture: Political Attitudes and Democracy in Five Countries* (Princeton: Princeton University Press, 1963), pp. 103–04.
[13] Van den Berghe, *Race and Racism*, p. 54. The Revolutionary Institutional party (PRI), which dominates post-revolution Mexican politics, continues to struggle with the unfulfilled pledge to the rural citizenry, especially the Indians. During the last presidential election campaign it was noted that while national per capita income doubled between 1950 and 1970 and now amounts to almost $600 per year, many rural peasants, especially among Mexico's three million Indians, live on less than $100 per year. *New York Times,* December 2, 1970.

In Cuba the Indians were long gone, but the Negroes generated an intellectual movement that seeded Cuban radical critiques of the society's colonial vestiges and American overlordship. The Afro-Cubans, like the mainland Indians, symbolized a search for national identity and legitimacy free from indebtedness to Europeans. Once again, however, the eventual revolution was not exclusively or even primarily ethnic. As in Mexico, intermarriage had blurred racial identities; mulattoes were found on all rungs of the social ladder. Afro-Cubanism, which had its literary blossoming in the 1930's, emphasized Negroes' cultural, rather than racial, contribution to Cuban life. The Negro brought together recognition of economic exploitation and a non-European cultural alternative. As in Mexico and Bolivia, these two awarenesses formed a base for later political mobilization. Juan Marinello, a Cuban critic, argued that Negro art was distinctively Cuban: "Here the Negro is marrow, and root, the breath of the people. . . . He may, in these times of change, be the touchstone of our poetry." [14]

Discrimination against Negroes, who comprised one-third of the population, did exist in pre-1958 Cuba, though it was never sanctioned by law as it was in the United States. Their disproportionate concentration among the unemployed and lower-paid workers was one factor bringing them into the ranks of Fidel Castro's anti-Batista revolution. Negroes had been prominent in the Cuban Communist party and in the labor movement even before Castro. On the other hand, political leaders for several decades had gained electoral support by claiming that they would promote Negro interests; yet the results were always disappointing. This produced political disillusionment among Cuban Negroes and made them initially cautious or even cool to the Fidelistas.[15] Still, despite discrimination, Cuban Negroes were far more tightly integrated into their nation's political and economic system than were Bolivians and Mexican Indians. By 1958, Negroes were the mainstay labor of Cuba's principal commodity crop, sugar. Overall,

---

[14] Quoted in Franco, *The Modern Culture of Latin America,* p. 134.
[15] Maurice Zeitlin, *Revolutionary Politics and the Cuban Working Class* (New York: Harper Torchbooks, 1970), pp. 72–73.

in fact, Cuba, was more homogeneous and integrated and more capitalistic than either 1952 Bolivia or 1910 Mexico. Consequently, Cuba's revolution was less motivated by the land hunger of remote indigenous people than by a mobilized and disaffected proletariat, a large part of which was Negro. Perhaps because of their economic deprivation, Negro workers were especially supportive of Fidelista class movement. In an attitude survey, Maurice Zeitlin found that Negroes were more likely than whites to favor the revolution, though the majority of workers in each racial group supported the revolution.[16] In other words, to Negroes the dysfunctions of the current system were most blatant, but the working class as a whole was ripe for revolution. Class antagonism, racial disaffection, and cultural nationalism all were operating to the advantage of Castro and his guerrillas. Castro and his chief lieutenants were not Negro, and their revolutionary platform was based not on an ethnic ideology but on a loose notion of socialism and anti-imperialism. But Castro made explicit appeals to Negroes and mulattoes (though Batista himself was a mulatto). If there was a racially defined enemy, rather than a class defined enemy, it was the whites, who still commanded most property. Racist America was not only the principal foreign exploiter, but the local whites' savior.[17]

Since the revolution, Castro's regime has made deliberate efforts to open beaches, hotels, schools, and skilled jobs to Negroes. Although evidence of racial discrimination persists, it appears to most observers that Negroes were indeed among the prime beneficiaries of an essentially class-motivated revolution.[18] Again, in contrast with the other two Latin American

---

[16] Ibid., pp. 77–79; pp. 86–87.

[17] Ramon Edvardo Ruiz, *Cuba: The Making of a Revolution* (New York: Norton, 1968), pp. 25–26.

[18] Joseph A. Kahl, "The Moral Economy of a Revolutionary Society" in Irving Louis Horowitz, ed., *Cuban Communism* (Chicago: Aldine, 1970), p. 102. Also Zeitlin, *Revolutionary Politics and the Cuban Working Class*, p. 75. Elsewhere Zeitlin has singled out Cuba and Chile as the only Latin American countries with mobilized working classes. See Maurice Zeitlin, "Chilean Revolution: The Bullet or the Ballot," *Ramparts* 9, no. 9 (April 1971): 23.

A dissenting opinion concerning the persistence of racism in post-revolution Cuba is in Geoffrey E. Fox, "Cuban Workers in Exile," *Trans-action* 8, no. 1 (September 1971): 21–30.

revolutions, it may be that the Afro-Cubans' high degree of integration into the society assured them of rewards from political upheaval.

Here is an essential dilemma for ethnic groups. If they are to preserve their ethnic distinctiveness and communal integrity, they may have to remain peripheral to any major political movements or accept the role of just being allies — allies who are easily dropped once the revolution has attained the political goals. If they are an integral part of the revolution, though with certain special complaints, they will add to the momentum and will gain more from the revolution's success. But they are likely to lose their ethnicity. Not all ethnic groups regret this; in a generation or two the Negroes in Cuba may disappear as an ethnic group, with no communal regrets at all. Whether this is the desire of most Latin American Indians is highly questionable.

PHASE 2: MOBILIZATION AND WARFARE

The leap from conditions sufficient for revolution to revolutionary warfare itself is a perilous one. Conditions that are perceived as depriving authority and institutions of their legitimacy must become springboards to popular, purposeful action. The dislocations that subvert the status quo may produce withdrawal instead of collective involvement; this can encourage cynicism instead of commitment to an alternative vision. These possibilities are especially likely to frustrate revolution in multi-ethnic countries divided by communal hostilities and isolation.

Organization and ideology have been most effective for bridging the gap between condition and mobilization. Organization provides the disenchanted with an alternative course of action outside the decaying legal institutions, a new way for men to relate to each other in common pursuit. It serves as a means of communication, a structure for command and division of labor. Ideology complements and reinforces organization with a set of explanations of the root causes for revolution and with clear definitions of friend and foe. Ideology also presents a blueprint for an alternative social system, a goal for which men can risk their lives in violent combat.

No revolution thus far has reproduced the neat ideological-organizational models so carefully drawn by leaders before-hand. Some upheavals — for instance, the American, Mexican, and Cuban — have been particularly vague and fluid. Even the most explicitly designed revolutions — the Vietnamese, Russian, and Chinese — have been experimental and eclectic in practice. But none has been devoid of ideology and organization for effective mass mobilization. The existence of ethnic pluralism has been a principal factor compelling revolutionary leaders to modify their formal ideological and organizational designs. Frequently these steps have been taken on an ad hoc basis without a clear notion of the long-range problems created by such deviations.

Whether tightly or loosely constructed, ideology and organization must accomplish five essential tasks in the warfare phase of revolutionary development: recruit revolutionary soldiers and cadres, channel the energies of groups and the newly politicized, justify leadership and coordinate operations, pacify the groups that reject active opposition to the government, use violence in a way that fully exploits the incumbent government's weaknesses.

Individuals easiest to recruit into a revolutionary movement are those who have the least stake in the status quo and the most poignant complaints against the current elite. Members of persecuted ethnic minorities share these conditions. Historically, they indeed have provided workers for revolutionary causes: Russian Jews prominent in the Menshevik and Bolshevik parties, Berbers in the Algerian National Liberation Front, Negroes in the American Continental Army; Meo tribesmen in the Pathet Lao guerrilla force. However, it is one thing to recruit individual revolutionaries among persecuted groups; cooptation of entire ethnic communities is something else. Persecution or minority status can motivate other Russian Jews, American Negroes, and Laotian Meos to eschew any involvement in national political movements or even to accept the overtures of the counterrevolutionary regime. Weak or peripheral ethnic communities are just as likely to suspect the motives of majority group rebels as majority group officials — and often with good cause. As we have seen already in the case of the Meos, an ethnic group with very limited political resources may be squeezed between two stronger contending forces in a revolution.

One solution is not to choose sides at all but to try to calculate the probable victor and give him at least minimal cooperation while staying out of battle. Michael Moerman, who studied and lived with the Thai-Lue, one of Thailand's lowland minorities, reported that when news came to their village of the probable invasion of Communist Meos from neighboring Laos, the Thai-Lue fell back on a traditional strategy. They told Moerman:

> About 60 years ago we were conquered by the Central Thai. We offered them candles and flowers [signs of respect and loyalty]. They became our Caw Naj [officials or rulers] and we pay them taxes. When the communists come, they may conquer the Central Thai. Then we will offer them flowers and candles and call them Caw Naj. We will pay them taxes and all will be as before. We are the common people; what happens to officials does not concern us. If there is war we must leave for a while in order to avoid vandals and stray bullets. Whatever side wins, we will return and call them our leaders.[19]

The strategy is most applicable in ordinary warfare, but when conflict takes the form of a revolution, with its high degree of political ideologization, it may prove harder for pragmatic noncombatants to preserve their autonomy with "flowers and candles." Alternatively, the realists among the revolution-

---

[19] Michael Moerman, "A Minority and Its Government: The Thai-Lue of Northern Thailand," in Peter Kunstadter, ed., *Southeast Asian Tribes, Minorities, and Nations*, vol. 1 (Princeton: Princeton University Press, 1967), p. 403. Moerman goes on to say (p. 409) that on this occasion one of the reasons the Thai-Lue villagers were so unenthusiastic about the potential invaders was that they were Meo, hill peoples "of whom lowland villagers are often fearful and contemptuous." Had they been other lowlanders, the insurgents might have been able to mobilize the minority's grievances.

Recently the Thai government has permitted remnant Nationalist Chinese soldiers — who fled the Communists in China in 1949 and now engage in the opium trade — to move into Meo regions in northern Thailand. Bangkok hoped that the Chinese troops would act as a buffer between pro-Communist Meo insurgents and lowland Thais. *Washington Post*, March 21, 1971.

ary forces will deliberately play down their ideological platforms in order to permit a marriage of convenience between
local ethnic communities and the rebels.

Other ethnic "outsiders" will decide that their best interests
lie in affiliation with the regime rather than trying to maintain a precarious neutrality or taking the risk of backing the
insurgents. Once again, however, counterrevolutionary ethnic
groups usually choose sides on the basis of communal interests
rather than ideological preference. In the American revolution, the first and second Indochinese wars, and the abortive
second Bolivian revolution of 1967, rebels found themselves
at war not only with their principal political enemies but with
their ethnic allies as well. Che Guevara's Bolivian diaries include repeated references to the guerrillas' inability to win
the confidence of the Indians, much less their cooperation.[20]
Bolivian Indians were far from securely integrated into the
established political system, but they had gained at least
enough from the revolution of 1952 to be disinterested in
Guevara's movement. Besides, the general at the head of
Bolivia's military junta spoke both Indian tongues, but Guevara's guerrilla band was filled with outsiders who could not
even communicate with the Indian peasants in their own language.[21] In the American revolution the ethnic groups backing the status quo went beyond hostility to active participation
on behalf of the English. Their choices were based on perceptions of the likely result of a colonist victory, plus their own
past relations with the English Crown.

During the revolutionary war in America the dominant English community in the colonies was represented on both
sides. But a high proportion of non-English colonists leaned to
the Tories and England. Among them were most Indian
tribes, the Dutch, French-speaking Calvinists (though not

[20] Robert Scheer, ed., *The Diary of Che Guevara* (New York: Bantam
Books, 1968). See entries for April 1967 (p. 105), May 1967 (p. 120), June
1967 (p. 134).

[21] Robert F. Lamberg, "Che in Bolivia: The 'Revolution' that Failed,"
Problems of Communism 19 (July–August 1970): 25–36. Also John
Womack, Jr., "The Bolivian Guerrilla," *New York Review of Books*
(February 11, 1971), pp. 8–12.

English-speaking Calvinists), many southern Negroes, and the Scots. As disparate as these groups were, each was relatively unassimilated into the colonial society's mainstream or had reason to fear the aggressive mobility of English colonial patriots should they win independence. It seemed better to cast one's lot with king George III, whose rule was distant, than to suffer the expansionist intrusions of neighboring American settlers. The pro-Tory minorities had accurately gauged the nature of nationalist revolutions — and without any help from political theorists. Revolutions and their supporters are inherently expansionist — not just territorially but culturally and politically — because of their grounding in abstract ideals and their escalations of popular mobilization. It is not coincidence that many Tory sympathizers were frontiersmen or Indians who foresaw a flood of new arrivals if England was defeated.

Ironically, then, the aggressive Anglo-Americanism of the rebels led non-English communities to side with the English; the Tories were by no means more English than the patriots. One historian points out; "Canadians of the St. Lawrence Valley were suspicious of the revolution, not only because they lived far outside its physical homeland, but also because they were French and Catholic, and the revolution seemed to them English and Protestant." Likewise, "the two most purely English provinces, Virginia and Massachusetts, were the strongholds of the Revolution, whereas, it was in the patchwork societies of Pennsylvania and New York that the Tories were the strongest." [22] On the other hand, few ethnic groups, English or non-English, reacted uniformly to the revolution; response depended on several factors, only one of which was ethnic identity. Ethnic groups at any time are more than merely cultural communities. Their members live in concrete circumstances, and their behavior in part will be determined by these circumstances.

The Scotch-Irish of Pennsylvania and those of the southern

[22] William H. Nelson, *The American Tory* (Boston: Beacon Press, 1964), pp. 88–89. Nelson goes on to say that the Dutch and Germans who supported the revolution were those who were most Anglicized, who had not held on to their distinctive languages and religions.

colonies took different stances toward the revolution. The northern Scotch-Irish, a group scorned by many English colonists and thus allotted lands out in the wilds of the frontier, had long been irritated by the Pennsylvania Quaker aristocracy's neglect of their interests, especially its failure to provide protection against Indian attacks. They joined the revolution hoping that it would upset the colony's proprietary regime. However, that they accepted the ideology of the revolution only in part is indicated by their opposition to Pennsylvania's abolition of slavery in 1780. By contrast, Scotch-Irish in North Carolina pledged loyalty to the Crown. Though they too were frontiersmen, they perceived their enemies to be the coastal colonists, who also happened to be the state's spokesmen for the patriot cause. Moreover, most of them were recent immigrants and feared that they would lose their British-bestowed land grants if independence was won.[23]

Although the Indians had perhaps the most to lose if English rule ended and the restraints on westward migration were lifted, even they were divided. A majority of the tribes backed the English, but two tribes within the Iroquois League — the Tuscarora and the Oneida — sided with the colonists. Meanwhile, the other Iroquois tribes — the Mohawk, Onondaga, Cayuga, and Seneca — joined the British in battle under the leadership of Joseph Brant, a Mohawk chief. Their selection of the losing side was costly and again underscores the vulnerability of minorities during revolutions. After sharing British defeat at Oriskany, New York, in 1777, Brant and his Indians were the objects of a punitive American expedition into Iroquois country. When peace finally came, the worn-out and pro-English Iroquois followed Brant into Canada, where they established new homes. The six nation Iroquois League had been divided for the first time.[24]

The British were backed by an impressively diverse set of

---

[23] Maldwyn Allen Jones, *American Immigration* (Chicago: University of Chicago Press, 1960), pp. 55–57; see Chapter 2, "Ethnic Discord and the Growth of American Nationality," pp. 39–63, for an excellent discussion of the role of various ethnic groups in the revolution.

[24] Alvin M., Josephy, Jr., *The Indian Heritage of America* (New York: Bantam Books, 1969), pp. 314–15.

sympathizers, but they never coordinated them. Like so many other counterrevolutionary regimes trying to thwart a revolution, the British lacked what the American rebels had and exploited: mass mobilization.

The French and the Americans fighting in successive revolutionary conflicts in Vietnam suffered from a similar handicap. They too have had the assistance of certain ethnic minorities, in addition to superior technology and numbers, but neither was able or willing to integrate heterogeneous supporters into a well-coordinated force. The French and the Americans were skillful in exploiting ethnic peculiarities, but they stopped short of integrated mobilization. Various mountain tribesmen, Vietnamese Cambodians, foreign allies, and Vietnamese troops all supposedly were fighting for a common counterrevolutionary cause, but there was scant integration except for coordinated command at the top. This may be adequate to cope with ordinary warfare, but it is less effective in political conflict.

The task facing the rebels is harder. It is necessary for them to win not only fair-weather allies among strategic ethnic groups but long-term political converts who later will promote societal change. Usually this is accomplished with patience, careful cultivation, and minimal emphasis on formal orthodoxy, at least at the outset. One technique used to allay communal suspicions of the rebels is to employ men of identical ethnic background as liaisons between the main revolutionary organization and the particular community. Or majority group members may have to learn minority languages and customs; they may even live among the potential recruits to inspire confidence and to learn what issues bother the community most. The introduction of radio to revolutionary warfare adds other possibilities for contact. Native language broadcasts from clandestine transmitters aided the Viet Minh, and later the Viet Cong, in establishing contacts with hill tribesmen.

Revolutionary programs also may have to be expanded to include appeals directly relevant to a given ethnic group — despite the fact that linguistic freedom or racial equality seems inconsequential to insurgent leaders themselves. For instance, though most American Indians eventually sided with England, the colonial rebels were fully aware that the Indians held strategically critical positions along the frontiers. So the Continental Congress took steps in 1775 to "secure and preserve" the friendship of the Indian nations. Some among the American revolutionaries were eager for freedom to move into the western wilderness, but the Continental Congress on July 12, 1775, resolved "that the securing and preserving the friendship of Indian nations, appears to be a subject of the utmost moment to these colonies." It then sent to the Iroquois League a message "modeled after the best Indian oratory of the period," in which the Congress asked the tribes to view the revolution as "a family quarrel between us and Old England," and thus "we desire you to remain at home, and not join on either side, but keep the hatchet buried deep." [25] The Iroquois clearly were not persuaded that neutrality finally would be rewarded by protection of their lands.

Members of the dominant ethnic group also have to be disciplined not to look down on or socially ostracize alien recruits. Many Great Russians, for example, shared anti-Semitism with their czarist adversaries and expressed contempt for the Muslim peoples of the eastern provinces. Similarly, American white patriots from southern colonies were not free from racial bigotry, their support of the Declaration of Independence notwithstanding.

Reliance on such tactics assumes that the ethnic group being cultivated is reluctant to join in radical political action because of a sense of its foreignness or vulnerability once it becomes involved. But there are instances in which ethnic communities are on the brink of political mobilizaton after generations of quiescence. In these cases the task facing insurgent leaders is not so much stimulation as direction and cooptation.

A revolutionary movement can be "underdeveloped" just as an established political system can. A critical task of devel-

[25] Quoted in Harold E. Fey and D'Arcy McNickle, *Indians and Other Americans: Two Ways of Life Meet*, rev. ed. (New York: Harper and Row, Perennial Library, 1970), p. 55.

opment for any insurgent movement is the creation of channels coterminous with streams of newly activated mobilization.
Grass-roots organization will be especially important for handling ethnic minorities because they often are village or tribally based.

If the recently radicalized community has been stimulated
by nationally defined goals and grievances, then cooptation into
the revolutionary movement is feasible. Bolivian Indians, for
example, were mobilized prior to the 1952 revolution by the
Chacao War against Paraguay (1932–1935), as well as by economic development that brought many of them out of their
ancient psychological and geographical isolation.[26] Indians
who left the peasant villages to become laborers in the mines
were already organized by the labor syndicate, while peasants
in the highlands, though less organized or politicized, nevertheless were activated by promises of land once Spanish haciendas were broken up. Their nascent activism had two
channels: first, a national labor movement; second, a national
revolutionary party, the Movimiento Nacionalista Revolucionario (MNR). However, the MNR was never an "Indian
party"; rather it was a labor party, and the Indians integrated
into its ranks were those farthest from the mines, their traditional regions. In other words, the radical organization could
most easily absorb the "de-Indianized" Indians in Bolivia.[27]
Consequently, although Indians comprised a majority of the
Bolivian population and had shown growing awareness of their
stake in political change, they in fact played only a peripheral
role in the revolution led by the MNR. The party appealed to
the Indians with promises of land, citizenship, and the vote,
but organizationally it left them on the sidelines. "By the end

[26] The Indians had a new perception of themselves as a result of fighting for the nation against Paraguay (though Bolivia lost), and non-
Indian Bolivians gained a greater understanding of Indians after joining
in common cause with them for the first time. Whites and mestizos who
had associated with Indians before 1932 found themselves dependent on
the allegedly "primitive" Indian foot soldiers. Richard Patch, "Bolivia:
U.S. Assistance in a Revolutionary Setting," Richard Adams et al., eds.,
Social Change in Latin America (New York: Vintage Books, 1960), p. 115.

[27] Robert J. Alexander, *Organized Labor in Latin America* (New York:
Free Press, 1965), pp. 121–26.

of 1957 the Indians were still playing a minor role, insofar as the leadership of the National Revolution was concerned." [28] Mobilization had begun, however, and continued despite the revolutionary elite's inability to confine it within controllable vehicles. When land redistribution was not undertaken quickly enough after 1952, Bolivian Indian peasants began forming their own peasant syndicates, expropriating land from below. With the specter of an Indian-white civil war before them, the newly installed urban authorities took belated steps toward agrarian reform in order to prevent the spread of violence.[29] In 1956 a peasant syndicate leader, Jose Rojas, was elected to the national senate. For the first time in Bolivian history the senate conducted its affairs in a native language when the speaker could not use Spanish.[30] The MNR and non-Indian radicals could hardly claim full credit; they ran behind the Indian mobilization, not ahead of it.

A principal reason for the success of the Bolivian upheaval, despite scant Indian participation, was its concentration in the metropolitan center. Revolutionary wars fought mainly in the developed part of the country can get by with minimal support from remote ethnic groups. The Russian revolution was more prolonged than the Bolivian, but it too was confined largely to the developed urban centers in the west. The Red Army could overthrow the czar without aid from Asian minorities. Whether the army could thereafter consolidate Bolshevik authority without the aid of Asian minorities was another matter, but at least the old regime was toppled. Such

[28] Ibid., p. 83.

[29] Patch, "Bolivia," p. 119. Although its "revolution" was peaceful, Chile experienced Indian land grabs after the electoral victory of Marxist president Salvadore Allende, especially in Cautin province, where traditionally oppressed Mapuche Indians are a rural majority. In other provinces non-Indian peasants also ran ahead of the radical government in seizing land. *New York Times,* January 28, 1971.

[30] Ibid., p. 129. Currently there are reports that the farms carved out of hacienda estates by land-hungry peasants are not proving capable of supporting the Indians on them and Indians in some highland areas actually have become poorer since the revolution. Businessmen in La Paz worry that radicals will seek to exploit what they see to be the growing disillusionment with the revolution among Indians. *New York Times,* January 25, 1971.

is not the case in guerrilla-type revolutionary wars. The greater the reliance of insurgents on guerrilla techniques, the more imperative it is somehow to incorporate nonurban minorities, often those groups furthest removed from the mainstream of political conflict. Bolivia's MNR did not have to rely on highland Indian support; Che Guevara did. In Malaya, the mainly Chinese Malayan Communists were badly hurt when Chinese squatters were resettled by the British and the guerrillas were left to seek aid from unfriendly Indian rubber tappers and Malay peasants who made up most of the rural population. The Algerian National Liberation Front was greatly assisted by the cooperation of the non-Arab Berbers, whose mountain homes provided refuges that French soldiers could not penetrate.

Two cardinal tenets of guerrilla warfare make ethnic group support necessary. The first is popular assistance; the second is mobility to offset the enemy's superior firepower. In other words, a guerrilla force relies on the local populace for food, shelter, and information and looks for a sanctuary beyond easy reach of the enemy, where guerrillas can retreat for rest and training. In three of the most famous cases of revolutionary guerrilla wars sanctuaries have been in territories occupied by ethnic minorities — Algerian Berbers, non-Han Chinese, and Vietnamese hill tribes. The revolutionaries' "minorities policies" were the product of strategic necessity; if they did not win the support or at least the tolerance of the remote minority communities, they faced the unhappy prospect of going back to the lowlands where the government's military assets were hardest to combat.

The Chinese Communist party and its young Red Army retreated northward in its historic Long March of 1933, after being driven out of their Kiangsi soviet by Chiang Kai-shek. They headed for the northwest, where they could recoup without Kuomintang harassment. But northwest China was populated largely by non-Han Chinese, cool toward other Chinese who had tried with contempt to dominate them for centuries. To win their trust the Chinese Communist party, led by Mao Tse-tung, offered minorities freedom to determine their own political allegiance, including the right to select total independence. Even before deserting the Kiangsi soviet in the south the party in 1931 passed a formal resolution promising the "toiling masses of these nationalities" self-determination or incorporation into the new China, whichever they wished.[31] Later Mao, operating out of the caves of Yenan in the north, publicly pledged to the people of nearby Inner Mongolia a choice of independence or inclusion:

> We are persuaded that it is only by fighting together with us that the people of Inner Mongolia can preserve the glory of the epoch of Genghis Khan, prevent the extermination of their nation, embark on the path of national revival, and obtain the freedom and independence enjoyed by peoples such as those of Turkey, Poland, the Ukraine, and the Caucasus.[32]

In other words, the approach of the Communist guerrillas was to convince strategically placed minorities that their best guarantee of future independence lay in actively supporting the revolution against the Nationalist regime of Chiang Kai-shek. As the war progressed, however, Mao stopped talking of independence and referred instead to the possibility of "autonomous states" for minorities. During the revolution — the first half of which ran parallel to China's war against Japan — the Chinese Communist party showed considerable flexibility in dealing with the northern minorities. It dealt with conservative communal leaders when convenient; it left the promise of future self-determination vague enough to permit several interpretations; it promoted the overthrow of native landlords when that was feasible. Minority group members from both north and south China joined units of the Red Army.[33] The main objective was to keep the minorities at least neutral

---

[31] Walker Conner, "Ethnology and the Peace of South Asia," *World Politics* 22, no. 1 (October 1969): 62.

[32] Quoted ibid., p. 63. The symbolism of Genghis Khan has continued to have significance for Mongolians. While the Socialist People's Republic of Mongolia (Outer Mongolia) has been wary of recognizing Genghis, the Inner Mongolian Nationalists, who are faced with Chinese pressures, have used the great conqueror to remind Mongolians of their golden age. See Chapter IV, pp. 43–7, for Chinese ideology and the treatment of contemporary Mongolian nationalism.

[33] See Edgar Snow, *Red Star over China* (New York: Grove Press, 1961), pp. 283, 347–48.

so that Communist guerrillas could move with ease in the western and northern provinces. But it was hoped that the Communists could inspire positive action by playing upon natural ethnic hostilities between the minorities and the Han Chinese, represented by Chiang's army. In the same way Mao played upon Han Chinese nationalism to mobilize political peasants against the invading Japanese. "It is therefore evident that the Chinese Communist leadership fully appreciated the close interrelation between peoples' wars and ethnic psychology, and once having adopted the strategy of gaining power by conducting such a war, they continuously ascribed the greatest importance to the exploitation of ethnic attitudes." [34] The problem would come after the revolution, when a new Communist government tried to reconcile its wartime promises to minorities with its nationalist pledges to the majority.

The most celebrated victory of guerrilla forces over a conventional modern army occurred not in China but in Vietnam. The French defeat in 1954 at Dienbienphu, a saucer-shaped plain surmounted by the highlands of North Vietnam, alerted the world to the extraordinary potentials of guerrillas. It also marked the end of France's efforts to forestall the nationalist-Communist revolution led by the Viet Minh. Although the main actors at Dienbienphu were French and lowland Vietnamese, a decisive role was played by minority hill tribesmen. They fought on both sides, but in the end it was the Viet Minh who proved more skilled in using them in political warfare. And, due to the internal pressures of French politics, this was a political victory of the first magnitude, even though it left a huge French army in the field.

The population of North Vietnam and South Vietnam is more than 85 per cent ethnic Vietnamese, but almost one-half of its combined territories is occupied by ethnic minorities who are either isolated from or unfriendly toward the majority community. It was among these minorities, especially the tribal hill peoples, that the Viet Minh had to concentrate their wartime maneuvers. To have tried to match the French in the rice paddies below would have given all the strategic advantages

---

[34] Connor, "Ethnology and the Peace of South Asia," pp. 67–68.

to the colonial army. In the hills, on the other hand, guerrillas could exploit their physical mobility and tactical ingenuity. The occupation of Dienbienphu by French paratroops in 1953, less than a year before the decisive battle took place, was essentially a futile attempt by the French army to use traditional military tactics in an untraditional war in the highlands.[35]

The Viet Minh had begun cultivating hill tribesmen in the early years of World War II, starting with the Tho peoples in the northeast. Their situation near the Red River delta and along the route between south China and Vietnam had put them into contact with lowlanders for generations. Not only were the Tho the largest of the northern hill tribes, but they were most subject to assimilationist pressures by ethnic Vietnamese. The French pursued a similar policy. Upland tribes such as the T'ai continued to enjoy considerable autonomy during the colonial period, but the Tho felt the French impact more directly. They staged a revolt against French rule in 1940, when French administrators were diverted by invading Japanese. Communists, seeing in the revolt a chance to establish links with a hill tribe, supplied the Tho with an organizational structure through which to channel their frustrations.[36] The Tho became the minority most closely integrated into the Viet Minh organization. This was a result of the Tho's assimilation into Vietnamese society, their sensitivity to political changes in the lowlands, and their location along the important China-Vietnam route. Tho guerrilla units helped the Viet Minh take over Hanoi after Japan's surrender, and the minister of defense in the first government organized by Ho Chi Minh in 1945 was a Tho named Chu Van Tan. By the end of the first Indochina war, in 1954, there were three Tho generals leading revolutionary forces, including Chu.[37]

Dienbienphu was to the west, toward Laos, outside the Tho

---

[35] For an exhaustive account of the battle of Dienbienphu, see Bernard B. Fall, *Hell in a Very Small Place* (New York: Vintage Books, 1968).

[36] John T. McAlister, "Mountain Minorities and the Viet Minh," in Kunstadter, *Southeast Asian Tribes, Minorities, and Nations,* vol. 2, pp. 792–93.

[37] Ibid., pp. 795–96.

homelands. As the war progressed, the Viet Minh had to penetrate other, less assimilated tribes, which had had French protection and had fought with the French against the Japanese.
On the eve of the northwest military campaign, Ho Chi Minh
instructed his officers about the importance of cultivating
friendly relations with the local minorities, the most important of which were the T'ai:

> The government has issued policies concerning the national
> minorities; you and the troops must implement them correctly.
> This is a measure to win over the people, frustrating the
> enemy's scheme of "using Vietnamese to harm Vietnamese."
> We must so do that each fighter becomes a propagandist. You
> must behave in such a way that the people will welcome you
> on your arrival and give you willing aid during your stay and
> miss you on your departure.[38]

What this meant in practice was exploiting internal grievances among the T'ai. For the French policy toward the upland T'ai had favored the so-called White T'ai over the Black
T'ai, generating disaffection among the latter. The Viet Minh
penetrated the Black T'ai, although they were never so fully integrated into the revolutionary movement as were the Tho.
Rather, Black T'ai formed their own units and assisted the Viet
Minh against the French and their White T'ai clients in return
for promises of autonomy. French commanders apparently were
unaware of the intracommunal factionalism they had created
among the T'ai, or perhaps they simply overlooked its significance for war in the highlands when they chose to seize and
fortify the mountain plateau known as Dienbienphu, located
in the traditional homeland of the Black T'ai.[39]

The French made one disastrous military miscalculation:
they had not counted on the Viet Minh's being able to put
heavy artillery in the surrounding hills to shoot down at
them. That aside, the ethnic configuration that crystallized at
Dienbienphu was the result of several calculations. It was not

---

[38] "Teaching at the Meeting of Officers for the Preparation of the Military Campaign in the Northwest [September 9, 1952]," in Bernard B. Fall,
ed., *Ho Chi Minh on Revolution* (New York: Signet Books, 1968), p. 228.
[39] McAlister, "Mountain Minorities and the Viet Minh," pp. 804–16.

just a case of French manipulating the White T'ai while the
Viet Minh pulled the strings on Black T'ai and Tho puppets.
Rather, the various hill tribes were making their own judgments, trying to discern where their best interests lay. The
White T'ai changed their outlook when Dienbienphu's fate
became sealed. T'ai made up the bulk of government troops
who managed to escape without being taken prisoner. Some
ten thousand men were captured, while only seventy-eight
escaped through the jungle. Of the seventy-eight, a mere nine-
teen were Europeans, while twelve of the fourteen noncom-
missioned officers and thirty-two of the forty enlisted escapees
were tribal T'ai.[40] Once France withdrew from Vietnam, the
political position of its former allies was all the more precarious. Among the several thousand tribal refugees migrating to
South Vietnam after 1954 were two thousand T'ai.[41]

As the White T'ai moved southward, the Viet Minh were
making contacts with the hill peoples native to the southern
highlands. They had less success there than in the north, in
part because the southern tribes were less developed and because of the strong ties of paternalism binding minorities to
French administrations. That is, the Viet Minh were able to
coopt tribal minorities into the revolution most easily when
they were affected negatively by French policies or when the
tribes possessed a stable set of institutions that permitted negotiation and mobilization. The Viet Minh, and later the Viet
Cong, were far more successful in cultivating southern tribes
after the French had departed and the Saigon regime of Ngo
Dinh Diem, with its American university advisers, started
pressing for centralized control in the highlands. Resentment
against Diem's policies of land transfer, lowlander settlement,
and administrative intervention gave Communist insurgents
an entree they lacked in the first Indochina war. They made
contact with the non-Communist tribal autonomy movement,
Front Unifié de Lutte de la Race Opprimée (FULRO, United
Front for the Struggle of the Oppressed Race), took tribal dis-

---

[40] Fall, *Hell in a Very Small Place*, p. 442.
[41] Bernard B. Fall, "Commentary" on Frederick Wickert's "The Tribesmen," both in Edward W. Lindholm, ed., *Vietnam: The First Five Years*
(East Lansing: Michigan State University Press, 1959), p. 193.

sidents north to be trained, then returned them to organize their own peoples and broadcast messages in tribal languages. Communist held out to southern hill tribes the example of northern minorities who had at least a semblance of self-determination in the form of the T'ai-Meo and Viet Bac[Tho] autonomous regions.[42]

Appropriately, Hanoi chose the first anniversary of its Dienbienphu victory to make a significant announcement. On May 7, 1955, Ho sent a letter to T'ai and Meo tribesmen congratulating them for their revolutionary participation but reminding them that the revolution had been fought for autonomy within a larger socialist state:

> For one year now, the Northwest area has been completely liberated. This is owing to the close unity among all nationalities and their enthusiastic participation in the Resistance War, to the valiant struggle of our army, and to the clear-sighted leadership of the Party and Government. . . . The Thai-Meo Autonomous Region is an integral part of the great family of Viet Nam, making with other brother nationalities a monolithic bloc of unity. It will always enjoy the education and leadership of the Party and Government and the assistance of other brother nationalities.[43]

PHASE 3: CONSOLIDATION

In the last years of his life, bed-ridden and unable to attend party meetings, Lenin became occupied with the problems of Russia's minorities. His revolution had succeeded only in part. After the abdication of the czar in March 1917, Lenin returned to Russia and the following November pushed aside Alexander Kerensky's liberal provisional government in favor

[42] For discussions of Diem's policies toward the hill tribes, their implications for the Viet Cong, and the later modification of Diem's approach, see Fall, "Commentary," pp. 135–40; George M. Kahin and John W. Lewis, *The United States in Vietnam*, rev. ed. (New York: Delta Books, 1969), pp. 106–07; Larry R. Jackson, "The Vietnamese Revolution and the Montagnards," *Asian Survey* 9, no. 5 (May 1969): 313–30. A critique of Diem's American-funded land reform program and its impact on the Montagnards is contained in Al McCoy, "Land Reform as Counter-Revolution," *Bulletin of Concerned Asian Scholars* 3, no. 1 (Winter–Spring 1971): 14–49.

[43] "Letter to the Compatriots in the Thai-Meo Autonomous Region [May 7, 1955]," in Fall, *Ho Chi Minh on Revolution*, pp. 260–61.

of the more radical Bolshevik regime. But the final phase of the Russian revolution remained unfinished, for a genuine revolution requires not merely the collapse of an old authority but the erection of a new system. This means a period of consolidation, and in Russian it precipitated a civil war.

Lenin's troubles with his own Communist party and with Georgians and Asian minorities are similar to problems found in most revolutions launched amidst ethnic diversity. Only after the ancient regime has fallen and the insurgent movement starts to assert its own authority do the consequences of its early strategies come to the surface. To build the broadest popular base and appease strategically placed groups, revolutionaries have made promises and have built organizational structures that later frustrate consolidation of the new system. In Phase 1 and Phase 2 insurgents promise various ethnic groups full equality or communal autonomy or both — that is, first-class citizenship with an end to autocratic imperialism. They nurture or tolerate communal organizations and assertive ethnic leadership.

What was functional during the mobilization phase becomes dysfunctional in a period of consolidation. The problem is one of political development in general, but the explanation for the gap lies in the modernizing impetus of revolutions. Typically, modernizing revolutions expand the arena of political participation. They raise expectations of equality and of a wider distribution of society's benefits while they drive for a political system that can employ science and technology for the sake of growth. If a revolution — regardless of its particular ideology — is to fulfill its modernizing potential, then it must culminate in the creation of a strong central government. Privitism, claims of autonomy, and identification with subnational cultural tradition all become suspect during consolidation, despite the hopes of autonomy and cultural freedom that inspired political activism among ethnic groups.

Resistance against the drive for political cohesion and national mobilization can come from several quarters. Those committed to individualism, along with supporters of minimal government and localized control and regionally based power groups, will oppose schemes for a strong central government with broad authority. They also will question efforts to direct citizens' identities and energies toward national objectives. Ethnic pluralism is not needed to make the job of revolutionary consolidation difficult. Yet because the demands of ethnic groups threaten the fragile unity of the new system and highlight the embarrassing inconsistencies in the revolution's program, they are especially troublesome.

The severity of tension aroused by ethnic demands during the consolidation period varies according to four factors: the extent to which any community was recruited into the revolutionary movement through separate ethnic organizations, the importance of communal and cultural goals in mobilizing members of any ethnic group, the lengths to which the national leadership went to guarantee that the communal goals would be fulfilled, and the extent of overlap between ethnic and general expectations, especially with regard to their "modern" content.

Not all members of distinct ethnic groups join revolutions for communal reasons; many are motivated by broader class causes. Such men are ideal liaisons between the mainstream movement and their respective communities. They even may be harsh critics of parochial ethnic claims in the consolidation era. Joseph Stalin, himself a Georgian, was appointed commissar of nationalities charged with resolving the conflicts between the Bolsheviks and the various nationality groups. He took account of nationalities and demands for autonomy but was eager to forge ahead with integration of the state. Stalin therefore rejected the arguments of his Georgian compatriots in favor of broad powers for non-Russian peoples. Despite Lenin's own belated misgivings, Stalin overrode Georgian nationalists inside and outside the Communist party. He himself was a member of a minority, but the revolution had made him a party member and class ideologue first and an ethnic nationalist second.[44]

44 Moshe Lewin traces the post-1917 dispute between Lenin and Stalin over how fast to centralize the Soviet state in his *Lenin's Last Struggle* (New York: Vintage Books, 1970). According to Lewin, in his final years, when Stalin was on the ascent, Lenin continuously warned the party not to "hurry" toward unification so fast that it rode roughshod over the national minorities. His views were not accepted.

The Georgians were not the only group to resist merger within a centralized state. The conditions that undermined the czar had also stirred cultural and political nationalism outside of Russia proper. After March 1917, when a moderate provisional government replaced the czar, the nationalities question became acute. By the time of the Bolsheviks' October revolution (which took place in November by the Western calendar) non-Russian mobilization had proceeded even further and had taken more politicized forms. Bolsheviks were more cognizant of these nationalist stirrings than either the provisional government or the White Russian counterrevolutionaries. For this reason, national movements did not bolster the White forces in the 1917–1921 civil war, though they did retard consolidation of power in the hands of the Bolsheviks.[45] In their efforts to bring down the provisional government the Bolsheviks had used the minorities, but in doing so they created obstacles to governing on their own later.

At the end of 1917, Russia was threatened by White counterrevolutionaries, possible intervention by European powers, and minority secession. When the czarist system was overthrown, the Romanov empire began to disintegrate. Communists did not want to be tainted with imperialism, but for several reasons they could not accept the fragmentation of the Russian empire. The non-Russian regions annexed by the czars contained natural resources valuable for the development of the Russian — or Soviet — state. If the Bolsheviks renounced the empire or even just the southern areas containing Asian peoples, Central Asia and Transcaucasia would be open to attack by Britain, placing the new nation's security in jeopardy. For generations, Russian settlers had migrated to these distant parts of the empire, and Moscow did not feel it could desert them. Marxist-Leninist theory asserted that oppressed peoples were defined by their material class status; to have acknowledged the legitimacy of minority nationalisms would have weakened the new government's ideological foundations. Perhaps we should also note that the Bolsheviks were

---

[45] "The preservation of a united Russian State was a symbol of my faith," wrote White general Denikin. Robert Conquest, *Soviet Nationalities Policies in Practice* (New York: Praeger, 1967), p. 21.

overwhelmingly Russian and that it would have been natural for them to share many of the czarists' messianic feelings about the benighted non-Russians.[46]

The Bolsheviks had to deal with minorities that were just beginning to flex their political muscle; there had been little nationalist mobilization prior to the revolution. The first organizations, such as the All-Russian Muslim Congress, were cultural in orientation, but they soon became more political and called for territorial autonomy to match cultural freedom. So Bolsheviks confronted numerous national governments and nationalist parties that could not be mollified with mere linguistic or religious guarantees. They included:

West Russia	Ukrainian Central Rada
	Byelorussian Rada
South Russia	Bessarabian Sfatul-Tseri (Regional Council)
	Crimean Kurultai (General Assembly)
	Azerbaidzhani Mussavat
	Armenian Dashnak
	Georgian Menshevik
East Russia	Autonomous Muslim Government of Turkestan [47]

No two of these organizations or the nationalist movements behind them could be handled in exactly the same way by the party leadership. Factors such as vulnerability to foreign penetration, numbers of Russian settlers, and strength of local Communist parties varied from region to region and shaped Moscow's policies. One reflection of these differences is the complexity of the ultimate federalist pattern, which includes autonomous republics and regions, union republics, and people's republics. Nevertheless, the trend following the 1917 coup was

[46] Geoffrey Wheeler, *Racial Problems in Soviet Muslim Asia*, 2d ed. (London: Oxford University Press, 1962), p. 10.

[47] Conquest, *Soviet Nationalities Policies in Practice*, p. 21. One of the most complete accounts of the various nationalist organizations and their relations with the Bolsheviks is Richard Pipes, *The Formation of the Soviet Union: Communism and Nationalism, 1917–1923* (Cambridge, Mass.: Harvard University Press, 1964).

unmistakable. While Russian Communists softened their hostility toward a federal solution, they moved steadily in the direction of political centralization. They made treaties and agreements with minorities, assuring them of autonomy, while overlaying the federation with a centralized party structure invested with primary decision-making authority. There was also, of course, the presence of the Red Army, which spread east and west after 1917 and represented not only Communist but Great Russian hegemony.[48] The weakness and fragmentation of the nascent nationalist movements, however, were also to blame for their short lives. In the Asian regions, for instance, the czarist system had not produced a native civil service, and literacy was confined to a small elite. Both conditions made it almost impossible to establish durable government, even given the opportunity afforded by the revolution. Foreign support in these areas was nonexistent or fleeting. Furthermore, minority regions were far from being internally homogeneous, and nationalist movements were plagued by incoherence. The presence of Russian settlers, who were among the most urban and educated inhabitants, intensified the fragmentation. In Turkestan, for instance, their presence was decisive, for by the end of 1919 Turkestan was under the control of Russian colonists.[49]

In Russia the period of consolidation lasted seven years. Not until 1923 was the Union of Soviet Socialist Republics established. During this time the Bolsheviks by trial and error devised a formula for undercutting federalism while simultaneously sanctioning it. The formal distinctions between autonomous regions and republics, union republics, and the people's republics were artificial. Richard Pipes concludes that "the centralization in all those areas occurred simultaneously

[48] At the end of the civil war in 1924, the Red army was reorganized to permit more participation by minorities. The Ukrainians, Byelorussians, and Transcaucasians — peoples subject to military service under the czars — were the first to be recruited into the new nationality divisions and regiments. Less progress was made with the other nationalities. On the eve of World War II the nationality units were disbanded on the grounds that they contradicted proletarian values articulated in the more centralizing "Stalin constitution" of 1936. Conquest, *Soviet Nationalities Policies in Practice*, pp. 52–53.

[49] Wheeler, *Racial Problems in Soviet Muslim Asia*, p. 14.

and, even before the formal establishment of the USSR, they were (with the exception of the People's Republics) reduced to a status which was, for all practical purposes, identical." [50]

Nevertheless, consolidation was not smooth. Disputes between Russians and non-Russians and between Communists and non-Communists were bitter. Especially disillusioned were minority nationalists who had either joined the Communist party or assisted in the overthrow of the czar in the belief that revolution would further their nationality's pursuit of independence. Even with centralization, the official doctrine remained ambiguous, for the right of autonomy was still acknowledged in theory. The ambiguity of the Communist revolutionaries derived from two misconceptions. First they ignored nationalist claims within the Russian empire for too long, putting off serious consideration until late in the revolutionary war. Perhaps they did not realize the extent to which White Russian chauvinism, not the appeal of Marxism, had driven nationalists into the arms of the Bolsheviks. Later, when they did focus on minority aspirations, they assumed that those claims were essentially cultural; language and religion were thought to be the Ukrainians' and the Kazakhs' chief concern. In fact, however, the revolution itself had helped to politicize minority nationalism to the point that cultural tokenism was not enough. Had minority politicization started earlier, had the revolutionary war been more widespread and less confined to cosmopolitan western Russia, and had the White counterrevolutionaries been less parochial, the Bolsheviks might have needed much longer than seven years to complete the consolidation phase of their revolution.

Where ethnic groups are just as diverse as in Russia but more integrated into the revolutionary war itself and not mobilized by explicitly communal appeals, the four determining factors operate rather differently. Postwar consolidation proved

[50] Pipes, *The Formation of the Soviet Union*, pp. 246–47. The people's republics were exceptional, for they enjoyed at least a brief period of self-rule. There were three in 1922: Bukhara, Khorezm (Khiva), and the Far East. But as soon as the Red army entered Vladivostok on the heels of the evacuating Japanese, the Far Eastern People's Republic was abolished. In Bukhara and Khorezm the Communists steadily increased their power. In 1924 the two remaining people's republics were abolished and replaced by five new republics.

easier in the American colonies, for instance, than in Russia. In America the revolution did not degenerate into civil war — at least not immediately. It was first an anti-colonial war, and thus the nationalist intent was visible almost from the start. There were fewer grounds for disillusionment than in Russia, where Marxism and Great Russian chauvinism were often hard to disentangle. Various American colonies, it is true, did not expect the revolution to breed so strong a central government as was ultimately created in 1789; still the notion of a united America was central to the revolution by 1776.[51] The anti-foreign animus cementing the Chinese, Yugoslav, and Vietnamese revolutions served a similar function, though revolutionaries in all three instances did make promises to autonomy-seeking ethnic groups.[52] But in the American revolution the ethnic groups least assimilated were precisely those that stayed neutral or supported the British — for example, Indians, Scots, French-speaking Calvinists. American revolutionaries did little to disguise the nationalist orientation of their cause, and this prompted communities most anxious to maintain their distinctiveness to resist the revolution.

The basic document of the American Revolution was the Declaration of Independence. In it all men were defined as equal, but one glaring exception emerged to unsettle consolidation efforts after Yorktown. This was the status of the Negro. The Declaration did not take into account the thousands of Negro colonists who were held in slavery, and most slave-owners who fought on the side of the revolution had no intention of sacrificing their slave property. Much as Chinese and Russian revolutionaries committed to Marxist egalitarianism

[51] The growth of community and identity as "Americans" was slow. Not until the late 1760's was there a society in the Atlantic colonies that one could accurately refer to as "American." Richard Merritt traces the evolution of this identity through analysis of patterns and content of communications in the colonies in *Symbols of American Community, 1735–1775* (New Haven: Yale University Press, 1966).

[52] China's Communist revolution slipped into civil war most clearly after the party seized the central government and drove out the Nationalists. In 1950 the Communist Red army invaded Tibet, whose government continued to insist on Tibetan independence. Not for another six years was Tibet subdued and declared an autonomous region within the People's Republic of China. See Tsepon W. D. Shakabpa, *Tibet: A Political History* (New Haven: Yale University Press, 1967), pp. 299–317.

could not conceive of dismembering Imperial China or Russia, certain American insurgents overlooked the blatant contradiction within their cause. The articles of capitulation signed after the battle of Yorktown in 1781 declared that any American property held by British troops was subject to recovery. Though silent concerning slaves, American Virginians were especially anxious that British ships should not sail with stolen slave cargo. General Washington himself issued orders to assure its return.[53] Many blacks stayed with the British, some as slaves, others as free men. But in America the promise of the revolution stopped short of the Negro.

Negroes were included — or at least not explicitly excluded — within the formal pledge of the revolution. It did accelerate scattered movements in the colonies to abolish slavery. Pennsylvania was the first to do away with slavery, in 1778; Massachusetts followed in 1781, the year of Yorktown. Negroes were active participants in the revolution, not simply symbols of a cause. Some slaves sought freedom by enlisting in military service. In the north reluctance to recruit Negroes into the Continental Army and state militias declined as the conflict progressed, especially as obtaining sufficient white soldiers became difficult. The practice of substitution was common, and many Negroes took the place of white draftees. New England state governments took the lead in enlisting black manpower to fill their military quotas. In the south only Maryland authorized slave enlistments. Southern colonies feared the consequences of arming and training Negroes.[54] The southern states did feel pressed enough for recruits to enlist free Negroes; yet the rationale was often questionable in light of the war's professed principles. Governor Thomas Nelson of Virginia wrote to Washington in 1777 that, though he agreed with Negro recruitment, he did not concur with the widespread idea that "they could best be spared." He said, "After they have risked their lives and perhaps may have contributed to save America," it would be unjust if they were not "entitled

53 Benjamin Quarles, *The Negro in the American Revolution* (Chapel Hill: University of North Carolina Press, 1961), pp. 158–59.
54 Ibid., pp. 53–56.

to the privileges of Freemen." [55] This, of course, was before the invention of the cotton gin made a slave economy seem indispensable to southerners.

In the north the revolution precipitated the abolition of slavery, but abolition was not established as a nationwide policy — and never was until the American Civil War. Consolidation focused instead on the unification of white Americans. The task took almost a decade and stimulated tense conflict. But Negroes were left out of the consolidation *for the sake of consolidation.* In other words, only by overlooking the most profound discrepancy between principle and practice did pragmatic American politicians believe they could assure political unity among thirteen jealous states.

In 1792, Benjamin Banneker, a Negro mathematician and almanac compiler, wrote to secretary of state Thomas Jefferson, reminding him of the revolution's incompleteness and the high price of post-revolution consolidation:

> Sir, suffer me to recall to your mind that time, in which the arms and tyranny of the British Crown were exerted, with every powerful effort, in order to reduce you to a state of servitude. . . . Here was a time in which your tender feelings for yourselves had engaged you thus to declare, you were then impressed with proper ideas of the great violation of liberty, and the free possession of those blessings, to which you were entitled by nature; but, sir, how pitiable is it to reflect, that although you were so fully convinced of the benevolence of the Father of Mankind, and of his equal and impartial distribution of these rights and privileges . . . that you should at the same time counteract his mercies, in detaining by fraud and violence so numerous a part of my brethren, under groaning captivity and cruel oppression.[56]

PERSPECTIVES OF ETHNICITY AND REVOLUTION

The radical character of revolution makes it unlikely that any group can escape its impact. Yet ethnic pluralism per se is

---

[55] Thomas Nelson, Jr., to George Washington, November 21, 1777, quoted ibid., p. 74.

[56] "Letter from Benjamin Banneker to the Secretary of State, 1792," in Milton Meltzer, ed., *In Their Own Words: A History of the American Negro, 1619–1865* (New York: Crowell, Apollo Editions, 1968), pp. 14–15.

neither a promoter of revolution nor a hedge against it. It can lead a revolution along paths that will define problems of national development for generations afterward.

When revolution parallels the disaffection of a major ethnic community, mobilization will be particularly intense and consolidation least hazardous. In such cases nationalism and radicalism nourish one another. Development becomes less a matter of integration than of promoting social and economic growth. However, when ethnic groups are mobilized outside the revolution or autonomously within, development hurdles can be formidable. The viability of the polity is jeopardized, not just its growth. If ethnic groups are significant in numbers as well as in the social roles they play, then revolutionary movements may have to elevate communal claims to the status of a central concern or else risk defeat.

No revolution ever has managed to obliterate preexistent ethnic identities. At most, it redefines them and accelerates assimilation processes begun before the old system decayed. Revolution had this effect in both Mexico and Cuba and among the Tho in North Vietnam. But it has been more common for revolutions — unintentionally — to *accentuate* collective ethnic identities and politicize communal aspirations. Revolutions, in other words, do foster mobilization and politicization. But neither of these guarantees national cohesiveness; each could widen gaps between culturally distinct groups. For newly installed authorities, the latent effects of revolution create unexpected problems — questions not taken care of earlier by plans or orthodoxy. For the outside observer, ethnic factors expose dimensions of the revolutionary process otherwise obscured. First, the perspective of ethnicity reveals revolutions to be more ad hoc than often presumed. Too many accounts of modern radical movements are set down after the struggle; a revolution often appears more like a programed scenario than in fact it was. In reality, for example, Che Guevara's Bolivian diary may shed more light on the character of revolution than do his careful *post facto* writings on Cuba's guerrilla war. Ethnic group cooptation or pacification is precisely the sort of critical matter revolutionary strategists neglect until they confront it head-on; then they resort to improvisation. Improvisational agility may be at least as important for radical leaders as theoretical acumen.

In addition, the ethnic vantage point clarifies the relationship between revolutionary wars and civil wars. Warfare launched in the name of system transformation may end under the banner of state unification. The likelihood of civil war depends on the intensity of ethnic or regional separatism, the extent to which revolutionary mobilization supersedes it, and on the ability of counterrevolutionary forces to create alliances with ethnic dissidents. If a nation is vulnerable to foreign intervention at the time of internal upheaval, the revolutionaries will be inclined to brush aside promises of autonomy or equality, even if they risk civil war.

Closely related is the importance of the constructive phase of revolution. System change demands creation of a vacuum and then the filling of that vacuum with alternative values, institutions, goals, and relationships. The relevance of ethnic conditions may not come to light until the third phase. If the consolidation period is considered an integral part of revolution, few revolutions are overnight phenomena. They drag on for perhaps a decade after the demise of the old regime, during which time ethnic conflict intrudes into all sorts of difficulties.

Finally, analysis of ethnic groups highlights the fact that how revolutions are fought can shape their ultimate consequences. Choices made for the sake of tactical expediency in the heat of battle can haunt insurgents long after they have attained power. Warfare, while accomplishing the ouster of a government, can create new problems for developers. The kinds of appeals made to strategically located ethnic minorities and how closely they are integrated into regular revolutionary organizations will have long-range political repercussions. Though offers of autonomy may seem consistent with radical objectives during wartime, they can become totally unacceptable when thoughts turn to growth and modernization. But promises are not easily forgotten, and the political slate is not simply wiped clean when guns are traded for slide rules. The means of reconciling wartime ethnic pledges with peacetime necessities is usually ambivalence — that is, formal decentralization combined with uneasily practical centralization. Thus revolutions, remarkable for their starkness and militancy, have on many occasions concluded on a note of deliberate vagueness.

If the result of revolution is a reordering of social roles and a redistribution of political power, then history has witnessed even fewer genuine revolutions than we suggested at the beginning of this chapter. Most of those listed actually achieved fundamental transformation only within the dominant ethnic community; weaker ethnic groups remained ill equipped to shape their own destinies. If we judge revolutions not just according to their impact on the dominant group, but on *all* communities, then most revolutions in multi-ethnic societies have fallen far short of their ideals.

CHAPTER X

Conclusion: Beyond Modernity?

DEVELOPMENT THEORY postulates a peculiar image of human nature, usually only tacitly expressed. Basically, development theorists presume that men are highly malleable, not like puppets but insofar as they can willfully alter their values, allegiances, and even self-identities. When this potential is untapped, as often is the case, a society is destined for perpetual underdevelopment. National leaders must fashion institutions and policies that can exploit this human potential, thereby prompting individual citizens to redefine their roles, aspirations, and associations. This is a "positive" portrayal of human nature: men are seen as more than pawns in an impersonal universe; they are deemed capable of acting in ways — through reason, science, organization — that transform nature and adjust societies to meet new conditions.

It is a nuisance, even a danger, when certain human circumstances stubbornly persist despite their "dysfunction" to modern life and mobile man. Religion, superstition, fatalism, familialism, nostalgia, passion -- all are obstacles that development theorists must analyze so that public officials can reduce their negative influence. Ethnic loyalties fall into a similar category. They, like religion and passion, can be useful in the short run, but eventually they curb progress and blind individuals to their true capacities. Like a midwife, an ethnic group may assist at birth but should be ready to depart soon afterward. Groups founded on ethnic allegiance compete with the nation-state. Such competition is intolerable because the nation-state is the principal vehicle for development. According to development theorists, ethnic groups are not acceptable if they siphon off emotions and energies crucial for national planners.

Political development, even in periods of expanding social mobilization, does not lead inevitably to centralized authority or to the unitary state. It is true that development in the modern era does put a premium on coordination, planning, and maximization of scarce resources. But structural fragmentation and decentralization are not the stigmas of underdevelopment. In a multi-ethnic nation political efficacy should be measured not by degrees of centralization but by the *appropriateness* of any structural formula to the quality of the given ethnic diversity (numerical balance, territorial concentration, developmental disparities) and the nonethnic demands upon the political system. Each of these conditions is subject to change. Ethnic communities migrate, scatter, recluster, disintegrate, propagate — sometimes without a conscious plan but at other times according to deliberate calculation. Nonethnic demands in the form of requisites for economic well-being, citizen expectations, and external threats are equally fluid and will alter politicians' judgments of the jurisdictional patterns that are most functional.

An essential element in the elusive concept of development is preparedness. A political system must be equipped with antennas sensitive to change, not just changes in immediate popular desires but in fundamental relationships. As the quality of ethnic pluralism is transformed and nonethnic situations need change, political leaders must be ready to consider the impact of transformation and willing to design new political patterns if existing ones prove inadequate. Reevaluation is most troublesome when the existing jurisdictional pattern is integrally tied to the legitimizing ideology — for example, the way federalism is linked to democracy in America and centralism is linked to party authority in most Communist countries. In these instances, political engineers need the assistance of the political philosopher or ideologue; mechani-

cal tinkering alone without changes of mind will provide a
shaky foundation for genuine development. Reassessing patterns of communication and authority is also difficult when
the established structure supports the dominance of one ethnic group over others. Once again, development calls for more
than engineering skill. Groups will have to confront hard
choices, usually between continued growth and international
competitiveness on the one hand and redistribution of society's rewards on the other.

We usually talk about nation-building in terms of values,
identities, and associations. In a swing away from traditional
political analysis with its focus on formal institutions, legal
relationships, and explicit political acts, we now devote most
of our attention to analyzing implicit dimensions of politics
and nonpolitical variables. The swing in this direction was
necessary and fruitful, but there is a danger that observers
will underestimate the amount of self-conscious calculation
that goes into creating and maintaining a nation-state,
especially when it shelters numerous ethnic communities. Revisionists within the social sciences are doing us a favor when
they remind us that nations are not natural, that they are
artificial collectivities often sustained by oppression or manipulation. Nowhere is this more evident than in multi-ethnic nations currently experiencing the strains of transition.[1]

American social scientists generally have assumed that, with
modernization, ethnic groups will fade away of their own accord. In fact, the prominence of ethnicity in public affairs has
been a popular measure of modernity in comparisons of cities
or states. Chicago and New York City appear, at least in this
respect, less modern than the allegedly deethnicized cities of
Dallas and Los Angeles — though actually urban southern
California is becoming more "ethnic" because of the rising

[1] Elliott Currie argued for a new appreciation of the role of repression
in the maintenance of political systems: "The concept of repression directs
attention to all of the ways in which societies are maintained or imposed
instead of permitting us to take for granted a condition of stasis, of normal
social function. It alerts us to the active measures through which given
arrangements are forcibly created, extended or secured against the possibility (or probability) of change." Elliott Currie, "Repressive Violence,"
Trans-action 8, no. 4 (February 1971): 14.

numbers and political confidence of blacks and Mexican Americans. Still, the overall assumption stands: while they might be necessary cushions during periods of transition, ultimately ethnic groups lose meaning and utility for their educated, urbanized, industrialized members.[2] In this belief the current social science establishment and revisionists concur, though for quite different reasons. The mainstream pluralists acknowledge that ethnicity is a basis for group asociation, but they see its political salience fading rapidly in any country that fosters democratic — that is, individualistic — participation together with wide distribution of the fruits of modern development. In analyses of the United States and other nations, ethnic attachments are judged "primordial," an attribute of "traditional" society, in which men's horizons are narrowly circumscribed and opportunities unnaturally curtailed. If the national elite would conscientiously cultivate popular civic involvement and rationally plan for economic growth, ethnicity soon would be no more worrisome than it is among the assimilated third-generation immigrants in America. The current, perceptive critiques of the social science establishment, oddly enough, do not depart radically from this older view.

The revisionists' principal disagreement is with the assertion that a steady dilution of parochial attachments has occurred in the United States.[3] Instead they see a persistent gap between the considerable power and benefits enjoyed by the Anglo-Saxon or white majority and what is possessed by less-

[2] A study of voter turnouts in American cities revealed that between 1940 and 1950 a high proportion of recent European immigrants increased turnouts, but by 1960 the proportion of immigrants in a city's population had little effect on turnout. Daniel N. Gordon, "Immigrants and Municipal Voting Turnout: Implications for the Changing Ethnic Impact on Urban Politics," *American Sociological Review* 35, no. 4 (August 1970): 676. Gordon goes on to note (pp. 678–79), however, that where cities switched from partisan to nonpartisan elections ethnic motivation also declined. Party competition helps sustain ethnic interest in elections. Many newer cities such as Los Angeles have nonpartisan elections.

[3] Essays representing a variety of revisionist perspectives are in Philip Green and Sanford Levinson, eds., *Power and Community* (New York: Vintage Books, 1970); Marvin Surkin and Alan Wolfe, eds., *An End to Political Science* (New York: Basic Books, 1970); William E. Connolly, ed., *The Bias of Pluralism* (New York: Atherton Press, 1969).

fortunate groups, especially the non-European minorities. That is, the quality of life common to blacks, Chicanos, Puerto Ricans, Indians, and sometimes non-English European immigrants reveals the falsehood of pluralist melting-pot portrayals. The continuing exclusion or deprivation these groups suffer has been glossed over by optimistic historians and social scientists in their eager search for continuities and consensus in the American experience. The story of the annexation of Hawaii and what it meant for native Hawaiians gets lost; the Turner thesis about the democratizing influence of the frontier overshadows the treatment of Indians; the patriotic fervor of the American revolution hides the ethnic character of the loyalists; the dynamism of the industrial age masks the stability of many European-derived neighborhoods.[4] The second target of contemporary critics is the notion that in the United States national integration "just happened" or was brought about by essentially benign, though hard-headed, policy decisions. Revisionists are less likely to concentrate on socialization and canal-building as the American way to nationhood and more inclined to look at coercion and oppression used in the name of national unification. The Indian reservation, the slave-holding plantation, and the Japanese relocation camp all take on new significance in revisionist explanations of American political integration. Nevertheless, the presumption remains: ethnicity's continuing prevalence is proof of underdevelopment.

If American modernization and democracy were as widely distributed as so many social scientists assume (especially when they use the United States as an index of *other* countries' progress), then ethnicity would not continue to intrude upon political decisions or to separate citizens from one another. Consequently, when ethnicity is declared an enduring fact of American life, the "underdeveloped" sectors of society — the lower middle class and the poor — are cited. To be ethnic is to be deprived in some way of mobility and power. In this sense

[4] Historical reexamination of the role and treatment of ethnic groups is contained in Paul Jacobs and Saul Landau, eds., *To Serve the Devil*, vols. 1 and 2 (New York: Vintage Books, 1971).

there seem to be two sorts of underdeveloped ethnic stratum whose presence testifies to the incomplete modernization of the United States. The first is composed of groups most clearly subject to discrimination, largely on the basis of race (though race is often defined quite broadly): blacks, Mexican Americans, Indians, Japanese, Chinese, and Puerto Ricans. These groups have been involuntarily "ethnicized" by outsiders and thus excluded from society's benefits. Only recently have they begun to take this negative situation and transform it into a powerful weapon for positive action. Blacks, Chicanos (the politicized term by which Mexican Americans now identify themselves), and others are declaring that ethnicity is "beautiful," not just aesthetically but politically. Ethnic solidarity provides a foundation for mobilization, the goal of which is destruction of barriers limiting social mobility. The second underdeveloped ethnic stratum includes lower-class white, European-derived ethnic communities: Poles, Italians, Jews, and scores of others.[5] In their cases, ethnicity seems less a product of external imposition than a result of communal desire. If Boston's Irish families become angry about an urban renewal project that will raze their neighborhood and scatter them among outlying suburbs, they are displaying their unwillingness to accept the inevitabilities of modernization. Urban renewal is a good example of how underdevelopment and ethnicity relate differently to nonwhite and white "ethnics" in the United States: slum clearance and freeway construction are said to produce forced concentration among blacks and Puerto Ricans; they are presumed to break up the closely interwoven neighborhoods of Irish and Italians.

For mainstream as well as for dissident social scientists ethnicity represents unfinished business for political modernizers:

5 The Catholic Church, which includes many of these groups, has led the way in reviving interest in the white ethnic. But it too has made "lower middle class" and "ethnic" almost synonymous. For example, see a paper by the church's leading exponent of ethnic mobilization, Geno C. Baroni, "Report of Community Development Task Force" (Conference on Urban Ethnic Community Development, Washington, D.C., June 15–19, 1970). Also Andrew M. Greeley, "White Against White: Enduring Ethnic Conflict," in Louis Kapp Howe, ed., *The White Majority* (New York: Vintage Books, 1970), pp. 111–18.

if modernizers do their job well, ethnicity should lose its salience. Mainstream and revisionist writers disagree not about the relationship of modernization to ethnic survival; they both imagine them, in the long run, to be inversely related. Rather, their disagreement is over how far the United States in particular has progressed toward achieving popular participation and equal opportunity, the hallmarks of modernity. Those who hold up this nation as an example of completed modernization perceive ethnic groups as vestiges of the past; when ethnic loyalty does arouse emotion, the stimulus must be artificial. On the other hand, social scientists who reason that the United States is far from being a model of modern development consider ethnic mobilization convincing evidence of the gap between ideal and reality. Thus, by taking black or Chicano militancy seriously, a student of political development might accurately pinpoint the status of the United States on the scale of modernity. The fundamental analytical question, however, is: if Americans and their government do wake up to the fact of incomplete modernization and do work toward its achievement, then will ethnic groups finally disappear? Researchers on both sides of the academic barricades seem to answer "yes."

The United States, of course, is not alone among allegedly modern countries puzzled by the outbreak of ethnic militancy. Canada, the Soviet Union, Belgium, Great Britain, and Switzerland are experiencing ethnic mobilization while struggling with *post-modern* problems such as leisure, pollution, and suburbanization. There are at least two ways to explain this phenomenon. We may have overestimated the extent of modernization in these advanced nations; perhaps they are not as far ahead of others as we thought. Or they may be developed as a whole but still contain pockets of traditionalism that social scientists, in their fascination with nation-level analysis, have overlooked.

In either case, the basic premise regarding the inverse relationship between development and ethnic allegiance still holds. All we have to do is readjust our time schedule a bit. In the future, though not so soon as we predicted, development will permeate all sectors of Britain and Canada, and then ethnicity will slip into the wings, where we mistakenly presumed it to be already. Naturally, the salience of ethnic politics in places like Africa and Asia is to be expected. Tribal clashes in Nigeria or communal riots in Malaysia do not upset our established notions about development; we were fully aware that these countries were still casting off the shackles of traditionalism. Ethnic salience in advanced societies subverts traditional development theory.

There is a third way to explain the surprising vitality of ethnicity in advanced countries. It is conceivable that development and ethnicity are not inversely related. They may not be related at all. Underlying this alternative proposition is a modified view of man and society — as well as modified notions of development and ethnic identity. This view perceives the adaptability of individuals to be limited not to the extent that people are irrational or "slaves of nature" but at least to the extent that they have needs that cannot be sloughed off like passing fashions. Among these needs — which are no more mystical than environmental needs in ecological theory — is a basis of social relationship more enduring and less instrumental than occupation, status, and legal right. Ethnic groups may be one kind of collectivity that fills this need, and thus ethnicity survives long after its traditional functions have been taken over by more impersonal, secular groups.

If development does not mean the inevitable demise of ethnic attachment, perhaps the reason is that ethnicity is qualitatively different from what we believed it to be. It appears to be more adaptive and resilient and less tradition-bound than many social scientists have suggested. For instance, Chinese in Malaysia who have never set foot in China, speak little Chinese, and are at home in cosmopolitan cities, still may evaluate the policies of the Malaysian government from the point of view of Chinese communal interests and be dismayed over the gradual suppression of Chinese schools. Or consider the prominent ethnic communities in New York City. Nathan Glazer and Daniel Moynihan found, upon reexamining their study of the New York "melting pot," that numerous ethnic groups displayed remarkable adaptive capacities. Generational distance from the mother country did not necessarily diminish the meaningfulness of ethnic identity. Glazer and Moynihan describe four conditions shaping the survival of white ethnic groups in New York: the declining merit of certain occupational identifications that used to give individuals a sense of personal pride and identity; greater concern with domestic affairs than with foreign affairs; disillusionment with the Catholic Church because of its liberalization; a resurgence of racism, which has intensified feelings of insider and outsider among New Yorkers.[6] Ethnic groups are not surviving by holding tightly to old modes of behavior or tradition-encrusted forms. At first glance, in both Malaysia and the United States, ethnic communities seem to shrug off much of what we have considered ethnicity: language (though it may remain symbolically important), ties with the mother country, old styles of living, formal religion. Ethnicity may be a much *sparer* phenomenon than we believed — cultural and associational, yes, but not rigidly so.

A look at the Indian youths who occupied Alcatraz or the French Canadians who support the FLQ inclines us toward a similar reevaluation of the minimal requirements for ethnic identity.[7] In other words, even though modern development brings with it tradition-rending changes such as the rational division of labor and secularization, ethnicity per se may be equipped to adapt to the new conditions. Whether any particular ethnic group can manage to survive is another matter. Survival will depend on the attributes of the culture and group setting. To suggest that ethnicity and modernity are not

[6] Nathan Glazer and Daniel P. Moynihan, *Beyond the Melting Pot*, 2d ed. (Cambridge, Mass.: M.I.T. Press, 1970), pp. xxxiv–xxxvii.

[7] American Jews and Italians may offer two of the clearest examples of just how spare ethnicity can be. There is a growing movement among young Jews to find a Jewishness that relies on neither the synagogue nor Zionism. I saw a notice on a bulletin board in Washington not long ago inviting Jews to come to a meeting to discuss "the search for a Jewish counter-culture." In the Italian community the Italian Defense League, organized in 1967, has provoked considerable controversy, but its style and goals are not coated in tradition. The league has taken on Paramount Pictures for its production of a purportedly anti-Italian film, *The Godfather*, and has picketed F.B.I. offices in protest over the bureau's discrimination against Italians in anti-crime campaigns. *New York Times*, March 20 and 23, 1971; April 4, 1971.

antithetical is not to say that each and every ethnic group will survive. However, some aspects of modernity may sustain ethnic communalism. For example, certain labor unions in England, the United States, Guyana, and elsewhere bolster ethnic loyalties. Suburbs do not always dilute ethnicity but frequently reassemble members of ethnic groups in new residential patterns. Radio stations can permit wider and faster intragroup communication than the community grocer ever did. Democratic elections create new rewards for ethnic solidarity. Universal literacy stimulates new interest in communally oriented literature, magazines, and newspapers. Cable television is likely to multiply the number of channels available and encourage ethnic programing similar to that now on radio. Nationalist ideology provides a means for politicizing what was formerly only a cultural affiliation. The modern positive state, with its penetration into citizens' private lives — family, education, morality, housing — generates new interest in cultural issues and thus culturally defined groups.

The proposition that ethnicity and development are not inversely related requires a redefinition of ethnic identity. It also calls for a redefinition of development. Specifically, it implies that development, modernization, and nation-building are analytically and empirically separable. In the preceding chapters we have described instances in which national regimes lost the ability to meet citizens' expectations because of accelerated development at the subnational level. The political development of an ethnic group often has proceeded at such a pace that national stability has been undermined. In these cases we are witnessing political development, but it is not strictly national. The nation-state is a relatively new polity. Contemporary political scientists may have confined their studies of development to the national unit to such an extent that they mistakenly equate political development with nation-building and thereby overlook political development occurring on other levels.

Two trends are going on simultaneously, each modifying the utility of using the nation as the chief reference point for all political investigation. First is the movement toward supranational bodies, which, though they have national inputs, are systems of behavior larger than nation-states. When Europe's farmers marched on Brussels in March 1971 to protest the farm pricing policy of the Common Market, we witnessed a political event that defied simple national analysis. Likewise the proliferation of multi-national corporations challenges our conventional modes of investigation. Robert Heilbroner is among those trying to evaluate the impact of "multi-nationals" on development. He concludes that they might easily widen rather than bridge the gap between the world's rich and poor.[8]

Perhaps the emergence of supranational systems has been responsible for our neglect of the second trend, the political mobilization of subnational communities. Because international organizations usually possess commercial influence plus at least the trappings of power and because they appear to offer an alternative to destructive conflict among jealous nations, they are given considerable attention by political scientists. Subnational groups, on the other hand, often represent the powerless; they seem to generate impractical economic programs and to multiply the violence that already plagues most of the globe. Thus subnational movements are relegated to the status of problems — that is, problems for national elites — and frequently are considered so pathological that they are handed over to pyschologists and sociologists for investigation, while political scientists devote themselves to wielders of power at the center. But subnational mobilization — whether urban, regional, or ethnic — is so prevalent that it justifies direct study by political scientists. It may be a harbinger of a new form of political community, one more open to extrapolity relationships and more tolerant of localized power. Jean-Jacques Servan-Schreiber led a campaign against the Gaullists in a recent French municipal election under the slogan "Region and Europe." Servan-Schreiber is not a nostalgic or parochial politician. He argued that rebellious French in Canada and Basques in Spain were bearers of a message that had import for all people concerned with future political development. Their message is that the nation-state is reliant on wars and depen-

8 Robert L. Heilbroner, "The Multi-national Corporation and the Nation-State," *New York Review of Books* (February 11, 1971), p. 24.

dent industries; as wars are limited and industry gains autonomy, the nation-state will atrophy and new forms of polity will
have to be created. Servan-Schreiber emphasized his conten-
tions by flying two flags over his party's meeting hall — the
flags of Lorraine and Europe, but no French Tricolor.[9]

Change prompted by ethnic militancy could take either of
two directions — toward greater national cohesiveness, based
on more equal distributions of power; toward a devolution of
power to appease groups that cannot be absorbed by national
institutions. If ethnic groups are as immune to the assimilationist tendencies of modernization as we have suggested and
if they are capable of significant political development, the
latter course may become most probable. Devolution of power
can take several forms. It can lead to decentralization, various
types of which are being tried in the People's Republic of
China, Italy, the United States, Britain, and elsewhere. Or it
could produce autonomy for smaller political units. The
difficulties of translating paper autonomy into effective autonomy are evident in the cases of Rumania's Hungarians, North
Vietnam's T'ai tribesmen, and the Zulu in South Africa.
Americans who are attracted by the concept of community
control are sensitive to these difficulties and make a careful distinction between decentralization — where authority remains
vested in the center while functions are sent downward — and
autonomy — in which authority as well as functions devolve
upon the local community. Italians, Puerto Ricans, Chicanos,
and blacks have been among the American ethnic groups
speaking out in favor of community control.[10]

American Indians propose a form of devolution that would
even more radically alter the character of the nation-state and
the meaning of citizenship. Vine Deloria, a Standing Rock
Sioux and a chief critic of federal and state policies regarding
the Indian, has proposed that the United States Constitution
be rewritten so that groups, not individuals, are recognized
as the critical members of the nation. Instead of pressing for

9 James K. Glassman, "Reports and Comment: France," *Atlantic* (February 1971), pp. 6–14.
10 Alan A. Altshuler, *Community Control* (New York: Pegasus, 1970).

reforms to accelerate modernization and thus make ethnic groups obsolete, Deloria starts from the premise that ethnic groups are functional and enduring and that only a covenant acknowledging this can provide a firm foundation for a polity. Groups would relate to the larger political entity by treaty, but treaties having surer safeguards than those once foisted upon Indian tribes by dishonest white men:

> The contemporary interpretation of "we the people" in reality means "we the peoples," we definable groups, and thus admits minority groups into Constitutional protection which they should have received as groups a century ago. . . . To continue merely on the basis of an abstract individual contracting with other individuals would be to court disaster.[11]

Cases made in favor of devolution of political power vary in their enthusiasm for modernization. Some communal advocates see decentralization and autonomy as the only ways to loosen the grip of an alien elite whose control of national policy prevents weaker groups from gaining resources they need to compete in modern society. Scores of other ethnic spokesmen in old and new nation-states, however, view modernity with extreme skepticism. Not only does modernity challenge the values and bonds the ethnic groups prize, but it seems to offer little to individuals who forsake ethnic affiliation.

Common among the grievance charges leveled at modern society are alienation and centralization. Persons living in modernized societies (or in the modern sectors of transitional societies) often feel ineffectual, unable to control their own lives. Paradoxically, men enjoy a wider range of contacts than ever before but feel integrated only in terms of a functional role, not in terms of personal belonging. The other side of this coin is institutional centralization, the removal of decision-making to remote councils for the sake of coordination and mobilization. Modern societies prize rationality and growth; development theorists have looked for this or have tried to explain its absence. But rationality requires abstraction and high levels of analysis, in which many variables can be taken into

11 Vine Deloria, Jr., "The New Constitution," in *We Talk, You Listen* (New York: Macmillan, 1970), p. 52.

account. Growth, which was thought to be the only guarantee of satisfying rising popular expectation, depends on this exalted level of rationality, for growth is the result of coordination and maximization of resources, including manpower. Now in both modern and quasi-modern countries people are asking: what is the price for rationality and growth, and is it worth paying? They are questioning whether centralized decision-making is the best way to achieve those ends. What looks rational and growth-producing in the Canadian capital of Ottawa, for example, looks unjust to French-Canadians in Quebec. Ethnicity has become a major lever for forcing doubts about modernity into the open. Ethnic spokesmen are challenging the close connection of modernization and development. If modernity leads to alienation of the individual and to centralized injustice in the name of rational planning, then perhaps modernization is antithetical to genuine development. Maybe the concept of political development has to be neutralized and the nature of political community reassessed. Historical psychologist Robert Jay Lifton has said:

> Our sense of the continuity of life is profoundly threatened. There is a strong undercurrent of imagery of death and technological annihilation, and it becomes increasingly difficult for people . . . to give significant form to their ideas, their actions, and to themselves. They are no longer certain where anything begins or ends.[12]

Loss of a sense of boundaries, not just territorial but social and psychological, may be at the core of the current outbreak of communal versus nation-state tensions. The fact that the struggle to establish new boundaries for meaningful political action is going on in countries at several different stages of modernization warns against relying on the inevitability of the nation-state or assuming that political development leads to modernity. The mobilization of ethnic groups may reflect the traumas of casting off tradition, but it may also portend innovative political forms for the future, beyond modernity.

[12] Robert Jay Lifton and T. George Harris, "The Politics of Immortality," *Psychology Today* 4, no. 6 (November 1970): 70; emphasis added. See also Robert Jay Lifton, *Boundaries* (New York: Vintage Books, 1970).

Index

275